D0712900

KARACHI VICE

KARACHI VICE

LIFE AND DEATH IN
A DIVIDED CITY

SAMIRA SHACKLE

MELVILLE HOUSE
BROOKLYN · LONDON

KARACHI VICE: LIFE AND DEATH IN A DIVIDED CITY
First Melville House publication August 2021
First published in Great Britain by Granta Books, 2021

33614082408369

ISBN: 9-781-61219-942-9
ISBN: 9-781-61219-943-6 (eBook)

Library of Congress Control Number: 2021937674

Printed in the United States of America
1 3 5 7 9 10 8 6 4 2

A catalogue record for this book is available from the Library of Congress

For my grandparents Ahmed and Sabiha Husain,
who never saw how their Karachi had changed

CONTENTS

Maps	viii
Political Groups	xi
Timeline of Major Events	xiii
Prologue	xvii
1 Safdar	1
2 Parveen	22
3 Siraj	44
4 Jannat	65
5 Zille	86
6 Ashura	105
7 Lyari	125
8 Anarchy	143
9 Sahiba	161
10 The Karachi Operation	174
11 Bahria Town	196
12 Aftershocks	214
Author's Note	239
Acknowledgements	241
Glossary	245

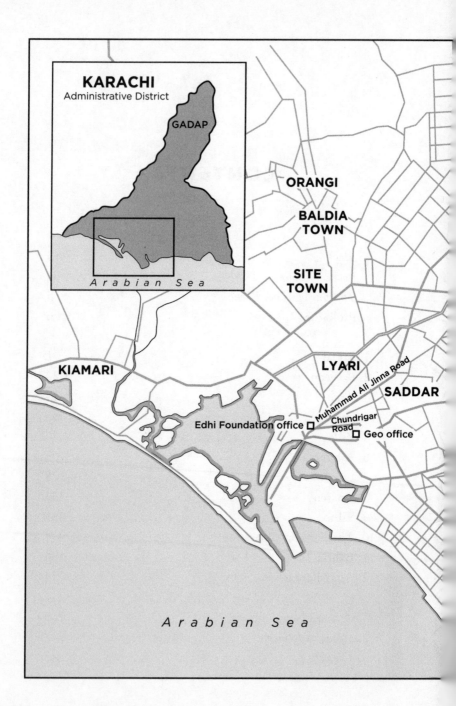

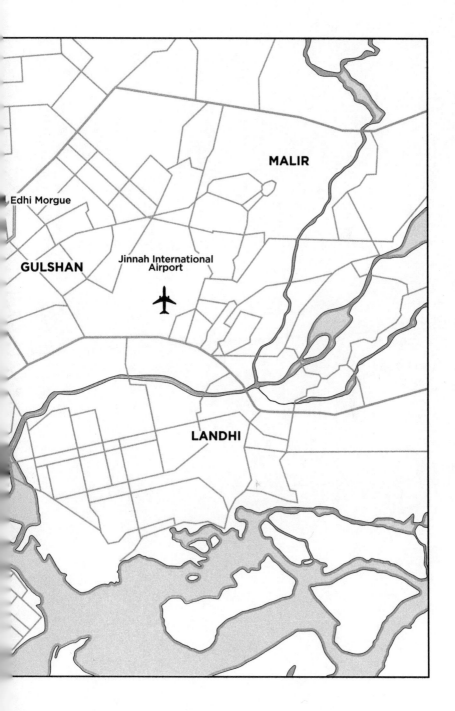

POLITICAL GROUPS

Awami National Party (ANP): a Pashtun nationalist party with broadly secular and leftist politics

Inter-Services Intelligence (ISI): Pakistan's main intelligence agency, an all-powerful entity

Muttahida Qaumi Movement (MQM): a secular and left-leaning party that represents the Mohajir community

Pakistan Muslim League (Nawaz) (PML-N): one of Pakistan's main parties of government, led by the Sharif family – centre-right and conservative, with a staunch belief in free market economics

Pakistan People's Party (PPP): Pakistan's other main party of government – a centre-left, social democratic force headed by the Bhutto family

Pakistan Tehreek-e-Insaaf (PTI): a centrist political party with a strong anti-corruption platform and support from the country's emergent middle classes

People's Aman Committee (PAC): a politico-military body set up by Lyari's gangsters in 2008, affiliated with the PPP

Rangers: a paramilitary law enforcement agency, administered by the army, that sits somewhere between the police and the military, and is often deployed in cities to assist policing

Tehreek-e-Taliban Pakistan (TTP): an umbrella organization formed in 2007, bringing together a number of extremist terror groups based in north-western Pakistan

TIMELINE OF MAJOR EVENTS

June 1992: Operation Clean-up is launched in Karachi by Nawaz Sharif's conservative government, aimed at stopping ethnic violence and cracking down on the MQM. Led at first by the army, and later by Rangers and police, it lasts until 1996. Thousands are killed or disappeared.

July 1993: Prime minister Sharif is ousted. Fresh elections are held and left-leaning Benazir Bhutto returns to power.

February 1997: Elections are held. Bhutto is ousted and Sharif returns to power.

October 1999: The army stages a coup d'état. Sharif is removed and army chief General Pervez Musharraf takes over.

June 2001: Musharraf formally appoints himself as president.

October 2002: Musharraf holds elections. A pro-Musharraf political party wins a majority and forms a coalition with, among other parties, the MQM. This ramps up MQM control in Karachi after years on the back foot.

2003: Lyari is divided by a brutal turf war between gang factions led by Arshad Pappu and Rehman Dakait.

March 2007: Mass protests, known as the Lawyers' Movement, are held in Pakistan after Musharraf unconstitutionally suspends the chief justice. Eventually Musharraf bows to pressure and calls elections.

December 2007: Benazir Bhutto, leader of the PPP, returns to Pakistan after eight years in exile. She is assassinated at a campaign rally in Rawalpindi.

February 2008: A general election is held. The PPP is elected to national government and Bhutto's widower, Asif Ali Zardari, becomes president. In Karachi, the ANP/PPP win some city seats and the MQM steps up its attacks on these rivals.

2008: In Lyari, the People's Aman Committee is formed as part of a truce between Rehman Dakait and Arshad Pappu. Zardari strikes a deal with Dakait to shore up PPP votes in Lyari.

August 2008: Rehman Dakait is killed by police in Lyari. Uzair Baloch takes over as kingpin of the area.

December 2009: A huge bomb blast at a Shia religious procession kills more than thirty people.

July 2010: Flooding in Sindh pushes people from rural areas into Karachi in search of work and shelter.

April 2012: Police launch the disastrous eight-day operation in Lyari to root out the gangsters. It fails.

December 2012: The MQM's London offices are raided as part of a murder investigation. The MQM calls a strike in Karachi in response.

March 2013: Arshad Pappu is kidnapped and killed. Uzair Baloch and Baba Ladla are videoed playing football with his head.

May 2013: A general election is held. The PPP loses and the PML–N takes over. Nawaz Sharif becomes prime minister for a third time. The MQM wins a majority in Karachi, but is threatened by the PTI.

September 2013: Sharif gives the Rangers – who had maintained a presence in Karachi since 1992's Operation Clean-up – the go-ahead to launch a new targeted operation in the city.

2014: Construction of Bahria Town Karachi, a massive development on the outskirts of the city, begins.

June 2014: Karachi's Jinnah International Airport is attacked by ten TTP militants. Thirty-six people are killed. In response, the army increases strikes on terrorist hideouts in North Waziristan and ramps up its urban operations.

March 2015: Rangers raid Nine Zero, the MQM's headquarters, and arrest sixty party workers.

July 2018: Another general election is held. This time the PTI wins, breaking the two-party deadlock, although the election takes place in a climate of increased censorship and army control. Imran Khan becomes prime minister.

December 2018: The Supreme Court orders a stay on construction at Bahria Town Karachi and finds evidence of illegal land appropriation. The decision is reversed a few months later.

PROLOGUE

I moved to Karachi in the aftermath of riots, arriving to smashed shop windows and the smell of burning tyres. It was 2012 and the city had been engulfed by protests against a YouTube video that made offensive statements about the Prophet Muhammad. The city's few remaining cinemas had been attacked, and churches had taken extra security precautions, lest the mob hold Pakistan's Christians accountable for the crimes of the American film-makers. The scale of destruction was disproportionate to the offence itself. I was a Londoner moving to my mother's hometown, a place I had visited only once since childhood. This was an immediate introduction to the discontent that bubbled beneath the surface of the city, always ready to erupt into violence.

I walked out of the airport into a heavy, humid night and was collected by my aunt, my mother's cousin, with whom I planned to stay. We got into the back of the car; up front was the driver. (This felt unnatural to me to begin with, although I knew that it was common for well-off families in Pakistan to employ a full-time driver; many companies do the same for their office staff.) Karachi is a web of flyovers and highways, the sides of the roads dotted with battered colonial facades, concrete monstrosities, improvised shacks and half-built shells of buildings. Ornate plasterwork sits below poorly constructed high-rises designed only to maximize the space.

To travel on these roads is to be confronted with the massive population of this heaving city. We drove through traffic sprawling into multiple lanes. Motorbikes, sometimes bearing up to five family members, wove in and out between the cars, and men clung to the tops and sides of minibuses. As we drove, my aunt dispensed some safety advice. If a man on a motorbike stops by your car window and flashes a gun, don't ask questions, just hand over your cash and phone. Change your timings, routes and vehicles frequently to minimize the risk of kidnap. If you pass through a dangerous district, don't stop – not even if someone crashes into you.

Over the following weeks, I realized why most of this advice was predicated on being in a car: travelling around the city was when Karachi's wealthier citizens were most vulnerable to the violence that surrounded them. Like most affluent residents of the city, my relatives were somewhat insulated. They lived behind high walls, protected by twenty-four-hour armed guards. Even the cafes and shops they frequented were surrounded by metal detectors and bored security guards with AK-47s slung over their shoulders. There was good reason for this. Karachi was in the throes of one of the worst outbreaks of violence it had seen since the 1990s. Every day, some fifteen to twenty people were killed in targeted attacks by rival ethnic groups or political parties, and whole neighbourhoods were frequently off-limits due to rioting or running street battles. But the city was so big that even as this was happening, life in the more affluent districts could go on more or less as normal. The areas of Clifton and Defence, where most of my relatives and friends lived, formed a city within a city, their wide streets, lush greenery and palatial houses a world away from the urban warfare of Lyari or Orangi. Here, the backdrop of violence quickly became mundane: perhaps a day trip to the beach would be impossible due to a security alert, or dinner plans would have to be rearranged because of a citywide strike. For all Karachi's vast sprawl, most of its citizens live in a tightly constricted geography, not venturing too far from their locale lest they stray into danger.

Each morning, I sat with my aunt in a marble-floored living room overlooking a luxuriant garden where blooming coral trees spilled over a pagoda. The pet parrot, who was loud and surprisingly vicious, squawked in the background, picking up the odd word from conversations. Tellingly, one of his favourites was *tamasha*, the Urdu word often used to mean 'commotion', referring to a protest or riot. Over breakfast, I would look through the English-language news-papers, reaching first for the *Express Tribune*. It published a crime map every day in its Karachi edition, under headings like 'Shootings and raids' and 'Mishaps and bodies found', a half-page infographic mapping out the violence consuming areas of the city. I would skim through the daily accounts of targeted killings of political workers and gang battles, the latest convulsions in the multiple conflicts that have racked Karachi for decades. From the vantage point of the comfortable living room, the street war unfolding a few miles away felt unreal and distant, just a headcount on a page.

The violence had deep roots. Karachi's history is one of migra-tion and rapid expansion. In 1947, Karachi was a port city with a population of fewer than 500,000 people. Today, there are closer to 20 million, more than triple the population of London. When Pakistan was formed out of the bloody Partition of India, trainloads of Muslims crossed the border in search of a new homeland, arriving exhausted and brutalized. Karachi was the final stop on the train, and as the refugees were turned away from everywhere else, it was their destination by default. These migrants, who became known as Mohajirs, settled first in sprawling refugee camps and then took up the government jobs left vacant by the Hindus and Sikhs who had fled in the other direction. My grandparents married in 1948, a few months after Partition; the wedding celebrations had to be scaled down because Mahatma Gandhi was assassinated that week. Soon afterwards, my grandmother left her home in a Muslim part of northern India to live with my grandfather's family in Karachi. Immediately, she began to volunteer in the refugee camps that engulfed swathes of the city. Two years later, in 1950, my mother was born. Despite these harsh beginnings, as the capital of a new nation, Karachi was infused with a feeling of hope and possibility – Pakistan was a new country, forging a national identity, and this was the city at the centre of it all. This was the Karachi that my mother and grandmother had told me about: a cosmopolitan place full of energy and action.

In the decades since Partition, Karachi has been home to a series of complex and ever-evolving conflicts, with sectarian and ethnic resentment mingling with politics and organized crime. First was the tension between the Mohajirs and the local Sindhi population. The Sindhis were broadly less educated and resented the newcomers dominating them in business and public sector jobs. The optimism that was Karachi's mood music in the early days of nation-building hardened into mutual suspicion, hostility and aggression. In the 1970s, my grandparents and their four children – my mother, two aunts and my uncle – moved to the UK, making a new life among the tree-lined avenues of north-west London. It was after they left, through the 1970s and 1980s, that the tensions between Karachi's different groups flared into riots and led to the formation of noxious ethnic political movements. Later, people flooded into Karachi from Afghanistan, displaced by the war, and from Pakistan's north-west and elsewhere in the country because of violence or natural disaster. These subsequent waves of migration followed the same pattern, with a growing number of ethnic groups fiercely competing for physical space and economic resources. Even today, when earthquakes or bombs, floods or gunfire have displaced people from their homes in Khyber Pakhtunkhwa or Balochistan, they still flock to Karachi, attracted by that sometimes arrhythmic but perpetually beating heart of economic promise. All of Pakistan has converged here, along with the tensions and rivalries that automatically follow.

Many of the parties that dominate the political landscape today have their roots in ethnic identity. The Muttahida Qaumi Movement (MQM), which has long dominated Karachi's politics, represents the Mohajir community. It evolved from an angry student movement during the riots and ethnic tension of the 1970s and 1980s. The Awami National Party (ANP) represents Pashtuns, from the north-west of the country. The Pakistan People's Party (PPP), traditionally one of the main parties of national government, is grounded in the heartlands of Sindh, the province in which Karachi sits. While the party aspires to speak to a wider audience with its message of social justice, it relies on rural Sindh for its core support. The Pakistan Muslim League (Nawaz) (PML–N), the other main party of government, barely features in Karachi because it focuses almost entirely on its ethnic Punjabi base. In recent years, there has been some disruption of this old order. Imran Khan's Pakistan Tehreek-e-Insaaf (PTI) was elected to national government in 2018, its anticorruption message appealing to young and upwardly mobile city dwellers rather than to any single ethnic group.

Compounding the pressure of multiple migrations and deep-rooted ethnic allegiances is the fact that the city can barely keep pace with its constant, dizzying expansion. Buildings, half-buildings and makeshift shacks have sprung up to accommodate the steady stream of newcomers. Services have not developed quickly enough. Vast areas of Karachi have no proper sewerage system, no connection to the mains water supply or electricity, and scarcely any police presence. Always ready to fill the gaping holes left by the state are criminal gangs, with mafias trading in these utilities as well as in weapons, extortion and drugs. Many of the gangs are intimately connected to political parties, which are active participants in the street wars that afflict their constituents. Most have militant wings that, at different points, have brutally intimidated opponents – through abduction, torture, even murder – and ties to the criminal gangs that for a long time ran the city. Extortion, after all, is a handy way to raise funds, while controlling the sale of land is an efficient way to shore up your voter banks.

Karachi's politics have particularly high stakes, but they play out against a tumultuous national backdrop. Successive politicians and military rulers have sought to exploit the nation's ethnic divisions for their own gain, the consequences of which are marked in blood on Karachi's streets. Pakistan has spent almost half of its seventy years under military dictatorship, with successive elected governments overthrown by an army which plays a disproportionate role in public life. Even when civilian politicians are in power, the army and intelligence services continue to pull the strings. This means that many state institutions are weak and ill-equipped to meet the needs of a wildly expanding population. And the army is capricious, sometimes supporting violent movements, sometimes brutally suppressing them.

When I moved to Karachi, the country was experiencing a new democratic moment. In 2008, the most recent military leader, General Musharraf, had stood down and called an election, after losing public support following a clash with the judiciary. During the campaign that followed, Benazir Bhutto was killed by a suicide bomb at a rally in Rawalpindi. But her party, the centre-left PPP, went on to win a majority and her widower, Asif Ali Zardari, became president. They were Karachiites, but also – like every mainstream politician in Pakistan – notorious for corruption. As far as I could see, their government hadn't brought any tangible improvements to the city. I covered the 2013 election, when power swung back to the other main party, the centre-right PML-N, headed by Nawaz Sharif. It was the country's first ever democratic transfer from one civilian government to another: every other elected administration in Pakistan's short history had been ousted by the army. This was cause for celebration, as was another election and change of government in 2018 – but certain factors have remained constant: the dominance of the military in public life and the nexus of corruption and power that controls basic resources such as water, electricity and land.

The city I moved to in 2012 bore little resemblance to the one my family had left behind in the 1970s. I spent months disoriented by its scale, trying to understand not only the physical web of streets, but the second layer of geography – the corners where one set of allegiances switches to another, the blocks where hostile forces huddled. It would take more time to fill in the blanks, to turn the pencil outline of the city's layout into a shaded image in full technicolour, showing where each of its multiple warring elements sat.

In 2013, after a year in Pakistan, I returned to London. But I continued to make regular visits to Karachi, drawn back by its complexity. At home in the UK, people saw Pakistan as a lawless, terrifying place. It was there in the awkward silence when I discussed upcoming trips, or in well-meaning comments about my 'bravery'. Travelling around Pakistan, I noticed that many people elsewhere in the country had a similar feeling about Karachi: that it was lawless, dangerous, impossible. On the face of it, they had a point. Karachi is polluted and violent, and in many ways a difficult place to live, or even to visit. But despite these challenges, the city has an almost gravitational pull. Rightly or wrongly, millions of people around Pakistan continue to see it as a place where they can make their fortune, or escape the inequalities of their rural homes. Like the vast numbers who pack up and move to the city every year, I found myself unable to escape Karachi's orbit. My urge to return, and to keep returning, was not just about family ties. Sometimes I told my relatives I was coming, sometimes I didn't – my work as a journalist was not always compatible with their safety concerns. For people who had no option but to live among the threats and try as best they could to avoid danger, it was difficult to see why I would choose to spend time in the very localities that had become synonymous with violence, the slums whose names appeared in news broadcasts and on crime maps. But to me, understanding Karachi felt crucial to understanding Pakistan. The gang wars and political battles may be geographically contained, but they reflect and anticipate nationwide shifts. Unpicking the minutiae of the daily struggles taking place on these dusty streets reveals something about Pakistan and its place in the world. *Karachi Vice* follows the lives of five Karachiites, whose disparate lives converge during a terrifying crime wave.

Over the decade that I have spent going regularly to Karachi, the city has changed. The violence reached a terrible crescendo when the international airport was attacked in 2014. After that, a paramilitary-led security crackdown reshaped the lines of power in the city. As people in different parts of Karachi shared their stories of conflict and crackdown with me, I began to understand how they found snatches of normality in extreme circumstances and reserves of courage in the face of fear. Karachi's citizens have had to learn to navigate a complicated and ever-shifting web of criminality and violence, of state neglect and police brutality, and to build their own networks of humanity and community. This is the front line of global urbanization at its most unforgiving.

1

SAFDAR

I was used to experiencing Karachi through the windows of a car, but not at such high speed. I was sitting in the passenger seat of an ambulance, siren blaring, clinging on tight as we lurched between lanes of traffic. The driver, Safdar, shouted through the loudspeaker attached to the vehicle, warning people to get out of the way. 'Son of a bitch – are you blind?' he yelled at a lorry driver; 'Hey you, long beard, move!' at a hapless pedestrian. We screeched to a halt outside an apartment block where a gas canister had exploded. Safdar ran inside. It was late 2016, December's cool breeze blowing through the streets, and I was in Karachi to research a story on the city's ambulance drivers. Safdar was my guide. He seemed to know every inch of Karachi, possessing an encyclopedic knowledge of the urban sprawl that I still struggled to navigate.

Safdar emanates an electric energy: he is constantly in motion. His boss introduced him to me, sarcastically, as 'our most polite driver'. He talks a million miles a minute, cracking jokes, jumping around to act out his stories, but dropping everything – leaving a drink half drunk, a story half told – if someone requires his help. Nothing is more urgent than getting to people in need. As we got to know each other, I learned that there was good reason for this: he had suffered the torture of waiting for help and being too poor to have other options.

When Safdar described his brother's prolonged sickness back in 2002, it did not surprise me to hear that what he had hated the most wasn't seeing his brother's pain or his mother's worry, although both were bad enough. It was the waiting. Minutes stretched into hours then into days as they waited in Karachi's Civil Hospital, a colonial-era building of weathered sandstone, its archways and circular turrets incongruous against the backdrop of exhaust fumes and honking traffic from the main road that ran alongside it. They waited to see the doctors with what felt like a hundred other patients. Ageing fans fitted on high ceilings struggled to move the still, humid air around the wards and corridors. When people tried to jump the queue and grab the attention of a passing doctor, a flash of injustice would overwhelm Safdar and he felt obliged to intervene. When the rage came over him, he was barely aware of what he was saying. Luckily, his outbursts usually passed as quickly as they arose.

His brother Adil was the reason they were there. His left leg was atrophied by polio, which meant he couldn't walk. Adil had contracted the illness as an infant and its effects had worsened over the years, so that now he couldn't bend his leg even when he sat down. When he prayed, when he used the bathroom, it remained straight, the knee joint locked in paralysis. The family had tried for years to manage Adil's slow deterioration, until there was no option but to submit to the doctors and the repeated surgery they recommended. Adil was in terrible pain, so bad that sometimes he momentarily lost his vision and cried out, his hands flailing for support.

The waiting did not end when they got to see a doctor. Some of the worst hours were when Adil was in the operating theatre. Safdar, his sister Amna and their mother would sit outside the hospital because there was no space to wait inside the already overcrowded building. Raised pavements ran alongside the roads in the dusty hospital compound. The women would jostle for a space to sit on the ground, together with the relatives of other sick patients who had come from all over the city. But Safdar preferred to pace back and forth, imagining he was doing something.

'Why don't you sit down?' his sister would ask.

'I am allergic to sitting still,' he would snap, unable to articulate the truth: that if he sat down, the worry might totally overwhelm him.

During that year of hospital appointments, Safdar began to recognize the other families who returned as often as they did. He'd see familiar faces in the crowd of dark hair and brightly coloured clothes, and wonder if they, like him, were consumed by a gnawing anxiety that the treatment for their loved one might not work. Even when the people were so tightly packed that it was hard to find a space to sit, Safdar did not resent the other families for adding to the wait. Instead, as he looked at them, he wondered what their stories were, who they were waiting for. Although he was only nineteen and didn't have a single qualification, he found himself wishing he could do something to ease this collective pain and make it so that poor people didn't have to wait so long for everything.

It was Safdar who communicated with the doctors when Adil was having surgery. His mother spoke the Pashto dialect of the village, and her Urdu – Pakistan's lingua franca and the main language of Karachi – was rudimentary at best. Although they spoke Pashto at home, Safdar could effortlessly move between the two. He was respectful in Pashto, the language of his parents. When he switched into Urdu, he cursed and joked like a born and bred Karachiite, with none of the telltale signs of being Pashtun – the distinctive accent or mixing up of genders – which could result in discrimination or worse. But though the doctors explained the procedures to him, Safdar had only a loose understanding of what they were doing. He had to put his faith in them. Just as Adil's illness was God's will, so God would decide whether the treatment would work.

When Adil came out of surgery, the next wait was for an ambulance to take them home. There was no way Adil could be crammed into a rickshaw for the long drive back to Landhi, an industrial area where they lived in the shadow of oil tankers, in a makeshift cluster of houses sandwiched between a truck stop and a loading bay. It was a forty-five-minute drive on a good day, and when it came to the traffic, good days were few and far between. Adil would come out of surgery stoical but dazed, visibly in pain as the anaesthetic wore off, with his stiff leg encased in plaster and a metal cage designed to keep it straight while it healed. There were no state ambulances, only those provided by the Edhi Foundation.

Although many aid organizations existed around the city, everyone knew the Edhi Foundation was the one that the poor could truly rely on. It filled many of the holes left by the state, providing free or low-cost services, including ambulances. It was a squeeze to fit the whole family into one of these small Suzuki Bolan minivans. Adil would lie on the stretcher, with Safdar perched on the side next to him, while Amna and their mother would take the small bench seat on the other side. But here at least Adil could be comfortable. The fee was fixed at fifty rupees (25p),* which they could just about afford. Sometimes, they left the house with only a hundred rupees for the whole day. It covered the ambulance to the hospital and back, and nothing in between. When the waiting went on for too long and darkness began to fall, Safdar would find himself irritable with hunger, his mouth dry with thirst, trying to hide it from his mother because he knew they did not have money to fritter away on snacks. Sometimes he would see her clenching and unclenching her fist

---

* Due to a credit crisis and an International Monetary Fund bailout, the Pakistani currency has rapidly lost value against the dollar and pound since 2017, so conversions can offer only an approximation of meaningful purchasing power.

around the crumpled fifty-rupee note that would get them home, scrunched up with the paper ticket bearing a number – their position in the queue for the ambulance. The whole family would keep their eyes and ears open for an Edhi driver – easily identifiable by their loose, bright red T-shirts – shouting out their number. Sometimes there would be people screaming in pain as their relatives begged the ambulance driver to take them instead. The drivers always stuck to the system, though, and ushered Safdar, Adil and the family into the back of the vehicle. Every time they drove away, Safdar felt overwhelmed by the scale of the need.

They had been living with Adil's illness for many years. It had struck before they moved to Karachi, when Adil was two. In the village, they had called it *burra bukhar* (big fever). He suffered high temperatures, headaches, shivers, vomiting, skin so tender he yelped when he was touched. He was in bed for over a week, sticky and hot, screaming with a pain he didn't have the words to describe. The adults in the village talked anxiously about what was wrong. Most thought it was typhoid. A few people mentioned polio, but for Adil and Safdar's parents, the idea was too much to bear. Typhoid was nasty but familiar; people had it, people recovered. There was no doctor in the vicinity, no hospital for miles, and so the family decided to deal with Adil's sickness at home. They kept him hydrated and tried to get him to eat, watching anxiously as he squirmed in bed and bawled with discomfort. The closest medical facility was in Peshawar, the big city, and given the distance and the state of the roads, it would take hours to get there, not to mention money that they didn't have. As the days passed, their mother grew more and more worried. She started to think about how to get together funds for the journey to Peshawar. But then, slowly, miraculously, the recovery started. Adil began to sleep peacefully instead of thrashing around, sweaty and fitful. He ate small bites of rice and dhal and soon he was running around with the other children again. Before long, however, it became clear that something wasn't right. While playing, Adil would be seized with such intense pain in his joints that he would scream out and his vision would blur. Sometimes his leg buckled under him.

Though Karachi was all Safdar could really recall of his childhood, sometimes he had flashes of a life before, a sensory memory of the village thousands of miles away in the north-western corner of Pakistan where he was born. Fresh mountain streams gurgling over pebbles. The taste of an orange plucked straight from a tree. An icy chill in the air slicing through clothing and hitting the skin, totally different from Karachi's warm sea breeze. They had all been family there. Safdar's paternal grandmother, *Dadi*, was one of five sisters who lived in the village with their children and their children's children. There were almost a hundred of them clustered in these houses on the side of a mountain. *Dadi*'s house was actually built into the hills, the courtyard and sections of the wall shaped from the rock. The land was fertile and green, while babbling brooks provided *meetha pani* (sweet water). But it was remote and work opportunities were few and far between. The children weren't aware that another life existed, but most of the adults lived under the shadow of perpetual anxiety about how to cover their basic costs. Safdar's father left for long spells of time, seeking work around the country. When he found a job in Karachi, thousands of miles away, it was decided. The family packed all the possessions they could carry and got on a bus, becoming tiny drops in the wave of migration of hundreds of thousands of Pashtuns to Karachi. The journey took more than twenty-four hours. They travelled over the bumpy, barely constructed mountain roads that surrounded their village. The children rocked around in their seats as the bus stopped and started, getting steadily more crowded as passengers were picked up along the way. The ride got slightly smoother as they hit the highway. Night fell. Dawn came. The landscape changed. The lush mountains of Khyber Pakhtunkhwa, Pakistan's north-western province, gave way to the flat greenery of the Punjab, and then to the starkly barren terracotta of Sindh, punctuated by occasional bursts of lush green agricultural land. Eventually they entered the densely knotted streets of Karachi. There were more people here than Safdar had ever seen.

They made their home in Landhi, out where the trucks stopped. The roads there were lined with low, thorny trees rising up from the heaps of trash amassed between the many petrol pumps that populated the area. On all sides of the main road were vehicles that threw up clouds of dust as they drove over the unevenly tarmacked surface: cylindrical tankers, diggers, rickshaws, brightly coloured trucks daubed with elaborate patterns in an art form that had developed over the years into a competition between truck drivers. Safdar's father had a job as a nightwatchman, standing guard over one of the many depots where tankers and trucks were deposited overnight on stopovers between different parts of Pakistan. The work suited him; he valued the independence. 'Getting a Pashtun to follow instructions is like getting a camel to sit in a rickshaw,' he once joked, alluding to the commonly held view that men from their ethnic background preferred jobs that allowed a level of freedom, working as drivers and guards rather than in factories or as house servants. Occasionally, he'd take a second job during the daytime hours, to bring in some extra money. He had a stint at a towel factory, working for 400 rupees a month. He didn't much like these jobs and the restrictions they involved. 'A lion cannot be caged,' he would say.

Behind the main road that cut through Landhi was a dense mass of houses and stores, a maze-like warren of streets where hole-in-the-wall shops that looked like cement caves sold jalebis – swirls of deep-fried batter seared in vats of oil and coated in syrup – or hot, fresh naan from a makeshift tandoor oven. Stalls stocked cheaply packaged sweets and household goods like lentils, rice and cleaning products. An old man tended a butcher's stall, swatting flies away from the row of pale pink chicken breasts that glistened in the heat. At first, the family lived in a single room – the parents, Safdar, Adil, Amna and a growing number of siblings. By the time Adil was having his surgery in 2002, there would be seven of them. As the family grew and the rent went up, they moved around Landhi too many times to keep track.

While most of the people in the streets that surrounded their house were Pashtun like them, Landhi as a whole was divided. Other parts were mostly occupied by Mohajirs, the Urdu-speaking people who had migrated from India at the time of Partition and settled in Karachi. After years of discrimination by more established ethnic groups – the Sindhis, indigenous to this province, and Punjabis, who made up the majority in Pakistan – the Mohajirs had formed a political party, the Muttahida Qaumi Movement, headed by a young firebrand called Altaf Hussain. Although they had only recently been migrants themselves, many Mohajirs did not like the influx of new-comers from northern Pakistan. When Safdar's family moved there in the early 1990s, Landhi was already one of the battlegrounds of a rapidly spiralling and intensely violent turf war between Mohajirs and Pashtuns.

The first few years after they moved to Karachi were the worst for Safdar's family, because they didn't know anyone and lacked the security that comes with being part of a pack. 'You know, they're killing Pashtuns, so don't let your kids out too much,' he heard a neighbour tell his mother. 'Don't let them out at all if you can avoid it.' They stayed inside after that, cooped up in their single room, playing and bickering and listening in on the discussions of the adults, leaving only to go to school. Gradually, his parents got to know everyone who lived nearby. Meanwhile, one by one, their relatives from the village began to make the journey south. Before long, there were more relatives in Karachi than in the village, like scattered fragments reassembling into a whole.

They were no longer strangers in the city, but the risks remained. At night, when Safdar's father was out at work, watching over the trucks, his mother sometimes stayed awake, her soft round face contorted with tension, heavy bags under her blue eyes. Death felt very close in those days, each morning bringing stories of someone shot down as they went about their daily business. More often than not, the TV news or the papers would say they were party workers, even if everyone knew that the murdered person had had no involvement in politics. Safdar's father took the back alleys when he walked over to the depot for his shifts, avoiding the main roads where he might be visible to a passing gunman. He had the pale skin common to Pashtuns, and even after years in Karachi, his Urdu was halting and hesitant, the Pashto accent obvious. Safdar picked up on his mother's fear, but could not conceive of the idea that his father might seriously be under threat. Everyone knew that Pashtun men had the courage of lions and Safdar was certain that his father was the bravest of them all. Perhaps that was why the Mohajirs didn't like them, he reasoned with himself. Perhaps they knew that if they allowed the Pashtuns to get too comfortable, they would dominate everything.

During the long, sticky days stuck inside, time took on a hazy consistency, formless hours punctuated only by mealtimes and prayers. More often than not the small TV with its bulbous glass front was set to the news on the state-owned PTV, which broadcast grim details of 'the Karachi situation'. When the army was sent in to restore order in 1992, Safdar was nine. He was captivated by the vision of these brave men in uniform, their tanks rolling in across the city that he now thought of as his own. Safdar began standing to attention when the army came on screen, practising his salute and making Adil do the same, even when he protested. Safdar vowed that one day he would wear that uniform and serve his country too.

By the time Adil was having surgery at the age of seventeen – six times over the course of a year – Safdar's dream of joining the army felt very far away. He had stopped going to school in the fifth grade, when he was around ten, because his parents could no longer pay the fees for the local low-cost private school. The nearest government school was further afield and the journey was too risky. This, combined with long gaps in schooling caused by the move from the village and the conflict in Karachi, meant that Safdar could barely read or write. He'd heard from friends that you had to sit a written exam to enter the army and so he pushed the thought of his impossible dream from his mind. He still felt a surge of pride and longing when he saw those brave men in their uniforms on his TV screen, but their life was not for him. One day, as Safdar paced around Civil Hospital, Adil's bone doctor asked him what he was going to do with his life. 'Some day I'll do something important,' Safdar replied. 'I don't know how yet, but I will serve the people so much that they will remember me. I promise you that.' The doctor told Safdar he would hold him to his promise.

Through that protracted period, there was one constant: the Edhi drivers, manoeuvring through the crowds, scooping people up and taking them to and from the hospital. One day, as Safdar and his mother waited outside, a group of Edhi ambulances pulled up, sirens blaring, and screeched to a halt. The ambulance drivers moved fast, carrying bloodied bodies into the emergency room, some people screaming, others unsettlingly still. There had been a bomb blast in the city. Safdar watched, horrified but unable to turn away. He was transfixed, not by the gruesome injuries, but by the drivers, wearing the red shirts with the white logo of the Edhi Foundation.

They moved efficiently and with purpose, like well-oiled cogs in a machine designed expressly to save people. That was when he knew the answer to the doctor's question.

The handwritten sign reading DRIVERS WANTED – APPLY NOW was permanently displayed above the kiosk at the Edhi Foundation's main office in Saddar, Karachi's old commercial district. It didn't take Safdar long to get there from Civil Hospital, travelling along the weathered tarmac of the city's jugular vein, Muhammad Ali Jinnah Road. In this area, battered colonial buildings with ravaged plasterwork and rusting metal window grilles have been repurposed as cheap cafes and all-purpose stores. Brightly printed signs, advertising Pepsi or electronics shops, are strung up below faded painted balustrades on old brick buildings in various states of disrepair. Vestiges of former colonial grandeur are visible everywhere. The part of Saddar where the office is situated is commonly known as Tower, after Merewether Tower, which is opposite the Edhi depot. This elegantly carved clock tower, a memorial for Sir William Merewether, the commissioner of Sindh from 1867 to 1877, stands tall at the intersection of two of Karachi's busiest roads. Once the bells on top of the tower rang on the hour. Now they are silent, coated in the dust kicked up by the roaring traffic, surrounded by a street symphony of honking horns, revving motorbike engines and vendors loudly hawking their wares.

The Edhi building sprawls along the pavement. When Safdar arrived that day, he saw an office fronted by a hole-in-the-wall kiosk where people could drop off donations, ask for work or request an ambulance. It was next to a glass-fronted control room where the Edhi staff manning the phones were just about visible. On the pavement in front of the office, rusting corrugated-iron sheets had been erected to provide shade for the people waiting outside or for drivers on breaks. Beneath this awning was a stone crib where mothers could leave unwanted babies, safe in the knowledge that the Edhi Foundation would care for them in one of their orphanages. Abdul Sattar Edhi, the great humanitarian who had come from India at Partition, had founded this organization from nothing at a time when the newly formed state of Pakistan was struggling under the weight of its growing population's needs. Starting with a single kiosk providing medicines in 1951, Edhi had rapidly expanded his work through donations from ordinary people. He had been there to help the poor when no one else would. Even now he sometimes sat under the awning with a begging bowl to solicit donations. Safdar admired the fact that he was not like other prominent people who lost their moral compass once they became successful. Despite his huge fame and the size of his foundation, which now spanned all of Pakistan, Edhi cared only about serving the common man. He still had the humility to sit cross-legged in the dirt, alongside the beggars and drug addicts, to encourage people to donate.

There was no sight of Edhi that day. Under the shade of the awning, a few ambulance drivers sat on stools, drinking chai and chewing paan – chopped areca nut coated in tobacco and wrapped in a betel leaf. The nut has a mild stimulant effect and is popular with drivers required to stay awake for long spells. Other drivers were napping inside their ambulances between shifts, languidly draped on narrow stretchers. Safdar nodded a greeting and walked over to the office. When he hammered on the front desk to attract attention, the manager on duty, Muhammad Liaqat, looked up.

'I want to be an ambulance driver,' Safdar said loudly, leaning his thin, wiry frame towards the metal grille to make sure he could be heard over the roaring traffic behind him.

Liaqat gestured for him to come in and Safdar walked round to the office's large, open door. It was dark inside, at least compared with the bleaching sunlight outside, which was so bright it made everything look overexposed and washed out. The air was humid and four electric fans whirred loudly, pointing at different parts of the room. This was a former colonial building with high ceilings and the manager, Anwar Kazmi, liked to remark that the British clearly hadn't been thinking of the Karachi heat when they built these excessively tall rooms. Kazmi was an old friend of Edhi's. The two men had bonded in their youth over their shared Marxist politics. Eventually, Edhi had convinced Kazmi that the revolution was not coming to Pakistan any time soon, so the best way to serve the people was to join him at the foundation.

'Can you drive?' Liaqat asked Safdar.

Safdar nodded. He didn't have a licence, of course, but that was a small detail.

'We'll need your national ID card and your driving licence, and then we can sign you up.'

'It's no problem,' said Safdar. His mind raced, trying to work out how to obtain these documents.

'It's very tough work,' Liaqat continued. 'It's easy to start, but not so easy to stay.'

Safdar puffed out his chest. 'Try me.'

It took several months to sort out the paperwork. First came the national ID card, the document that proved his citizenship and got him access to the world of formal employment. Then he had to gather money to buy a driving licence. Safdar had driven cars on visits to the village and was confident he knew what he was doing. His parents were unconvinced by his prospective new job, though: the pay was low and the risks were high.

'You could earn more money elsewhere,' his mother told him.

'Yes, but I need to earn virtue,' Safdar replied. 'I'll be earning my way into heaven.'

When Safdar returned to the Edhi office with his newly issued ID card and driving licence, Liaqat looked surprised to see him – but, Safdar thought, pleased too. Liaqat briefed him: as the only ambulance service in all of Karachi, they had to prioritize. They split calls into emergencies and non-emergencies. Emergencies were gunshot wounds, explosions, fires and collapsing buildings. Non-emergencies were people like Adil who had to get home after surgery, or go to hospital for an appointment. 'It's easy to sign up, but tough to stay,' Liaqat repeated. Safdar nodded, taking it all in.

On his first day, Safdar was assigned to work with a senior ambulance driver who would show him the ropes. Everyone called this driver Chiri Babu, or Bird Man, because he rarely sat still, hopping from place to place like a sparrow. One minute he would be sitting down and chatting, the next fixing his vehicle and the next at the chai stall. Chiri Babu loved to dance, shaking his shoulders and clicking his fingers whenever he heard even the hint of a tune. Safdar, whose exaggerated facial expressions and gesticulating hands gave the impression of movement even when he was sitting still, immediately liked his mentor.

It didn't take long for a phone call to come in on that first day. The body of a drug addict had been discovered near Kakri Ground in Lyari. Chiri Babu darted to his ambulance and Safdar followed, jumping into the passenger seat. Safdar had never dealt with a dead body before and had never been to Lyari, an area of the city notorious for gang violence. But there was no time to feel nervous. Chiri Babu drove fast, weaving in and out through lanes of traffic, past Karachi's port and into the dense web of streets and tightly packed apartment buildings that made up Lyari, a sprawling slum at the very heart of Karachi. As this was a poor area, there were fewer cars, the streets populated instead by motorbikes and rickshaws. The enormity of the city hit Safdar afresh. All these unfamiliar streets, occupied by different shades of the same conflict that had coloured his childhood.

He wondered how he would ever navigate such neighbourhoods alone. The ambulance pulled up by Kakri Ground, a large sports stadium where football and boxing matches took place, though it was also used for political rallies. Everyone knew, Chiri Babu told Safdar as he parked, that gangs and political parties liked to dump bodies in gunny bags – large hessian sacks generally used for grain – around the arena.

The smell hit Safdar as soon as he stepped out of the ambulance. The body had clearly been there for some time. A cloud of flies formed a buzzing halo and a teeming heap of maggots crawled over every visible part of flesh. The man's salwar kameez was drenched with fluids, the face rotting so the bone was partially exposed. Chiri Babu did not seem bothered. He walked over to the body as if it was the most natural thing in the world, scoping out the best way to lift it onto his stretcher. Trying to control his horror, Safdar followed. The smell filled his nostrils and a violent nausea rose in his chest. It was all too much. He sped away from the body and vomited onto the street. Chiri Babu heard the sound of his retching and walked over.

'Where do you think you are going?' he demanded.

'I'm sorry,' Safdar said weakly. 'I don't think I can manage. This body is in a really bad state.'

Chiri Babu's slap was sharp, leaving a hot sting on Safdar's face.

'What do you see over there? It is a human being,' Chiri Babu said. 'And what are you? You are a human being too.'

Safdar was silent.

'We need to lift this body together. It has to be taken away. So you get over there and help me.'

With that, Chiri Babu walked to the ambulance to get the plastic body bag out. Safdar took a deep breath and followed.

They went back to the body and put it into the bag so that the fluids didn't leak all over the ambulance, then lifted it onto a stretcher. Safdar had to look away from the squirming, glistening maggots, feeling vomit rising. He clenched his teeth. His pride wouldn't allow him to throw up again. They placed the stretcher inside the ambulance and drove back to the office. Although the body was encased in a bag, this did nothing to prevent the stench of death from filling the vehicle. Safdar opened the window, leaning his face out and inhaling the familiar smell of exhaust fumes from the passing cars.

Chiri Babu began to laugh. 'I don't know what all this fuss is about,' he said. 'The body doesn't even smell.'

Safdar looked at him in disbelief. Either Chiri Babu's nose didn't work or he had become impervious to death and decay.

The three days of training that followed seemed peaceful by comparison. There were driving lessons, which Safdar was silently relieved about given his inexperience behind the wheel. But these were no ordinary driving lessons. Safdar was taught how to weave the small ambulances in and out of traffic, and about the importance of being constantly aware of other drivers to avoid causing accidents. He was shown the location of all the major government hospitals, so that he would know where to take patients in a hurry. The mental map he had of his city changed shape, becoming a web of trouble spots all spinning out from the central locus of government hospitals. He learned how to identify life-threatening injuries, how to lift patients without causing harm, how to hold a badly injured body together until they reached the hospital. These were basic ambulances, equipped only with a stretcher, an oxygen tank and sometimes bandages. They were not set up to provide pre-hospital medical care, only to get people to the correct facility as quickly as possible while minimizing damage on the way.

The main thing, Safdar realized, was that he had done it. He might have vomited in the street and been slapped on the face like a child, but he had done the seemingly impossible and picked up a rotting corpse, got it to the mortuary and seen the death logged by the police. Anything was possible after that. He saw other young men who had trained with him drop out after a week or two. But the satisfaction Safdar felt when he collected someone and took them to the hospital, helping a family like his own, was like nothing he had ever experienced before. Even if he was drinking or eating when a non-emergency call came in – a routine transfer of a patient from hospital to home – he would drop the naan from his fingers onto the plate of dhal and rush to the ambulance. His colleagues laughed at him, this eager new guy who treated the most mundane cases like emergencies. But all Safdar cared about was making sure that the family who was calling for help didn't have to wait any longer than necessary.

Karachi was Safdar's city, the place where he had spent most of his childhood, but becoming an ambulance driver highlighted how limited his geography had been. The knot of streets he was driving through had appeared to him like a tangled ball of wool: incomprehensible. At first he felt a twinge of anxiety when he had to go into any unfamiliar area, particularly those whose names he recognized from the news. Lyari, Malir, Kiamari – all were known for gangs, drugs and violence. It wasn't just that he didn't know the streets themselves – where to turn left or right – but that he didn't know the dynamics that operated there. Perhaps this was how his parents had felt, moving into the centre of a battleground without any understanding of where the real danger lay. Over the months, the tangled ball of wool unknotted into neat strands, as Safdar developed an understanding not only of how the highways, streets and weaving back alleys connected, but also of people's loyalties and where the risks were.

Safdar knew he was doing the work that God had intended him to do. Everyone respected the Edhi Foundation and he detected a quiet appreciation of his graft among his neighbours and friends. His family was more difficult to persuade. He grew used to batting away their questions about his safety.

By the time I met Safdar in 2016, he had been an ambulance driver for over a decade and his answers to these questions were well practised. As we careered around Karachi at alarming speed, I looked in vain for a seat belt and asked if he worried about road safety.

'It's not that common for ambulance drivers to have accidents,' he told me. 'When we do, it is usually the public's fault.'

'What about gunfights or explosions?' I asked. 'Don't you think about your safety then?'

'I have never been afraid,' Safdar replied, with characteristic swagger. 'I will only be scared when my soul is being taken out of my body.'

Despite his nonchalance, his mother still worried. 'What kind of job is this, where you have to deal with dead bodies all day?' she often asked.

On the evenings when he arrived home with bloodstained clothes, it was hard to argue with her. She took the regulation red T-shirt and rinsed the rust-coloured blood splatters until the basin of water turned murky pink.

'The situation in the city is not good,' she would say, scrubbing at his clothes. 'Why do you have to go to all these unsafe places?'

Looking at his mother's anxious face, Safdar's mind was flooded by childhood memories of her pacing the room while waiting for his father to come home from work.

'I need prayers, *Amma* [mother],' he would say, too tired to fight. 'And I need your prayers most of all. Please pray for me.'

He had no intention of quitting. The level of need in Karachi had overwhelmed Safdar while Adil was having his surgery. Now that he was confronted daily with the violence and the poverty, there was no way he could step back. Safdar's job might not have paid particularly well, but it brought in some income to the household. His father still worked as a nightwatchman at the same truck depot, a job he would ultimately hold for forty years, and his salary increased only incrementally. Safdar's two youngest siblings, Fatima and Nadir, were getting close to school age, and Safdar was determined that they would make it all the way through to graduation.

Adil's treatment had dragged out over the course of a year, but it had been successful. Although he still had to walk with a crutch, a large wooden contraption that rested under his shoulder, his leg could bend and the pain was vastly improved. Where Safdar was impulsive and quick to anger, Adil was gentle and methodical. When he was fixing things, he was consumed by a total focus which shut out the constant low-level chaos of the house. A few years after Safdar had started work at the ambulance service, Adil got a job in the local market, repairing computers and mobile phones. Safdar – the eldest son – and their father sat him down and told him that the family did not need his earnings. Whatever he earned was his to keep. Safdar felt strongly that his brother, who was already so disadvantaged by his disability, should not have to take on the responsibility of caring for the family too. When he saw his brother set off for work, crutch under his arm, a wave of pride came over Safdar. Truly, Pashtun men were lions.

The ambulance drivers' shifts were long – typically eighteen, twenty-four or thirty-six hours – but that didn't matter, because the Edhi Foundation had become Safdar's second family. They would sit in the office under peeling paintwork, the fans whirring and moving the air around the room, drinking chai and smoking cigarettes as they idly chatted. On long breaks, some drivers napped, but Safdar didn't like the idea of lying on the stretcher. He took up chewing paan, enjoying the faint buzz it sent around his body.

Edhi, the head of the foundation, was usually in the office. In his free moments he was often immersed in conversation with his friend and colleague Kazmi. Their words about Lenin and the proletariat washed over Safdar, but he ached with admiration for this man who had started something from nothing. Edhi did not act like a high and mighty boss. He sat down with the drivers to eat, even though they were of a lower social status than he was. The foundation employed hundreds of drivers, but Edhi knew each one personally. He knew, for instance, that Chiri Babu was an excellent dancer and often asked him to perform a traditional Baloch dance. He would clap along for rhythm, cheering his appreciation. Edhi laughed easily, which was lucky given Safdar's penchant for practical jokes. Sometimes, egged on by Safdar, the drivers would take the small packets of nuts that Edhi liked to snack on and replace them with pebbles, or hide his hat.

'Yo, *Maulana* [a term of respect for someone pious or learned], what's up!' Safdar would yell when his boss arrived at the office.

Edhi would turn to Kazmi and say, 'Safdar is here. Take him away.'

It gave Safdar a warm sense of belonging.

In the mid-2000s, gang warfare in Lyari had erupted. After a certain time of night, Edhi drivers were not allowed to go to the areas worst affected by the violence. There was a high risk that it was a trap – that the drivers would be robbed, their vehicles stolen. Sometimes if a call came in from Lyari or Malir after 11 p.m., Safdar argued back, insisting that he knew the way and would drive quickly, and that it wasn't fair to make patients wait until morning. But this was one rule the foundation wouldn't bend.

After his first few call-outs, Safdar no longer worried about the sight of dead bodies. He got used to assessing a corpse's state dispassionately, thinking fast about how to solve the problem of lifting and transferring it with minimal damage. The first time he collected a dead body from Lyari on his own, without Chiri Babu's guidance, he concentrated hard on the physical navigation – driving through the knotted skein of streets, the apartment buildings packed so tightly that his vehicle could barely pass between them. He was collecting a victim of the gang war, a young-looking man pocked with bullets, his face frozen in an expression of horror, turning blue around the lips. Safdar lifted the corpse, put it in a shroud and transferred it onto the heavy metal-framed stretcher. He got back into the driver's seat and prepared to drive away. There was a banging at the window. A man pointed a gun at Safdar's face.

'Who are you?' he demanded. 'Where do you think you're taking this body? Is this your relative?'

Safdar spoke quickly, explaining he was only an ambulance driver and he had a responsibility to collect bodies.

'Whose side are you on?' the man demanded, but he lowered his gun and let Safdar pass.

Safdar drove quickly, his heart pumping. To his family, Safdar insisted that he was not afraid, that these no-good gangsters were as bad as terrorists. These cowards hiding behind their illegally procured guns were lower than the dirt on his shoe. He was not afraid. He was never afraid. But when his bosses said that he could not answer call-outs to Lyari in the middle of the night, he no longer argued back.

2

PARVEEN

They called it a slum, but Lyari was Parveen's home, in all its over-crowded glory. The area was as old as Karachi, not like the newer settlements that had sprung up on the periphery of the city as the population expanded. The history was there in the architecture – the tall and majestic old apartment blocks of a bygone era, painted in pastel colours with ornate but depleted plasterwork, like ageing aris-tocrats who had fallen on hard times. They stood cheek by jowl with squat concrete buildings, crammed in to accommodate a swelling populace, structures so close together that there seemed to be no gap between them at all. Some were topped with rusting corrugated-iron sheets held down crudely with bricks on each corner, others with half-finished plaster, the metal webbing still visible as if the buildings had been caught in a state of undress.

Throughout her teenage years, Parveen had seen street schools. One in particular stuck in her mind, a place she had spotted as she walked between two relatives' homes in the late 1990s. It seemed like a small oasis of order in an otherwise chaotic place. Students of all ages were squatting on a rug laid out on the street, squinting at the chalkboard through the afternoon sunlight and the clouds of dust kicked up by auto-rickshaws and motorbikes speeding past. The demarcations of the school were daubed onto the wall of the building behind it in paint, a crudely strung-up curtain on each side giving the impression, if not the actuality, of privacy. People crossed over the road to walk on the other side so as not to interrupt the lessons. In one form or another, street schools had been running in Lyari since the 1960s, free open-air teaching set up by the community to counteract endemic government neglect. Some kids were sent there to augment the teaching they got at underfunded government schools, or because their parents wanted to keep them occupied and away from drug dealers. Others – older teenagers, a few adults – had jobs as day labourers or in factories. Lyari was a poor area. Many people dropped out of school to work, only to find later that their career prospects were limited by illiteracy. Parveen, who had always wanted to do something for her people, knew she had to find out more.

In 2001, when Parveen was nineteen and had only just finished her own education, she got a teaching job. Although they called it a street school, the establishment on Lyari's Shah Baig Lane where she worked sat on top of a building a few storeys high, hemmed in by low perimeter walls and wooden boards painted bright green. From up here, you could see the familiar higgledy-piggledy buildings of Lyari stretching out on all sides. The school taught Urdu reading and writing, basic English and maths. Parveen loved teaching and finding out about her students' lives, but she also loved organizing and within a year she was involved in the day-to-day management of the school. Sometimes she and another teacher would take an auto-rickshaw out of the area, through the warren of congested alleys and under the cartoonish yellow arches that shouted WELCOME TO LYARI TOWN in English and Urdu. From here, the city opened out onto a wide freeway, a vast expanse of tarmac and cars, and they'd ride all the way to Urdu Bazaar, a hectic cluster of stalls and shops selling books and stationery on Muhammad Ali Jinnah Road. Here, they would seek out the second-hand stalls that stocked battered

textbooks, sometimes with pages missing or scrawls in the margins –
whatever they could find to supplement their teaching.

Nasir, a fellow teacher, caught Parveen's attention early on. She
noticed how he made the children laugh, how he always had a kind
word for everyone. But she also saw how the Urdu vocabulary stuck
in his mouth and tripped his tongue as he taught reading and writing.
Simple concepts seemed to vanish from his mind the moment he tried
to explain them. Nasir looked like a gangster, his passion for boxing
evident in his bulging biceps and broad chest, his dark skin draped
in fake branded T-shirts and jeans, but he had avoided the criminal
lifestyle that tempted so many of Lyari's young men. Parveen was
intrigued by him and they soon became good friends. Nasir told her
he had stayed in school till the tenth grade, hoping to get a job with
the Karachi Port Trust. Lyari was adjacent to the port, and the government jobs offered there, with their reliable salaries and permanent
contracts, were the area's best route to stability and relative prosperity.
Nasir had the qualifications, but time and again he had been refused.
His family was poor and didn't have the right connections. When he
talked about these thwarted ambitions, his face darkened with shame
and anger. That was how he ended up at the street school – he wanted
to keep busy and they always needed more hands on deck.

Every day for weeks, Parveen watched Nasir as he taught, hoping
he would improve. She felt a twinge of sympathy each time he
stumbled on his words or looked blank when he couldn't answer a
student's question, but she knew it wasn't right. The children should
not be getting substandard teaching, here of all places. This was how
it had always been for Parveen: the world was divided starkly into
right and wrong, and if she knew that a wrong was being done, it was
not a question of whether she should act, only when and how. This
compulsion had taken her into the homes of her students, arguing
that a girl should not be pulled out of school to get married before

she finished her education or that a son should not be sent to work before he had passed his exams. As a young teenager, Parveen had been disgusted by the piles of rubbish that gathered on the streets: potato peelings and banana skins turning brown in the sun, shiny plastic sweet wrappers that ripped and grew smaller but never actually decomposed, glass Pepsi bottles, plastic Mirinda bottles. Most people barely seemed to notice, and Parveen was just as bothered by the apathy as by the trash. She managed to convince a group of girls from her college to join her in a street clean-up mission, going out with brooms and sacks to collect the discarded debris. She felt a surge of pride as her neighbours, perhaps shamed into action, joined in. It hadn't lasted long. The very same people who had helped out one day were back to chucking their litter on the street the next.

But setbacks were no reason to stop trying to make Lyari better. As Parveen saw it, you had to try to do the right thing. And the right thing, now that she was in a management position at the street school, was to tell Nasir that he couldn't teach any more.

She waited till classes were done for the day, then asked him to come and talk to her. The evening sun beat down in a watery haze. Parveen looked out at the horizon. Other rooftops spread off into the distance, the grey concrete and brown rust of the corrugated-iron roofs broken up by bright snatches of colour of the billowing laundry strung up on rooftop washing lines. Plastic water tanks that perched on top of buildings stretched out like a string of bright blue jewels. Nasir looked nervous, his usually open and smiling face now tense.

'Nasir,' said Parveen, as gently as she could, 'you can't be a teacher, so what should we do about it?'

Nasir looked at her and nodded. He had known this was coming. His response was instant. 'I could open the school every day and clean up before the lessons start. When the teachers arrive, I could arrange tea for everyone.'

Parveen was surprised that he was suggesting his own demotion. 'You're willing to clean the school?' she asked, looking at his branded T-shirt.

Nasir nodded, looking almost relieved. It was agreed.

That evening, Parveen walked down the battered cement steps that led from the rooftop school to the bustling mayhem of Shah Baig Lane and began her journey home. When she was a child, she had hated walking to and from school on her own because of the men who made lewd comments or hung around on the streets smoking and selling *charas* (cannabis). In the eighth grade, Parveen had told her teacher, Miss Khan, that she was afraid to come to school. Every day for the next two years, until Parveen was moved to another class, Miss Khan walked her home, dropping her off before going on to her own place. It was people like her who made Parveen love Lyari: the feeling that if something bad happened, the community would reach out their arms to soften your fall. As she got older, the two most important men in her life, her father and *Mamoo*, her maternal uncle, had taught her to hold her head high and move with confidence even if she didn't feel it. Now, a young woman and a teacher, she walked to and from her job at the street school every day along narrow alleyways, between apartment blocks so close that it seemed you could put your hand out of the window of one and touch the building opposite. She wore her chador – a heavy cloth slung over her head that covered her down to her knees, the traditional dress for Baloch women – like it was armour.

Mamoo had one thing that Parveen's father didn't: education. When she was a teenager, he had given her books – Marx, Engels, textbooks on women's health. As Parveen read, the lines delineating right and wrong grew sharper and clearer. The fog of fear began to fall away and a righteous, towering anger took its place. She was angry when she saw the injustices perpetrated on women's bodies – her mother's friends, their bodies slack and iron-drained from multiple pregnancies. She was angry when she saw the bright young men she had gone to school with drawn in by the easy money and fast highs offered by the criminals who hung around on street corners, and angrier still that these drug dealers were allowed to do what they wanted in her area. The books gave her the language to express the inequities she had intuitively sensed all these years. Staying quiet soon ceased to be an option. The first time that Parveen really took a stand, she was sixteen. Her family had arranged a marriage for her elder brother Naeem. His wife, Saba, was younger than Parveen, a small teenager, young and slight and silent. She left school to be a wife and moved into their family house. Parveen watched in horrified silence as Saba struggled under the growing weight of her pregnant stomach. When the child was born with developmental problems, every fibre of Parveen's body throbbed with the injustice. She spoke to each member of her family separately.

'I might not be able to end child marriage in Lyari, but I can end it in my own house,' she said, her young voice steady and firm. 'If another woman in this family gets married earlier than she should, I will go to the police station myself and file a case against you.'

Parveen's father conceded immediately. He liked it when his daughters spoke up. Her mother was silent, which Parveen took as tacit approval. The biggest pushback came from *Nani*, her maternal grandmother. *Nani* had married off Parveen's own mother when she was just ten years old and twenty-five years younger than Parveen's father. It was an economic decision: *Nani* had been divorced and left with too many mouths to feed, and marrying girls off young was common practice.

In that case, it had worked out. Everyone agreed that Parveen's father was the kindest and most respectful man in the family. He had taken on responsibility for his young wife's relatives, making sure that her brother, Parveen's *mamoo*, had been able to get an education. *Mamoo* was a lawyer now, married to an educated woman. It was their influence that meant that Parveen and her younger siblings were raised with a more progressive ethos than her elder brother and sisters had been. This shift in values had indirectly led to this confrontation. But *Nani* was set in her ways and the history of her own decisions hung in the air, unspoken, when Parveen confronted her.

'You are threatening to send us, your own family, to a court of law?' *Nani* demanded, incredulous.

Parveen was almost surprised at how defiant her own voice sounded. 'Yes, *Nani*. You will be the first one I send.'

There were no more child marriages in the household.

Throughout Parveen's childhood, different women from the neighbourhood would visit her mother almost daily, sometimes sitting for hours, cross-legged on the floor, leaning against the cylindrical cushions that lined the walls as they poured out stories of abusive husbands and money troubles. Parveen's mother was gentle and caring and had a reputation as a good listener, someone who wouldn't judge. Parveen and her siblings – eventually, there would be seven of them, five girls and two boys – would squirm in boredom and discomfort as the women sobbed and ranted, but her mother never seemed to lose her concentration. 'Go and talk to your father,' she'd say, if one of the children was wriggling around in the corner too much and demanding attention. The children resented these women for taking up so much of their mother's time. But when she was alone, the women's words haunted Parveen – these stories of bad men, their violence and their urges.

The sense of omnipresent danger was palpable outside the house too. Parveen often felt uneasy in Kalri, the part of Lyari where she lived with her parents and siblings. The smell of *charas* hung in the air and boys lingered on the streets selling drugs – heroin as well as cannabis. Her father had built the house they lived in, a three-storey building, tall and thin, with a large step up from the unpaved street leading to an arched wooden door. Inside it was tiled in marble, with good-sized rooms, their doors lovingly carved from wood and with ornately beautiful metal grilles. Other relatives liked to joke at Parveen's father's expense: 'Usman built this big house, but he built it in Kalri!' On the narrow alley outside Parveen's house, the old neighbourhood women, sun-darkened skin deeply cracked with wrinkles, laid out rugs to sit on. Some smoked hookah pipes, sucking in deeply on the sweetly scented tobacco, the bubbling of the water adding to the background sounds of the chatter and movement that filled the streets. Others chopped onions, garlic, tomatoes and coriander for their evening meals. The smell of freshly cut herbs permeated the hanging miasma of stagnant water and decaying food scraps. Parveen would stop to greet her neighbours, their labour-worn hands rough to the touch, but the horrifying stories they had told her mother would always be in the back of her mind.

Sometimes Parveen wanted to escape from the closeness of it all, but Lyari was hers. She had grown up surrounded by local pride and it ran through her veins. *Karachi ki maa*, they called it: the mother of Karachi, the place where the city was born. Theoretically this was prime real estate, close to the port and a stone's throw from gro-tesque riches, the sparkling marble and high fences of Clifton and Defence. But Lyari had been neglected since long before Partition. The roads were narrow, barely paved, and everything was battered: the concrete bollards in the centre of the road, the weather-beaten fronts of apartment blocks. Yet despite the neglect, there was life in these streets. Each alleyway was a hive of activity. Hole-in-the-wall shops sold shoes, chai, pharmaceuticals, haircuts. Men walked with donkey carts stacked high with heaps of freshly chopped sugar cane or brightly coloured seasonal vegetables – carrots, onions, spinach. Carts selling snacks would drive around blaring out jingles from battery-powered loudspeakers: the cart selling *gol gappa* – a spherical fried crisp filled with a taste explosion of chickpeas in spicy tamarind water – always played a clip from an old movie song, 'Gol gappay wala'.

Parveen learned about politics from these rubbish-strewn streets, from the old men who gathered outside the chai hotels – so called, even though these tea shops did not have any guest rooms or beds. The old men would sit around plastic tables set up on the street, sometimes playing board games, while drinking cups of steaming chai, the sweet notes of cardamom, cinnamon and milk rising over the crowd, and sharing plates of spicy dhal slicked with oil, turmeric glistening yellow. The unspoken rule of these gatherings was that everyone should have read the political news so that they could analyse it together. Sometimes they even shared around a single tattered copy of one of the national newspapers, which were expensive to buy on their salaries. Shouting to be heard, the old men would give their interpretation of what the prime minister or home minister or provincial cabinet had said that day, and what they had really meant by it. More often than not, they'd argue about Baloch nationalism. Lyari was ethnically diverse but many were, like Parveen's family, originally from Balochistan, the neighbouring province – mineral rich but cash poor, home to a low-level separatist movement that had actually begun right here, in the heart of Karachi. Though most of them had been born in Lyari, they carried the wild frontiers of Balochistan in their hearts and cared passionately about its exploitation by the federal state. *Mamoo* had even spent time in hiding when he was younger, because of his involvement with the movement.

As the debates got heated, passers-by would gather round to listen, sometimes pitching in. There was no real hierarchy here and it didn't matter if you hadn't studied past primary school. From as far back as she could remember, Parveen loved to melt into these crowds and observe the debates. Sometimes she would speak up herself. 'One of our children is talking,' an old man said the first time she did so, shushing the crowd so they would listen. Her favourite times were when her father joined in, sometimes at the tables and benches set up outside his own shop, the Usman Ghazal Paan House. He sold not only paan here, but also snacks and chai, and at all times of day and night blasted out his favourite music, ghazals – Urdu poetry set to music, often used in film scores or sung by superstar performers. Sometimes the local hijras – transgender women – would gather outside to dance. Parveen's brother Naeem, who worked with her father at the paan shop and had the most exquisite voice, would sing for the dancers. That was usually late at night. Earlier on, the tables were mostly taken up by old men, swapping stories and debating. The way they wove their words together transformed any subject into a vivid blaze of colour, reminding Parveen of the Baloch folk tales she had grown up hearing. From the women at home to the men at the chai hotels, storytelling was so deeply embedded in their culture that sometimes it felt as if Lyari was built not from bricks and mortar but from stories.

Everything was so tightly packed in Lyari that there was even an intimacy to the criminality that lurked beneath the surface. Ghafar Zikri, the gangster who would end up controlling Kalri, the area around Parveen's house, lived just a few minutes' walk away. He was almost the same age as Parveen, an unremarkable boy she had only noticed in her childhood because he was so short. Rehman Dakait, or Rehman the Bandit, Lyari's most famous gangster, lived next door to Parveen's cousins in Kalakot, one of Lyari's more affluent neighbourhoods. His house was unimaginably grand – a smoothly plastered mansion behind a high wall, with an ominous balcony that looked like a military fortification looming over the street. According to Parveen's cousin Aisha, who shared the information in whispered tones, Rehman's house had seven rooms inside. Rehman had two wives and the second would often come over to drink chai with Aisha's mother, Parveen's aunt. She never volunteered much about her husband's work and no one ever asked her. Rehman was the most popular of Lyari's gangsters. Of course, he was shipping heroin and consignments of weapons – a business he had inherited from his father, formerly the area's top gangster – but the perception was that he invested in Lyari, and especially in Kalakot, his home. Aisha could reel off a list of neighbours who had been struggling to find cash to pay for household repairs, or a daughter's wedding, only to have Rehman quietly foot the bill. Parveen could not remember a time when Rehman had not ruled supreme. A truce with his father's main rival, Haji Lalu, had lasted throughout her teenage years and into her early adulthood, keeping the street wars mostly at bay. Parveen's parents talked with a certain nostalgia about times gone by, when gangsters fought with knives, not guns, and sold hashish instead of the heroin that came in shipments from Afghanistan, passing through port-side Lyari and on to the rest of the world. But everyone agreed that at least with Rehman in charge, the worst of the dirty business was mostly conducted outside Lyari.

It was in 2002, when Parveen was immersed in managing the street school, that the change came, a rupturing so abrupt that it threw into sharp relief how fragile the peace had been. A split between Rehman Dakait and Haji Lalu filled the streets almost immediately with the sulphurous scent of gunfire and the sharp staccato of shots and smashing glass. The parting of these two titans was like the shifting of tectonic plates, opening up a chasm under Lyari as lower-level gangsters saw an opportunity to assert their dominance over different clusters of streets. Suddenly, these were the only stories anyone was telling, and Parveen's friends and relatives shared every gruesome detail – some true, some false – of the gangsters' falling-out. The facts were shocking enough. It began with a quarrel over a kidnapping and a ransom payment, and escalated into all-out war when Arshad Pappu, Haji Lalu's son, desecrated the graves of Rehman's father and uncle, then kidnapped and murdered one of Rehman's relatives. Each personal act of violence and retribution between these men was enacted in their neighbourhoods. Narrow alleys became bloody battlefields. Different gangsters seized whichever streets they could. Ghafar Zikri, who ran Parveen's area of Kalri, was part of Arshad Pappu's faction, so it was impossible for Parveen to visit her cousins next door to Rehman.

Small children, some as young as seven or eight, were on the gangsters' payroll and loitered on street corners, keeping watch for rivals crossing into their territory. Others whizzed around transporting drugs, guns and payments on expensive bikes purchased for them by the gangsters. Once, walking home from school, Parveen saw a child she knew standing out in the searing sun, keeping watch. She felt the familiar force of her compulsion to speak. She went to find his parents to see if they knew what their child was up to. They were unconcerned, dismissing Parveen as if she was a madwoman. The father was a rickshaw driver. He told her that his already scant earnings were interrupted by the bouts of fighting and restrictions on movement, and besides, their son could make 500 rupees a day keeping watch or delivering packages. That was more than a rickshaw driver made even on a good day. It hurt Parveen to see children caught in this net of crime, but it hurt more when she understood that their parents were willing participants.

Though the familiar alleys on Parveen's route to school were now a mosaic of shattered glass and bullet casings, as long as there were children turning up to be taught she was adamant she would be there to teach them. By now the street school had relocated from the rooftop to the premises of a government school, where it ran its classes after hours. Nasir had adjusted quickly to his new role and Parveen respected him more and more each day, as she saw how hard he worked and the pride he took in doing his job well. Although he cared so much about his appearance, his muscles rippling under expensive-looking clothes, there was no real vanity to Nasir. If he experienced his demotion from teacher to menial support staff as a humiliation, he did not show it. He told Parveen what a good teacher she was. Before and after lessons, they would chat and laugh. 'I need to make my body strong. I need to build my body if I'm going to be a boxer,' he would say earnestly. Parveen made a point of ignoring the social conventions that restricted women's behaviour and she would jokingly demand that Nasir flex his biceps for her, sometimes kissing them and shrieking with laughter. He had an acute eye for women's clothes and would give her unasked-for feedback on her outfits. Parveen teased him, saying he was more interested in fashion and cooking than she was. He hit back that when he got married, he would expect Parveen to help select his bride's clothing.

The most nerve-racking time of day was in the evening, after classes had ended and the chalkboards were cleared away, when Parveen was ready to walk home. Ghafar Zikri had cemented his control over her neighbourhood and his boys stood watch on the network of streets around Parveen's home. They were armed with guns, often shouting intimidating comments or demanding to see the ID cards of any residents trying to pass through. Parveen recognized some of the boys – the sons of her neighbours, former students. At first, she refused to be afraid, walking as *Mamoo* and her father had taught her, with her head held high. She was so firm in her belief that these gun-wielding thugs were immoral and despicable that sometimes it felt as if nothing could touch her and she would be unable to stop herself from saying something, scolding them for disrespecting their elders or for taking the wrong path in life. When the winds of gossip carried stories of Parveen's behaviour back to her parents, they were alarmed, warning her to be careful.

Looking back on this time many years later, she told me she couldn't remember the exact moment that Nasir began walking her home every day. At first, she insisted she didn't need to be accompanied. 'I'll just walk behind you, then,' he said.

Nasir was on speaking terms with half of the boys standing out here in Kalri, linked to them by the tight bonds of lifelong friendship, even though he hadn't joined a gang. Sometimes he would shout a warning as they approached Zikri's boys: 'Get out of the way, hide what you're doing, *Baji* [older sister] is coming!' Other times, Parveen would turn around and see him waving his arms in the air in a silent gesture to alert them.

As they walked past the boys a sharp comment would sometimes fall almost inadvertently from Parveen's lips. But it was OK because Nasir was there to deliver Parveen to her door. Sometimes Nasir came in for tea or dinner. By now he was friends with the whole family and he liked to pay his respects to Parveen's mother, and to sit and discuss recipes with her sisters.

When they chatted before and after lessons at school, Parveen grilled Nasir about his friendship with the gangsters who lined her streets, demanding to know what they said about her behind her back.

Nasir laughed. 'They say, "Why does she have to scare us each and every day?"'

'And what do you say back?'

'I say, "You think you're scared? I have to work with her."'

That was on the good days. On the bad days, even Parveen had to admit defeat and stay inside the house. Then, the drumbeat of gunshots ricocheted around the narrow alleys, occasionally punctuated by the sound of distant voices shouting instructions or howling in pain. The streets were empty. Women chopped their vegetables inside, alone. The chai hotels were shuttered. The usual background noise of motorbikes revving and rickshaw engines chugging fell silent. There were no donkey carts selling fresh vegetables, no jingles from the snack sellers, no voices echoing around the streets. Occasionally, when Parveen peeped through the metal grilles that protected the insides of the windows in their house, she would see the figures of men darting between buildings, their bodies sometimes flattened against the wall to evade detection. She would see the flash of a gun or a small cloud of dust from a bullet or a fast-moving foot. But she didn't look out there too much. If you were spotted opening your gate to peer out, it might be seen as provocation. When she was stuck at home, Parveen worried about her students. Many had already lost relatives to the violence or to the gangs. Over a few short months, she had seen behavioural changes as formerly good-natured children became terse and withdrawn.

On days like these, when there was finally a break in the firing, the silence was so palpable that it seemed to have a physical form. Inside the house, Parveen and her family waited to see if the gunshots would start again. If they didn't, the tight drum of tension that had stretched over the area slackened in a collective sigh of relief. In the evening, the neighbourhood women would gather together at one of their houses and share chai and whatever food was left after days of being unable to go out and stock up – chalky biscuits in cheap, brightly coloured plastic wrappers or crunchy puri. Parveen and her sisters would join their mother as she sat with the neighbourhood women to compare notes. They would go over who fired the most rounds, which side had lost more lives, who was winning.

Parveen had grown up with these women and their voices were so familiar that they were soothing even if their conversation filled her with unease. They sounded as if they were discussing a football match, giving their post-game analysis and totting up the scores. Unlike the long evenings of Parveen's childhood when they would come, day after day, to confide in her mother about their personal upheavals, now that the whole area was practically up in flames there were no histrionics, no tears, apparently no fear, just matter-of-fact observations. This many dead today. These ones we knew. Those ones were strangers. Numbers, not people. Facts, not grief.

Throughout the violence, Parveen's father became more and more withdrawn. His paan shop had always been a 24/7 operation, but now, like so many other businesses, it stood closed for days on end. He spent an increasing amount of time at home, reading and shutting out the world around him. When he died of natural causes in April 2004, almost a year into the violence, Parveen felt that her whole world had shattered. Her father had been her defender, the one who supported her when she spoke out against injustice, the one who told her to shout back at the men who insulted her with lewd comments on the street. At the funeral, *Mamoo* cried harder for his brother-in-law than he had at his own father's death. Parveen was seized by stomach pains and dizziness, vomiting when she tried to eat. She lay in bed, the walls that her father had tiled spinning around her as time stalled.

Nasir visited her with some of the other boys who worked at the street school. They brought small cartons of the sweet, syrupy fruit juice that they knew Parveen liked and teased her about all the religious books she was reading. 'Have you replaced Marx with Islamic jurisprudence?' Nasir demanded, his tone light but disapproving. In her exhausted haze, Parveen was annoyed, but laughed despite herself. She sat with them and ate, and found that for the first time in weeks she did not throw up.

Grief enveloped Parveen's mother like a shroud. Although Parveen's father had said before his death that he did not want the women to wear white and mourn for forty days, as was customary, her mother stopped going out. For days at a time, it seemed, she would sit on the floor in the communal room, legs folded beneath her, slumped against the wall with only the cylindrical cushion for support, staring into space. She could not sleep at night. Parveen and her sisters would plead with her to eat something, to drink some water, but more often than not they got no response.

Outside the walls of the house, the conflict raged on. Unlike in days gone by, when Parveen could go to her relatives' houses in Shah Baig Lane to feel safer than she did in Kalri, now everywhere in Lyari was affected. The streets felt especially dangerous for women, with men making obscene comments and grabbing whoever they wanted. Parveen grew concerned for her sisters.

Around a month after her father's death, Parveen was sitting at home with her mother. Suddenly, her sister Noreen burst through the door and practically fell inside, screaming and shivering. Noreen was still a teenager, barely pubescent, but a man had groped her, right outside their home. Rage overwhelmed Parveen. She stumbled towards the front door, unlocking the metal grille, shouting at Noreen to point out the man who had done it. Parveen ran towards the man and grabbed him by the collar, hearing her own voice yelling, 'Do you want me to touch your crotch? How would you like it?'

Before she knew it, Parveen felt arms around her. It was Naeem and her mother pulling her back inside and away from the man's startled face.

Word spread quickly about Parveen's outburst. Whispers came via the neighbours that people were calling her a 'dangerous woman'. This filled Parveen with fresh fury. What made her dangerous, rather than the men who stared and grabbed? Noreen was too scared to go out, and when she did, she wore a burqa to cover her body entirely.

It had been a bad few weeks, with fighting between Ghafar Zikri's group and another gang in the web of streets around where Parveen's family lived. Each morning, the large concrete step outside their home was covered in bullet casings. The sisters took it in turns to sweep these remnants of battle away and onto the street below. One day, Samreen, who was between Noreen and Parveen in age, swept the step. She noticed the armed men who lined the street staring at her and tried to finish the job quickly so she could get back inside. The scarf loosely slung over her head slipped, exposing part of her chest. The men descended, grabbing at her as she screamed and ran back inside the house, slamming the metal gate behind her and, with shaking hands, securing multiple bolts and heavy padlocks.

Night fell, the starless sky clouded by dust and gunpowder. The electricity supply in Lyari was always patchy. Scheduled power cuts regularly plunged them into darkness and stopped the fan blades from turning. When the power went out around 8 p.m., as it always did for long stretches of the evening, darkness fell inside too. They switched on a battery-powered halogen light and placed it in the corner, illuminating the room with a watery blue tinge. There was a sound outside and Parveen peeked out of one of the windows. The men who had harassed Samreen earlier were gathered outside the house. 'We like that girl,' one of them yelled. 'Why don't you give her to us?' Parveen's heart beat fast. She checked and rechecked the padlocks and bolts. They barely slept that night.

When morning came, the gunfire ceased, giving way to silence. Nasir came over as soon as he heard what had happened. He listened to Parveen's account, his sweetly open face darkening in fury. He stood up abruptly, his stocky, muscular form seeming to take up more room than usual, and walked to the front door. He undid the bolts of the metal gate and pushed the door open.

'Listen up,' he shouted, as if to alert the whole street. 'Whoever fucks with the people in this house, watch out or I will fuck your mother.'

Every night for the next week, Nasir sat cross-legged on the concrete step outside the house, watching and waiting to make sure the men did not come back. If they approached, a stream of curse words gushed from his mouth and the men backed away. Rumours reached him that it had not been Zikri's boys who harassed Samreen but the rivals they were fighting off. When the immediate battle was won, Zikri's gang gave Nasir their word that no one would bother the sisters. But a seed of fear had taken root. The family began to talk more seriously about moving away from Lyari. When the topic had come up before, Parveen's mother had always steadfastly refused, but now she nodded when her children began to make plans. The streets had turned against them. Parveen's elder sister Nasreen was a nurse and could apply for government housing in Kiamari. This area, to the west of Lyari, stretched out along the coast, its ageing apartment blocks punctuated by rocky beaches and mangrove forests. Parveen felt almost feverish as she hatched these plans with her siblings, working out how they could orchestrate the move.

Whenever she could, she went to work at the street school. They were still running lessons, although on a much reduced scale and with smaller classes. One of her former pupils, a football enthusiast called Jango, had not only joined but was in charge of a gang, controlling some of the streets around Shah Baig Lane. Parveen felt a sinking sense of failure that she had not managed to save him through education. She and the other teachers tried to help their students as best they could, holding discussions about what was going on in Lyari and organizing social events to give the kids a break from thinking about violence. One of these, a picnic, was scheduled to take place at the beach outside Lyari a few weeks after Samreen was assaulted.

As the day approached, Parveen waited anxiously for signs of calm. The gunfire in her neighbourhood was so bad that it wasn't even safe to poke her head out of a window to see what was going on. She spoke on the phone to other teachers, who urged her to join them. 'The kids will really miss you,' they said. A bus had been hired to go round Lyari collecting people, but the shooting was too intense for Parveen to get safely to the bus stop. Besides, she had already drawn attention to herself when Noreen was attacked. Her family wanted her to lie low. On the day of the picnic, Parveen woke up feeling miserable and settled down with some reading. There was a knock at the door. She opened it and outside were two men – the founder of the street school and a stranger.

'We've come to take you to the picnic,' said the founder. 'Hurry up!'

Parveen was irritated. 'Are you crazy? Haven't you seen the shooting?'

The stranger looked her up and down. 'Hurry,' he said tersely. 'It's not a request.'

'Who are you?' Parveen demanded.

'Don't ask questions. Fetch your stuff and get out,' said the stranger.

The founder glanced anxiously at the street behind him before looking back at Parveen. 'Please, we don't have a lot of time.'

The decision had been made for her. Parveen put her shoes on, wrapped her chador tightly around her and stepped out onto the street. It took a few moments for her eyes to adjust to the sunlight after several days in the dim half-light of the house. Everything looked slightly different, slightly wrong. The narrow alleys were familiar underfoot, but were stripped of the people that made this area her home. In the near distance, Parveen could hear guns firing and bullets hitting buildings, together with the harried shouts of those in battle. As she walked behind the two men, she had the sense that she was watching herself through a glass. She did not know who the stranger was, but his rough manner, coupled with the ease with which they were passing through battle-strewn streets, made her absolutely certain that he must have gang connections. More than fear, Parveen felt shame and anger that she was walking in the care of a common criminal. She followed the two men, feeling like a prisoner of war.

When they reached the bus and Parveen jumped in, the other teachers and children cheered, delighted that she had made it. Parveen smiled, pleased to be there. But she could not shake her discomfort as they drove to the beach for the picnic.

'Who was that man?' she asked, as soon as she got the founder alone. 'Why was he sent?'

'Why ask?' he said in a joking tone. 'We just wanted you to join us. Come, enjoy the picnic.'

At the end of the day, the stranger returned to the bus stop to walk her home. Parveen had no choice. She acquiesced and walked with him.

The gunfire slowed to a halt that night. There was no telling how long the peace would last, but in the morning Parveen got dressed and went over to the school. There was to be a board meeting that day. All night, the questions had swirled around her brain.

'Yesterday you came to my house with a man I did not know,' she said to the founder, in front of the assembled board members. 'I have to ask you, who was that man, and why was it possible for me to reach the school despite all the fighting?'

An awkward silence fell. When the board members answered, they did not speak to Parveen, but about her.

'Parveen is emotional about Lyari and its deterioration,' said the founder. 'That's why she's asking so many questions.'

'It seems that Parveen is mentally disturbed,' said one board member.

'Perhaps she needs a break,' said another.

Parveen felt a surge of fury and humiliation pass through her body like an electric current. She would not allow these men the satisfaction of seeing her cry. She gathered all her energy. 'Maybe I do need a break,' she heard herself say. 'I won't come back for six months. You can divide my classes among the faculty.' Slamming down her pen and notebook, she stormed out.

Nasir, who had been in the next room, waiting to bring tea through to the board members, heard her voice and rushed after her, calling out her name. Parveen ignored him as she marched onto the street. She knew as she walked away from the school that she would never go there again. When she got home, the tears came – wrenching whole-body sobs. She cried for the job she had lost, for the father who had died, for the house that was no longer safe and for her disappointment in the people she had looked up to.

A few weeks later, Parveen's sister Nasreen heard that the apartment she was entitled to in Kiamari was available. It was time. They packed up their things and left Lyari.

3

SIRAJ

When Siraj started the Technical and Training Resource Centre (TTRC) in 1997, he rented a small shop on a high street. But the work soon expanded beyond the space and by 2002 he was looking for somewhere to settle permanently. He felt a pang of regret that his father had not lived to see him as the director of an organization with its own premises. *Abba* had been strict and wanted his sons to make a good living; he had never believed that this could happen through the social work to which Siraj was committed.

The new premises were in a modestly sized compound on a steep, bumpy alley off a main road. Like every other building in Orangi Town, it was built from concrete bricks, the colour of sand, which blended into the dust that billowed in the wind and clung to every surface. A metal gate separated it from the uneven road outside, and from the people and occasional goats that lingered there. Behind the gate was a small courtyard with a smooth concrete floor, surrounded by a low wall with shards of broken glass set into the top. There was nothing much of value here, but you couldn't be too careful – any street criminal with an allegiance to the Muttahida Qaumi Movement, the political party that dominated the area, could operate more or less with impunity, so it was best to avoid things being stolen in the first place.

Siraj's own office was a small, high-ceilinged room with a corrugated-iron roof neatly painted in white; a large, dark wooden desk – a gift from his former boss – sat in pride of place. The shelves were already stuffed with bulging cardboard files bound with string, while the filing cabinets were full of accounting books. Despite the chaotic appearance of the assorted papers, Siraj knew where everything was. He found written records reassuring: putting things down on paper meant you could prove they had happened. Documents were a vital line of defence against the tumult of the city.

The first time I met Siraj, over a decade after he had set up shop here, I got lost, which felt ironic on a visit to a map-maker. But I had never been to Orangi Town before and I couldn't find the right turning. Siraj is nothing if not a doer, so as soon as I called to explain, he jumped on his motorbike and drove around to find me and guide the car. Within minutes of parking up, he was deep into an explanation of the local criminal syndicates and the way they exploited the area, talking with the authority of a university professor. He often broke off to grab a specific document or diagram from the bundles of paper that surrounded him. I came to realize that this was how he made sense of his sometimes painful and chaotic surroundings: through evidence, order, information.

He showed me around the compound. The main room was fitted with a cluster of desks and computers, together with a large draughtsman's table, another gift from his former boss. On the walls were large, sketchily printed photographs of his mentors and former employers, showing them at work around the area. These people – Arif Hasan, Perween Rahman, Anwar Rashid – were pioneers who had both literally and figuratively put Orangi on the map: architects and planners who had got the area regularized and recognized by the authorities, in the process becoming famous for the way that they worked with the community. Siraj was trying to carry on this tradition. Alongside the photographs, the maps that he was working on with the TTRC were fixed to the walls with bright plastic tacks, the precisely drawn network of streets spreading out like a fine spider's web.

The office was in Ghaziabad, the part of Orangi where Siraj had spent most of his childhood and still lived. He told me that it was as familiar to him as his own skin: the houses made from unplastered concrete blocks with small slit windows to keep out the dust and heat; the higgledy-piggledy winding alleys, some of which looked as if they had been hacked out of the hills which made Orangi look so different from the rest of Karachi. Once, before the city had grown and swelled around it, Orangi had been at the very outskirts. Unlike Lyari, where the apartment blocks were so close together you could barely move, Orangi was punctuated by expanses of bare earth. For years, this had been the place where new arrivals to Karachi could find plots of land to call their own. The constant construction, as people built their homes on any spare inch of soil, meant that piles of rubble, brick and dust were a semi-permanent feature of the landscape. Clusters of people from all over the provinces that would become Pakistan were already living here when the Mohajirs came from India in 1947. But the area rapidly expanded after this point. Finding that no provision had been made for their arrival, many Mohajirs ended up in Orangi, carving a new settlement from the dust to replace the homes and businesses they had left behind. In the decades since then, as Siraj grew from child to adult, and Karachi's tentacles extended into the rural areas around it, Orangi had expanded so much that it was practically its own city, a web of bumpy *kacha* (untarmacked) roads and sharply angular buildings that looked like military pillboxes.

What Siraj loved about Orangi was that the people had built it for themselves. Most of the area's residents, his own family included, had been displaced from elsewhere. They did not have the ancestral ties to the soil that many people in Pakistan claimed, but they had still made it their own. Siraj himself had been born in Karachi, but migration was in his blood. After Partition in 1947, his family had uprooted themselves from their home in Bihar, India, to join the new Muslim homeland in Pakistan. Initially, they settled in the flat and humid landscape of what was then East Pakistan, but tensions steadily rose between Urdu-speaking migrants like Siraj's family and the local Bengali population, who were badly discriminated against by the West Pakistani central government. This culminated in a brutal civil war in 1971, which Siraj had grown up hearing about from his parents and grandparents. They spoke of the gnawing fear they had lived with, the crumbling of the world they had built. His maternal grandfather, *Nana*, had been a railway worker in East Pakistan. When the violence broke out, Urdu-speakers were targeted. One day, while *Nana* was out buying groceries, he was set upon by an angry mob. They killed him and dumped his body in the river. *Nani*, Siraj's maternal grandmother, told him that over the course of the war so much blood was spilled that the river ran red.

In December 1971, East Pakistan became the independent state of Bangladesh. What was once known as West Pakistan became simply Pakistan. Siraj's family was displaced for a second time. They arrived in Karachi to find a region that was not equipped to deal with them, or even willing to acknowledge their existence, despite everything they had already sacrificed in the name of Pakistan. Rather than being viewed as citizens, they were treated as newcomers. Many had problems getting official documentation and some were never able to get full Pakistani citizenship. There was no resettlement support or housing for the refugees from the Bangladesh war. Siraj's family, like so many others, were on their own. At first, the family lived in a rented house in Korangi, an industrial area of Karachi where

Siraj was born. A few years later, they bought a small plot of land in Ghaziabad and moved there in the early 1980s to construct their own house.

At first they built just one room, with an adjoining bathroom. Siraj's mother carefully cut hessian flour bags into sheets and stitched them together to create a makeshift awning that they erected on bamboo poles to cover a temporary kitchen. Under the shade this gave from the sun, Siraj's mother would make roti over a wood fire. At that time, different ethnic groups lived more or less side by side. The local Pashtun community controlled the building industry, running small brick factories that produced the ubiquitous concrete bricks used in the area. Siraj's eldest brother, Shamsuddin, was friends with one of these brick makers, who let the family have some on credit to hasten the construction of their home. Gradually, more rooms were added.

Because Orangi was an unplanned settlement, where waves of migrants to the city had simply built their homes with no regulations or support, there were no amenities. This meant it was not connected to mains water, electricity or gas supplies. At night, residents filled glass bottles with kerosene, dropping in a lit scrap of jute to create an improvised lamp. The pungent, oily smell rose over the area as night fell. The lamps gave the new homes a warm glow, but they were hazardous: once, Siraj's mother knocked one over and the hot kerosene splattered across her arm, permanently scarring her. Later, the area pooled their resources to buy a diesel generator which gave them some electricity in the long evening hours. It was shared between many families, so despite its loud clattering, it didn't give a huge amount of power to each household – sometimes only enough for a small tube light at Siraj's home. They would place it strategically in a doorway or on top of a wall so that it partially illuminated two rooms. In the evenings, Siraj did his homework in this half-light, fixated even as a child on order, routine and the importance of getting things done. When the generator wasn't working, he waited until the morning, using the hours between dawn prayers and the start of school to complete his assignments before setting off for his lessons on foot.

The lack of amenities gave the days and weeks a certain familiar rhythm. The family had two bicycles and every afternoon after school Siraj and one of his brothers (they were eight siblings, five boys and three girls) would hang blue jerrycans on their bikes and cycle off in search of water. There were public taps at the corners of some streets and they'd stand in line here to fill the cans. Sometimes, if the queues were particularly long, they'd go to the house of one family friend or another who had managed to dig a well near their home. They'd fill up there and cycle back to the house, jerrycans clanking against their bikes, trying not to splash too much water.

Shamsuddin, or Shamsu as he was known by the family, was eighteen years Siraj's senior. He had come to Karachi later than the rest of the family, having fought during the civil war with a pro-Pakistan militia and been held for several years in Bangladesh as a prisoner of war. During that time, Siraj's parents did not know if Shamsu was dead or alive. He emerged from captivity and arrived in Karachi with outlandish stories about his time in prison: he claimed that they had lived like kings, eating chicken *salan* (a tomato-based stew) all day, and that to entertain themselves the prisoners came up with ever more inventive ways to torment the guards. Within a year of arriving in Orangi Town Shamsu seemed to know everyone. He organized people in the community to demand better services. He worked the night shift in different factories, which freed up his days to agitate for change. He ran a small welfare association with some friends. They never registered it formally and used their own money to help people when necessary. He would sit at the chai hotels whenever he wasn't at one of the factories and make connections. Siraj knew from the way they greeted Shamsu when he moved around Orangi that people respected him, but he had only the vaguest understanding of what his brother did – something to do with getting people connected to water and electricity. When some locals rigged up wires to tap into the mains electricity supply in an adjacent area, Shamsu was not satisfied. He repeatedly wrote to Karachi's electricity board demanding that they put his part of Orangi Town on the grid. 'I am not a thief,' he would insist. 'I want to pay my bill.' His battle with the electricity board took eleven years of writing letters and pushing for meetings in the stuffy offices of local bureaucrats. But he did eventually get the area connected. The government erected the pylons and Shamsu organized local residents to pool their money for the cables to connect them. Electricity lines were strung up above the houses, a tangle of wires looping between tall poles, black lines etched across the sky. Through changes like this, life in Orangi had gradually improved. Now the houses had running water and mains electricity, at least some of the time. Gas cookers replaced the wood fires.

In spite of the respect Shamsu commanded in the area, their father was constantly berating him, particularly when he spent his own money on local improvements. 'How long are you going to live off your father for?' he would say. 'For God's sake, earn some money. Please let me help you set up a shop.' Siraj could see his father's point: his brother often struggled for cash. But he still admired Shamsu's selflessness, his hard work and his high status in the community.

It had never been in question that Siraj would finish school. If there was a single value that defined their community, it was a belief in education. There was a phrase he often heard repeated: 'Even if you can't put three meals on the table, get an education.' But in the mid-1990s, in his twelfth and final year of school, Siraj was drifting, uncertain about what he wanted to do with his life. The lessons were taught by strict old men who seemed to care more about scolding students than actually teaching them anything. Siraj heard about some boys from the neighbourhood going to Saudi Arabia and making a lot of money, so he'd begun to talk about that, without really knowing what it would entail. His father did not like the idea at all. Knowing that Shamsu was the person most likely to change Siraj's mind, he quietly asked him to intervene.

That was how Siraj found himself standing outside the office of the Orangi Pilot Project (OPP) one hot day in 1994. Motorbikes revved on the bumpy road and the sun beat down over heaps of uncollected rubbish and the haze of construction dust. The occasional elaborately painted truck roared past, a streak of colour through a monochrome vista. Siraj had brought a friend with him for moral support. He knew that Shamsu worked with the OPP, helping to coordinate their work in Orangi, but he also knew the people at the top were from outside the area and he imagined that they would be grand. The door opened and they were ushered in. Although they had not called ahead to make an appointment, they were taken straight to the director's room. A small woman wearing rimless glasses and a serious expression sat on a wooden chair, trying to bash a protruding nail at the side back in with a paperweight. This was not what Siraj had imagined. In fact, nothing in the room matched his expectations. There were none of the expensive trappings that he had anticipated: no glass door, no air conditioning, no servants hovering around.

'Excuse me, *sahiba* [madam],' said Siraj.

The woman looked up and smiled. The boys introduced themselves and explained that they were from the local area and had come on Shamsuddin's recommendation to find out more about the organization's work.

'Of course,' she said. 'Young people should always be interested in these things. I'm so glad you are here.'

The boys sat down and, for the next twenty minutes, the director – whose name was Perween Rahman, though she would always remain Sahiba to Siraj – explained the work they were doing at the OPP. She told them about how they had worked with local people to lay sewage lines, gathering small amounts of money from the community to get the funds together instead of waiting for money or permission from the government. She told them that the OPP provided the technical information – the angle of incline necessary to make the sewage flow downhill – but the street-by-street digging was done by the people themselves. '*Chota am, burra kam*,' she repeated, a phrase meaning 'The little man can achieve big things.' The best projects involved bringing in members of the community, she said – someone like her should only ever be a teacher, giving people the tools to help themselves. She told them that the OPP was mapping the area so that they could show the government what was here and get the services they needed. 'A map is like an X-ray,' she said. 'It lets the doctor see where the problem is.'

Siraj had never given sewage much thought, although throughout his early childhood disposing of human waste was an ever-present challenge and a cause of anxiety for the adults. In the absence of central systems, some people had concrete sewage tanks underneath their houses. A municipal truck came and emptied it once a month, for a cost of twenty-five rupees, the acrid stench filling the air. Others had tanks with permeable walls that allowed the waste to seep into the earth around it. Still others used the 'bucket system', where people relieved themselves into a pot that could then be passed through the bathroom to a ledge outside. Every day, someone would empty all the pots in that area. 'We are not dirty people,' Shamsu said once, in a characteristically blunt tone. 'We even keep our shit safely in boxes.' Siraj remembered walking through Rig Colony, one of the areas that used the bucket system, on a day when the guy who collected the waste wasn't on duty. Residents had protested and refused when he tried to raise his rates, so he had decided to show them how much they needed him by taking the day off. The area was a mess. Flies buzzed over the slowly baking faecal matter, the smell overwhelming the senses. The residents soon agreed to pay a higher rate.

When Sahiba explained the lack of resources and the push to get these basic amenities for Orangi, it was as if someone was putting words to Siraj's experiences for the first time. He left the meeting excited about what he had learned. As he sat in his unengaging lessons at school, Siraj thought of how Sahiba had spoken to him so candidly and wondered if there was a different way to learn. When he returned to the OPP after a few weeks, Sahiba greeted him as if he was already part of the team. She told him to stick around. 'This is a place where you can ask anyone whatever question you like,' she told him. 'People will always have time for you. But at first just observe and learn. Always look at what someone is doing, how they are doing it and, most importantly, why they are doing it.'

He started to spend almost every day at the office, watching people work. He was captivated by the precision of what they did. The draughtsmen worked on large tables, drawing diagrams of the streets outside. They mapped out areas of Karachi that had long existed in concrete reality but not on any city plans, in the process helping them to get connected to water and electricity services. Alongside this work, the OPP's architects gave practical advice to residents on how to modify their homes or schools. Siraj was particularly taken with the housing work; even years later, he vividly remembered the first time he was allowed to carry out a survey himself – he could still recall the exact dimensions of the house and the name of its owner. As Siraj watched the architects and draughtsmen work, the idea of moving to Saudi Arabia faded away entirely. The allure of the new and exotic dissipated, to be replaced by the deep satisfaction of making sense of the familiar.

Under Sahiba's guidance, he joined the OPP as a trainee. But within a few years, she began urging him to set up his own organization, despite the fact that he was still so young. For months, Siraj ignored the suggestion, preferring to stay with his mentors. Eventually, she had sent him packing with the large, dark wooden desk and a draughtsman's table, telling him that he would only be able to fulfil his potential if he started something of his own. And that is how he came to found the TTRC. Siraj described himself as a community architect, or – borrowing the term that both Sahiba and Shamsu liked to use – a 'social teacher'. When people were building their homes room by room, as his own family had once done, Siraj could advise them on how best to keep the heat out, or to stop the wind blowing dust in through the windows. Although he now ran an independent organization, he still worked closely with the OPP, sometimes carrying out their work on the ground and helping with mapping or surveying projects around the city. The success of the OPP in Orangi had made their work famous and Siraj started working on projects all over Pakistan.

Siraj was matter-of-fact about the limitations of what he did; he knew that getting an area mapped and recognized could achieve only so much. Although parts of Orangi were now connected to the mains supplies and, at least in Ghaziabad, people no longer had to cycle off with jerrycans for water, things were far from straightforward. For days or weeks at a time, the taps in every home or office would run dry. Then at regular intervals – in some areas every ten days, in others every fifteen and in the most unlucky only every thirty or forty – the local water board would open the valves that allowed water to flow. As soon as word spread that the water was on, Siraj and his family would twist the long-unturned taps. There would be spluttering and groaning as water gushed through the dry pipes and the frenzy to fill up water tanks would begin. Merely turning the tap wasn't enough. Most people had at least a basic suction pump. The next step up was a double pump. The biggest type – owned only by people with a lot of disposable cash – was actually designed for use on ships. You could spend a whole day trying to collect enough in your tanks to make sure you had water to last until the next time it came on. Recently, in Ghaziabad, the water had been coming on every ten days or so, which wasn't too bad – although often it felt like someone was playing a cruel joke on them, because the water would be on for ten or fifteen minutes, then, just as you were in full flow with your suction pumps, go off again for an hour. Siraj was so used to the water shortages that he could see the funny side. If the electricity was off in those precious moments when the water flowed, people would desperately plug suction pumps into their motorbike batteries, revving the bikes again and again to power them up. Things had moved on since Siraj's childhood, when he had to cycle to collect water, but people were still using bikes to access it.

By the time the TTRC was fully established, Siraj was well into his thirties, married with children. His relationship with his eldest brother had developed into a close friendship. On the face of it, the two men were very different. Shamsu was forceful and dramatic, often sounding as if he was addressing a public rally even in private conversation. He was sometimes crude in his humour and spoke Urdu with the sing-song lilt of Bihar, their ancestral home. He was most comfortable in a traditional white salwar kameez and prayer cap, and blended in as he travelled around on fieldwork in different localities in Orangi. He no longer needed to work all night in the

jute factory because the OPP paid him a wage to mobilize people for
their projects. Siraj was quiet and steely – just as firm in his opinions
as his brother, but with a more muted manner. For the most part,
he dressed in crisply pressed Western-style shirts and trousers, even
in the blaring heat. Although this was the professional uniform of
the city's aspiring middle classes, it meant he sometimes stood out
when he was in the field. But Siraj barely noticed this – as far as he
was concerned, he was simply part of the community he was serving.
He spoke Urdu with a neutral Karachi accent, except when he sat
up late at night talking with his brother – then the Bihari cadence
emerged. This was the best part of family gatherings for Siraj, after
the meal was finished, when he and Shamsu would sit over extra-
sweet chai and salted cumin biscuits, swapping ideas, voices rising in
debate, teasing each other, sometimes laughing so hard they couldn't
breathe. As soon as they started to talk about work, other members
of the family would leave the room, sometimes muttering about how
boring the discussions were for everyone else.

In spite of their apparent differences, the two brothers shared
many of the same views. They often repeated Sahiba's advice on how
to do community work: 'Suno, samjho, sikhao [listen, learn, teach].'
Shamsu made Siraj laugh recounting the story of the time, early on
in his work with the OPP, when he had complained to the organization's founder, Dr Akhtar Hameed Khan – whom they called Dr
Sahib (sir) – that people had sworn at him while he was working in
a particular neighbourhood.

'Do you think people should bow down to you and give
you enthusiastic salams [greetings]?' Dr Sahib had replied, in
Shamsu's telling.

'No, no,' Shamsu had protested. 'I don't want people to bow
down. But they talk shit about me – they use curse words.'

'You should be happy that people curse at you,' Dr Sahib had told him. 'People know that they can curse at you, because they don't see you as a thug or a gangster. They don't think you are more powerful than them. And to work in the community, you need to be their equal.'

Orangi Town had no shortage of thugs and gangsters. Everyone knew that you didn't want to get on the wrong side of the Party. Ever since it had emerged in the 1980s out of an angry student movement, the MQM and its charismatic leader, Altaf Hussain, had dominated local politics. At first, their messages had sounded good. During the ethnic riots of the 1970s, 'Mohajir' had coalesced as a common political identity for people who spoke Urdu as a first language and had migrated from India. The MQM promised to end the quota system that unfairly kept Mohajirs out of government jobs and universities. But their rhetoric about equal rights quickly hardened into something else. As the Party sought and gained political power in Mohajir areas, they tightened their territorial control. Young men wielding guns patrolled the streets as if they were running their own parallel state. Every family had a member who had joined – boys abandoning their schoolbooks to pick up guns, all for the promise of influence. There were even slogans daubed on walls around the area that made this trade-off explicit. One of the most common read: 'Sell your VCRs and buy weapons.' In 1992 the army instigated Operation Clean-up in response to the violence between Mohajirs and Pashtuns that was spiralling out of control across Karachi. In practice, it was essentially a crackdown on the MQM, intended to stop the Party from operating as a state within a state and to reassert government control. Officers uncovered the MQM's torture cells, bone drills and huge caches of guns. But Operation Clean-up was indiscriminate, the violence worsening over the two years that it ran. Tanks rolled into Mohajir areas and thousands of people were slaughtered. Men were rounded up, based more on their ethnicity and where they lived than on their involvement with politics. The MQM leadership was forced into exile; Altaf Hussain moved to London in 1992 and never returned, though he continued to run the Party remotely. The MQM suffered a brief dip in electoral support and, for some time, the most visible signs of their street power disappeared: there were no armed men patrolling outside their offices. But the Party had never really gone away. If anything, the harshness of the response had encouraged support from people who felt victimized by the state. Over the years that followed, the MQM continued to win seats across Karachi, wherever the Mohajir population was concentrated. When the military dictator Pervez Musharraf became president in 2002, he gave the MQM free rein in Karachi in return for their support. After that they were as powerful as they had ever been.

Now the Party was unassailable in Orangi Town, but this was Karachi and if Siraj knew one thing it was that anything could change at any moment. This was sometimes a worry, because the most important aspect of his work was consistency. Improving an area was not just about what you built or the maps you drew, but about your relationships with people, and those could be maintained only if you put in time and effort. The people of Orangi Town all had their ways of working around the constraints imposed by the Party, which had eyes and ears everywhere. In the streets around the MQM's offices, foot soldiers stood guard – often boys who had dropped out of school in pursuit of glory. In these more sensitive areas, getting a measuring tape out to map an area was unthinkable, since it looked highly suspicious. Sahiba had always told him, 'Think flexibly.' If he couldn't use his usual tools, he could still get an approximate idea of the size of a house or street by measuring his own stride and counting the number of steps it took to go past. So as the Party's iron grip tightened, that was what Siraj did.

Sometimes it felt as if the Party became more powerful and Orangi's different ethnic communities became more divided with every year that passed. Sahiba talked about the political parties that fought violently over the area as *peela naag* (yellow snakes) and *kala naag* (black snakes). The Awami National Party, which represented Pashtuns, were the yellow snakes and the MQM, which represented Mohajirs, the black. 'The black snakes are more dangerous than the yellow, but they're all snakes,' she would joke. When Siraj thought back to his childhood, he remembered the Pashtun brick makers who had given credit for materials to Mohajir families like his. The Pashtuns had a monopoly on the transport industry too back then, but he didn't remember it being a source of resentment until the MQM came onto the scene. He recalled days out with his family at Manora Island, a popular picnic spot some thirty kilometres away. Reaching the long sandy beaches and mangrove forests was like stepping into another world. They would catch the red government bus part of the way, then change to a privately owned yellow van. Both were always driven by Pashtuns. Once the MQM was in the ascendant, they told people to stop taking these buses and heavily promoted alternative, less reliable private coaches and motorbike taxis, so now even taking the bus was a political act. With each wave of violence, people became more divided. When anti-Mohajir riots in the neighbouring city of Hyderabad displaced hundreds of people in the 1980s, they moved to the Mohajir areas of Orangi, as did the steady drip of Urdu-speakers leaving Bangladesh. When people began to migrate in their tens of thousands from the mountainous region in Pakistan's north-west, they flocked towards the more heavily Pashtun areas – some of which were in Orangi. In this way, the demographics changed, hastened by each tragedy. When there were outbreaks of violence between Mohajirs and Sindhis, or Mohajirs and Pashtuns, people retreated into areas populated by others like them. The invisible lines separating people of different ethnicities became more obvious, sometimes physically demarcated on a map, where a single road might mark a sharp division. The Manghopir Road, a wide, traffic-choked thoroughfare in Orangi, was an example: on one side were the Mohajirs and on the other the Pashtuns.

Since the MQM had come to power in Orangi, people no longer had access to local government employees at the electricity or water boards, and the kind of activism that Shamsu had once done – personally lobbying for a power supply by repeatedly meeting local bureaucrats – was impossible. Instead, anyone with a complaint had to go to their local MQM unit, small party offices which were overseen by more senior bodies, known as sectors. Those party workers would solve the problem on your behalf – if you were loyal to the Party, or if they wanted something from you. Otherwise, you were stuck.

Siraj always liked to think in terms of solutions, but when Shamsu told him that he was being harassed by the Party, Siraj was stumped. For many years, Shamsu had sat on the board of a small local mosque. In the days before running water, he and the rest of the board sometimes arranged for tankers of water to be delivered there so that people could fill their jerrycans. Later, they used the mosque's loudspeakers to let people know when the water valves for the area had been opened, so they knew to switch their taps on. Shamsu told Siraj that someone from the Party had been to see him several times, complaining about access to one of the streets near the mosque. They had ordered Shamsu to destroy parts of the building to allow cars to pass through the intersection.

'I told them that I did not construct the mosque and I am certainly not going to demolish it,' Shamsu said. 'I told them, "It's an old mosque and you should talk to the people who built it." They insisted. They said, "You are going to pull this building down with your own hands.""

Shamsu openly supported the Pakistan People's Party and had never tried to hide that fact. The MQM didn't care about access to the street. They were making a statement, letting Shamsu know that his political views were not acceptable and that even religion wouldn't protect him. Siraj had rarely known his brother to back away from a fight, but this one seemed futile. Shamsu quietly stood down from the mosque committee a few weeks later.

The MQM was an inescapable, claustrophobic feature of life, its power even superseding that of religion. It was a tradition on Eid al-Adha, the smaller of the two Eid festivals, to sacrifice a goat, and Orangi – like the rest of Karachi – would turn into a meaty bloodbath, the bleating of the animals punctuated by the thwacking of axes, the smell of fresh raw flesh from people's yards mingling with the scent of cumin, garlic and frying meat from inside the houses. Most families would make *haleem* – a heavy porridge-like stew of lentils and slowly cooked meat, topped with slices of fresh ginger, green chilli and fried onions. There was always an excess, and whatever was left would be packaged and sent to the poor. The men of the house would dispose of the animal hide. Although this was a religious event, there was sometimes a small profit to be made by selling the goat skin to a local tannery – at least enough to go towards the cost of next year's sacrificial goat. But then the MQM had started hammering on the door during the Eid meal to demand that the skins be handed over. 'Give us the *bakri* [goat] skin, or I will skin you,' Siraj remembered one young man demanding, eyes bulging out of his head, gun in hand. Soon it was simply accepted that this was what would happen to the hides, and that any profit to be made from the tanneries would be for the Party and the Party alone.

As the MQM's stranglehold on Karachi's politics tightened, enabled by Musharraf, resentment grew among parties representing other ethnic groups and they protested against what they called 'state capture'. When Musharraf's grip on power began to slip in 2007 and the Pashtun population of Karachi increased with waves of migration from elsewhere in the country, the violence escalated. Sometimes the MQM would call a strike. This meant a total shutdown of the area, with MQM workers riding around Orangi Town on motorbikes, firing into the air to warn people to go home. If any shopkeepers stayed open, MQM thugs would burst in and tell them, 'Close your shop now, or stay closed forever.'

To Siraj, the situation felt so febrile that he was worried it would break into all-out war at any moment. When Musharraf's government fell and a new election in 2008 chipped away at the MQM's control, giving some provincial seats to the ANP, the battle for control of the city began in earnest. With the constant threat of strikes or random outbreaks of violence, it didn't seem worth the risk of the family going out to the cinema or for a meal in the evening. Their world constricted. Siraj focused on his work. One of the things he had in common with Sahiba was an almost single-minded focus on getting things done. Often, like her, he forgot to have lunch and would carry on working – either in the office or travelling around the area to catch up with contacts – long after everyone else had gone home and night was falling. Sahiba's attitude had always been that if you could get to work, then you had to be there. She herself lived outside Orangi, over an hour's drive away, so if she made it in when locally resident employees didn't, she was unimpressed. Siraj followed her example and clung to his routines. Occasionally, the gunfire was so heavy that he would tell his young staff to stay at home, but mostly they continued. Countless meetings took place with the staccato drumbeat of gunfire reverberating in the air outside the OPP office. The violence was quickly normalized; they came to call less intense outbreaks *hulki phulki* (lightweight) firing, a phrase more often used to describe a light snack or pop music than running gun battles.

When others at the OPP or TTRC did not want to go on field trips, Sahiba gave Siraj the bus fare and asked him to go. He never thought twice about whether it was safe, or whether he needed more secure transportation. These were his streets and the day he decided to stop using them his life might as well be over. If the people he was working with had to take the bus to get around, then he would too. Some months after the 2008 election, Siraj got on a bus to go home. The bus driver reminded him of the elders of his childhood: he was a Pashtun with a kindly face. Siraj paid his fare and nodded a greeting. Most of the other passengers were Urdu-speaking like him and it struck him that no one here had any issue with the bus driver. They all just wanted to live their lives. He stared out of the window, tired. It had been a long day.

He was almost home when the smell of diesel and gunpowder filled the bus. On the street outside, MQM workers were firing into the air and revving their motorbike engines as they drove around, warning people they were calling a strike. Suddenly the atmosphere on the bus became so tense that it was almost electric. People ducked beneath their seats and others ran down the aisle to push their way off. The gunshots were a half-hour warning for the streets to be cleared. Siraj looked up. He was most worried about the driver. He had heard stories of Pashtuns who did not make it home in time being shot on sight. It was a particular risk for bus drivers. Even if they did abandon their passengers and planned route, they were stuck on a slow-moving vehicle in lanes of stationary traffic as people tried to flee to their houses.

The driver leaned back towards the shrieking people on the bus. 'Please, sit down,' he shouted, in Pashto-accented Urdu. 'It is my responsibility to get you home. I will drop you at the right place.'

Tension grew in Siraj's stomach as the bus inched along to its planned stop. As he got off, he thanked the driver, who nodded nervously and looked at the road ahead. A few days later, Siraj heard that the driver of his bus had been killed before he made it home. It was just one death among hundreds, but it hit Siraj hard. He could think of only one thing to do. He sat down at the desk that Sahiba had given him and continued to map.

4

JANNAT

Driving down a dirt track so bumpy that the car swung wildly from side to side, I couldn't quite believe that I was still, technically, in Karachi. All around me was arid scrubland, covered in low thorny bushes and thick-stemmed cactus plants. It bore little resemblance to the flyovers and apartment blocks that made up the rest of the city. Once, this had been agricultural fields, but as more and more people flooded into Karachi through the 1960s, 1970s and 1980s, construction boomed in an unregulated mess. Quietly, the gravel and sand had been stripped from this district – Kathore – and other agricultural areas around the city. Over time, the soil had been left dry and stony, and near impossible to cultivate.

On this vast expanse of land to the east of Karachi, each settlement was far apart, remote. We eventually pulled up at our destination, a small village of a few hundred people called Lal Baksh Kachehlo Goth (*goth* means village). As I got out of the car, women and girls thronged around me, eager to introduce themselves to a newcomer. I noticed Jannat immediately. She was just as excited as everyone else to meet a stranger – an unusual occurrence – but her manner was more reserved. She pointed at my dictaphone. 'What's that for?' she asked. Before she opened up to me, she wanted to make sure that I wasn't going to use her words against her.

Later, Jannat told me that until it was time to go to secondary school, she had never really considered that there was a world outside the village. It was everything she knew and all the people she loved were here. Besides, as the village elder, Shafi Muhammad, often told them, this was their land. They were free here, and they should treat the land like their mother – with love and respect. Everyone who lived here was, like Jannat, a Kachehlo, a member of the same Sindhi tribe. They had been on this land for hundreds of years; their parents, grandparents, great-grandparents and great-great-grandparents were all buried here. The village even bore their name, although they usually abbreviated it to Lal Baksh. Like all the villages in this district, Lal Baksh was technically part of Karachi, but there was still barely any electricity, no running water, secondary school or doctor's surgery. However, this was home and, at least back in her childhood days, Jannat had felt safe here. She did not know then that one day the city that had rendered their land practically unusable would threaten to flatten their village altogether.

Everyone in Lal Baksh was related to each other to some degree, and on my visits there the younger girls would shriek with laughter as they tested me on whether I had remembered the multiple layers of relationships. The tradition was to marry within the extended family – first or second cousins – which meant that each person was bound to every other person in three or four different ways, the threads of these different connections plaiting together to form an unbreakable bond. Each family unit had their own home in the village – angular concrete structures, usually just one room, two or three for the more affluent – but no one ever closed their doors. Jannat's own childhood home had a few rooms. She shared one with her mother, her sister Bushra and her brother Rizwan. In the other rooms were their paternal grandparents, *Dada* and *Dadi*, and her two paternal uncles. Jannat's father had died in 1999, when she was just six years old, the same year General Musharraf seized power and returned Pakistan to martial law. Jannat had been so small when her father died that she could barely remember what he even looked like. If she tried to conjure up his image, she found there was a blur where his face should be. All she had to go on were the words of others. Shafi Muhammad and her uncles told her that her father had been very intelligent and particularly good at maths. She knew that he must have been clever, because he was a teacher at the big school in Kathore – the largest village in the area, about ten kilometres away. Working at a government school was the best possible job opportunity locally. It meant you were a public employee, with a regular salary and a permanent contract. Jannat's father had worked at the school for nine years before he died. Later, they realized that he must have been sick for a long time, as the hepatitis worked its way through his body and caused the fatal liver damage that killed him. He did not go to see a doctor until it was too late. The doctor in Kathore treated only minor ailments; more serious or complicated problems required a journey to one of the hospitals in Karachi. Unless you went by motorbike, this was expensive and, if there was bad traffic, it could take a couple of hours. Once Jannat's father got sick, there was nothing to be done. They buried him in their ancestral graveyard alongside the bodies of hundreds of other Kachehlos. After his death, Jannat's mother was always vigilant for the signs of hepatitis in others.

Dada, Jannat's grandfather and the head of the household, was kind and gentle and so paternal that Jannat and her siblings never felt the full impact of losing their father at such a young age. For most of her early childhood, he worked long hours; he owned a pickup truck that local people could hire for travel or to transport furniture and other goods. He sometimes came back from Karachi with special treats for the kids, such as biscuits that you couldn't get in the local shops, toy cars and dolls. Once, when she was still very young, Jannat had tried to set up a small shop, spreading out some of these treasures on a cloth and selling them to the other kids for a few rupees.

Jannat's childhood in the village was chaotic and glorious: running around barefoot on the scalding-hot dusty earth that separated the houses, splashing about when the rains came and filled the stony banks of the seasonal streams with gushing water. Rain was an event for the whole village. The adults, who had all been to the city and knew what its landmarks were, would rush over to look too, remarking, 'Who needs Sea View? This is our Clifton.'

Jannat was a thoughtful, serious child who usually did what she was told. She was the eldest sibling and felt it was her duty to behave well and help her mother, who was always extremely busy. She felt this responsibility particularly heavily because her two younger siblings, Bushra and Rizwan, were so naughty. The naughtier they got, the more Jannat tried to compensate by helping. Houses in the village were not equipped with a kitchen. Instead women from the same family unit – sisters-in-law, sisters, mothers – shared a kitchen space, an outdoor area protected by a low fence and a thatched roof, where they could build a small wood fire to cook roti and chicken *salan* or to heat the metal jug to make chai in the mornings. In the winter, the winds came, carrying clouds of dust which billowed in over the low fence. Even when she was too young to help with the cooking, Jannat sometimes lingered around outside waiting for her mother so that she could help to carry dishes back and forth to the house. There was a comforting familiarity to the smell of woodsmoke that clung to the clothes of her mother and the other women who cooked. When the men were away at work, the women did the laundry, took the goats and cattle out to pasture on the nearby stretch of land where they could roam freely, gathered firewood for dinner and led the goats back into the village as the sun set. Women had to work hard in the village. Jannat knew that one day, when she was married, she would have to do the same.

All the children in Lal Baksh played together, but Jannat and Bushra were close in the way that only sisters can be. They loved each other fiercely and drove each other to the brink of fury. Where Jannat was dutiful, quiet and calm, Bushra was wild and erratic. They shared a bed and often Bushra would kick Jannat, or flash her palm at Jannat's face, an offensive gesture in Sindhi culture. If Jannat complained to their mother, Bushra feigned innocence, insisting that she'd been asleep. 'You children are driving me mad, you never let me rest,' their mother would mutter. But this was nothing compared to Bushra's determination to avoid going to school. Each morning, the house became a battlefield. First, Bushra would try peaceful resistance, insisting that she had stomach pains or a headache. 'Have a paracetamol, then,' their mother would say. Next, Bushra unleashed the tantrums. She was small but her lungs were powerful. She screamed and shouted and wriggled out of the grip of her mother and uncles as they tried to pick her up and make her get dressed for school. Sometimes Bushra's strategy worked. The adults, too exhausted to keep fighting, would give up, leaving her to roam around the village as they headed off for their day's work – the uncles were both teachers, one at the village madrasa and one at the primary school in a nearby village. On other days, Bushra would bolt out of the house as soon as she woke up, hiding in someone else's home, or in the bushes and wilderness beyond the structures that made up the village, waiting until the adults were out of the way. Jannat quickly realized that there was nothing she could do to convince her sister to go to school, so in the mornings she would leap out of bed, wash her face, gulp down her morning chai and get away from Bushra's rages as soon as she could. Early on in her school career, she had figured out that Sakina, whose house was nearby, was the fastest at getting ready, so most days she went with her. The village school, a single-storey building on a big paved courtyard, was a short walk away. The sun bounced off the white marble-like surface, where gnarled trees were emerging from small square holes cut into the stone.

The government had built this school in the 1970s, long before Jannat was born, during the first Pakistan People's Party government. The Bhuttos, the dynasty at the helm of the PPP, cared about Sindhis; that's what Jannat had grown up hearing, anyway. Many people in the village were named for members of the Bhutto family – Zulfikar, Benazir, Bilawal, Aseefa, Bakhtawar. Jannat's classroom was dark, with a cement floor. The wooden window shutters and door were light blue, the paint flaking and bubbling in places. A large round stone propped the door open. The room was filled with dark wooden benches and desks. At the front was a chalkboard, an object of wonder that the children screamed and fought over every single break time, each of them desperate to scribble something on the board. In front of it was the teacher's desk, with various bits of rubber tubing lined up as a warning – they were used to whip misbehaving children. Usually it was the boys who got whacked, although sometimes the girls did too. The boys who were really rowdy faced other punishments, such as sitting in stress positions facing the wall with their hands behind their heads. The punishments didn't much worry Jannat. She was always top of the class. She loved going to school, loved the sense of glimpsing a new world through information and the gratification of doing well. The village teachers, two old men who also lived in Lal Baksh, even had a nickname for her. They called her 'Computerized', because she was as quick as a computer. Jannat didn't know exactly what it meant – she had never seen a computer – but the name made her glow with happiness. (When she told me about the nickname years later, she was a mother herself, her school days long since past, but she lit up and cackled with delight at the memory.)

Education was prized by Jannat's family. Although *Dada* hadn't been to school himself, he saw education as the most important thing in the world and visibly swelled with pride when he talked about the fact that all three of his sons had become teachers. He was determined that his grandchildren would be educated too. Long after everyone else had given up on Bushra, he tried, in his own gentle way, to persuade her to learn. In the dusky hours after he returned from work, he would call Bushra over to him and ask her to show him how to write his name, or her name. As the years progressed and Bushra still refused to learn to read or write, *Dada* and the two uncles put more and more energy into helping Jannat instead. *Chacha*, the uncle who taught at a school in a nearby village, helped her with her maths homework every evening, in the half-light before darkness fell.

While she was young, Jannat didn't think too much about what would happen after she finished the fifth grade. Most girls in the village stopped studying at that point, when they were around eleven years old, because that was the highest level you could reach in the Lal Baksh school. The nearest secondary school was in Kathore and it was too far to walk in the blazing heat. Without a public transport system, the only way to get there was on a motorbike. Girls weren't allowed to drive motorbikes themselves and could only go as a passenger with one of their immediate relatives – their father, a brother, an uncle. There was no other option; the tradition of intermarriage meant that anyone beyond the immediate family was a potential partner. This restriction did not get much better with age: once they were married, women still had to have a male chaperone to leave

the village. As Jannat approached the end of fifth grade, *Dada* sat
her down and told her that she was going to be enrolled in the big
school in Kathore. She immediately knew this was significant. 'My
granddaughter will be the first from Lal Baksh to graduate from the
tenth grade,' he announced. No one argued with him. By this time,
Dada had retired and sold his truck, and he did not own a motorbike,
but when people raised questions about how Jannat was going to get
to the school in Kathore, he said that he would handle it.

On Jannat's first day of secondary school, she went through her
morning routine with an unfamiliar knot of nerves in her stomach.
Dada and Jannat got onto the back of *Chacha*'s motorbike and he
took them to Kathore on his way to work. The motorbike kicked up
clouds of dust as it heaved and leapt over the road's bumpy surface.
At intervals along the winding track between villages there were
little banks of rubbish. Plastic bags and food wrappers were caught
on the thorny bushes that clung to the rocky earth, their shine turned
dull with dust. Jannat clung to her grandfather's back as their village receded behind them and Kathore loomed ahead. It was busier
than Lal Baksh, at once bigger and more compact. The houses were
closer together, spanning out from the main road, where the smell
of frying rose from stalls selling samosas and pakoras, nestled next
to carts of fresh vegetables. Along this road were small shops, one
selling children's clothes and leather shoes, another stocking basic
groceries and snacks. A chai shop and restaurant with turquoise
plastic chairs outside was blaring out religious music. Kathore was
adjacent to Super Highway, the enormous road that went all the way
from Karachi to Hyderabad, and sometimes traffic passed through
here. There was even the occasional car, alongside the motorbikes
and bicycles more commonly seen in the area.

At last, they reached the school. It was a small building set back
from the road, with only a handful of classrooms and an office for

the teachers, but to Jannat it looked huge. *Chacha* waved to *Dada* and Jannat as he drove off for his day at work in a different village. *Dada* smiled encouragingly at Jannat and squeezed her shoulder. She found his presence reassuring, but she knew that he wouldn't be able to come into the classroom with her. She sat outside with him as they waited for lessons to begin. Other students began to gather too. They were all different ages, boys and girls. Although many of them wore the Sindhi dress that Jannat recognized – the embroidery on their salwar kameez in geometric patterns – others were in unfamiliar clothes. Some of the surrounding villages were populated by Baloch people, many of whom had lived here for generations. They looked strange to Jannat. Even the other Sindhis – those who were not Kachehlos – scared her. When it was time for lessons to begin, *Dada* pushed her gently towards the classroom. 'Don't worry,' he said. 'I'll be waiting outside when you finish.'

Inside the classroom, Jannat was tense from her shoulders to her toes. She could barely look up at the chalkboard, let alone at her fellow students. This was the first time in her life that she had ever felt truly alone, so exposed in this new environment that it was as if her skin had been peeled off. She did not put her hand up to respond to any of the questions the teacher asked, even when she knew the answer: she didn't want to attract attention to herself. She thought of her nickname in the village school, Computerized, and felt ashamed.

Somehow, the day passed. When she walked out of the classroom, Jannat was flooded with relief to see *Dada* waiting on a bench outside, a big tree shading him from the sun. Before any of the other girls could try to talk to her, she hurried over to him. *Chacha* wouldn't finish work in time to collect them, so they had to wait and hitch a ride with whichever relative happened to be passing by. The fact that *Dada* was there as a chaperone meant Jannat had more flexibility about who she could travel with. They walked a short distance to the end of the *pukka* (tarmacked) road that cut through Kathore, to the point where it met the *kacha* (untarmacked) road that led to the village. Eventually, a cousin of Jannat's father passed by, and they hopped on the back for the drive home. Jannat felt the tension leave her body as they reached Lal Baksh.

Every day for the next year, *Dada* set off with Jannat in the morning and waited for her until it was time to come home. She didn't tell anyone in her family how difficult she found it going to school in Kathore. She had heard what people in the village were saying: 'Look how much effort her *dada* is going to, just for a girl to go to school!' In Kathore, she kept her head down and avoided talking to anyone. If other girls tried to strike up a conversation, she felt unable to even meet their eyes. When she was back in the village in the afternoons, she urged her friends to join her at the secondary school. 'I can't,' said Sakina, the friend with whom she had walked to the village school every day. 'There's no one to take me. Not everyone can do what your *dada* is doing.' Others were more blunt: 'My parents say it's useless for girls to study.' Jannat soon stopped trying to convince them. The easy confidence she had acquired by always being the best at the village school dissipated as she struggled to keep up and her grades fell. Her heart pounded every time the teachers asked her a question, and when *Chacha* tried to help with her homework in the evenings, she worried that he would notice her shortcomings.

In her second year at the school the anxieties began to lift. Although many of the other students had long since stopped trying to get Jannat to speak to them, one girl persisted. Mahfouza was Baloch, but like everyone else from this area, she could speak Sindhi too. When they came back to school after the long summer break, she asked Jannat how her break was. Jannat managed to answer, 'Fine, thanks.' It wasn't much, but it was a start. Mahfouza became

Jannat's first friend in Kathore and after that there were others. She began to speak up more in lessons. Her grades improved and soon she was back at the top of the class, getting As in every subject. *Dada* didn't say anything about it when she stopped running out of the classroom and straight into his arms, instead strolling out while chatting to the other girls. But she knew that he had noticed by the small smile that played around his lips when he asked how her day had been.

Dada was getting older and the journey each day tired him out. Although the school in Kathore was open six days a week, gradually Jannat began to attend on just three or four – whenever *Dada* was strong enough for the journey. She kept up with the work, studying pages in her tattered textbooks and asking *Chacha* for help when she got stuck. When Jannat's younger brother Rizwan was old enough to go to school in Kathore, she felt a glimmer of jealousy at how easy it was for him. He could hop on the back of anyone's bike, so he had no problem getting to and from school daily. This was her life and she accepted it, but how different things could have been – if she were a boy, if there were a school within walking distance, if there were proper roads or transport systems. Later, when she thought back to her days at school in Kathore, the memory was inextricable from the solid, steady presence of her grandfather, who was there every day, in the blazing summer sun, in the rain or in the cold dry wind that cut right to your bones, sitting under the tree, waiting to get her home safely.

When I started spending time in Lal Baksh, Jannat was married, and as we talked she was always tending to one of her children or rushing to get firewood or collect her goats. There is no sense of private space in the village, and the women freely passed in and out of each other's houses all the time, listening in, finishing each other's stories, cracking jokes. Culturally, it was not appropriate for anyone – particularly a woman – to boast or show pride, and Jannat downplayed her trailblazing school days. But they were clearly significant to everyone. Her sister Bushra, who still couldn't read or write, constantly interrupted our conversations, her jokes sometimes tinged with insecurity.

'You're talking to her because she's educated so she talks softly. But she might be filling your head with nonsense,' she would say, or, 'Jannat should give me her qualifications and literacy – I'd make better use of them.'

'I think the sun has baked her brain,' Jannat would mutter.

They were curious about my life in London and asked who was helping my mother with the housework while I travelled so far from home. But that was not their main preoccupation. All the women, Jannat included, always had the same question for me: 'Are you married yet?' I was not – and I was thirty-one.

'Just imagine,' Jannat murmured, shaking her head sympathetically when she first heard this news. 'This woman is so old and she is still unmarried.'

When Jannat asked if I had at least found my groom, I showed her a picture of my long-term partner. She grabbed the phone, flanked by a crowd of women and girls from the village, and scrolled through all the pictures of him she could find. They told me they approved and would pray for a swift marriage. As the months passed by and I returned to Lal Baksh, Jannat demanded to know if my wedding had happened yet, and whether my parents objected to the long delay. I tried to explain that I wasn't in much of a rush, that people got married at an older age in the UK, that parents didn't have much to do with it. But this didn't make sense to Jannat. Being a woman in the village meant accepting that you would not be making big decisions about your own life.

For as long as Jannat could remember, her mother had been

stitching and embroidering pillows and quilts for her dowry. This was what all the women did as soon as they had a daughter: prepare them to set up their households with a good stock of traditionally decorated homeware. Houses in the village were generally unfurnished apart from shelves built into or nailed to the walls and a bed, or the occasional roll-out mattress on the floor. The pillows and blankets were vital. They transformed a bare shell of a building into a home. Embroidery itself was stitched into the fabric of the village, a skill handed down from woman to woman, generation to generation. Whenever the women had a spare moment, between caring for their children and their goats, collecting firewood and preparing dinner, they would work on their embroidery together. As they did so, propped up on pillows that their own mothers had made for them, they gossiped and laughed, shared stories and jokes. Every so often, one of the men would take the women to a market in Karachi – Lyari's Leigh Market or the big one in Sohrab Goth – where they would brave the mass of customers and shouting street hawkers to pick up cheap ready-made salwar kameez or fabric that could be sewn into one by a tailor in Kathore. When they got home with their haul, the real work would begin, customizing these simple outfits with traditional Sindhi embroidery. The patterns were intricate and neatly geometric, often adorned with tiny mirrors. Jannat's mother was exceptionally good at embroidery and the other women often commented on how lucky her daughters were. She had set herself a significant challenge: providing Jannat and Bushra with fifty pillows and ten quilts each on their wedding day. This took up all her spare time. Year by year, the shelf against the back wall of their room steadily filled up with a growing pile of neatly stacked pillows, each meticulously embroidered into a blaze of glorious colour. She thought inventively about her designs. On the green pillows she stitched yellow squares, flanked by small mirrors encircled with blue and purple, surrounded by a larger yellow diamond. White pillows were, stitch by stitch, covered with opaque maroon teardrops. The red pillows had concentric circles populated with mirrors and a delicate white stitched pattern. As the pile grew, Jannat knew that her marriage was getting closer.

The identity of her future husband had never been a mystery. Jannat had been informally betrothed to Ghulam since she was small. Engagements were decided by parents, often when children were still very young, and although parents rarely sat them down to tell them who they were promised to, there were no secrets in the village and everyone knew everything. Ghulam was Jannat's cousin, the eldest son of her mother's sister and Shafi Muhammad, the village elder. He was ten or twelve years her senior – time was foggy in the village and no one was entirely sure of their own age. *Dada* approved of Ghulam because he had finished school all the way to the twelfth grade. When Jannat was growing up, playing with the other kids in the dusty ground outside their homes, sometimes one would yell Ghulam's name at her. Her cheeks would burn. As a result, she was generally faintly embarrassed in Ghulam's company. The engagement was formalized when Jannat was around sixteen. She was in the ninth grade, with just one year left before she could graduate from school. The wedding date was set for two months later.

Even though they had all lived together for their whole lives and knew each other's faces as well as their own, the tradition in the village was that a girl shouldn't be seen by her husband-to-be once the engagement was official. Girls would pull their dupattas (scarves) over their faces and turn their backs when their fiancés approached, or flee inside the house. Jannat, who already felt awkward around her future husband, was glad for the excuse to hide her face or run away if she saw him come near, shrieking and giggling if she found Bushra or her mother waiting. Everyone said that Ghulam was a good man, and Jannat had always found him kind and considerate, but she was not excited about marriage. She looked with growing dread at the hard daily slog that her mother and all the other women went through, and compared it to her own life: the trips to Kathore for school, sitting and studying and laughing with girls from all across the district, poring over her books in the evenings. She helped with the cooking and housework only when she wanted to – a bit of sweeping here and there, frying okra or chicken – and she did so in the full knowledge that it was ultimately her mother's responsibility, not hers. No one explicitly stated that she would have to stop going to school after the wedding, but Jannat knew that it was inevitable. She would be too busy with household duties, and *Dada* would no longer have the final say in what she did or didn't do. Yet even as the date of the wedding approached, every other day she and *Dada* continued to hop on the back of *Chacha*'s motorbike and make the trip to Kathore. They didn't talk about the fact that their journeys would soon come to an end.

Already, Jannat found herself with less time to do her homework after school, as she became increasingly immersed in wedding preparations. Her mother had finished stitching the pillows and now she was turning her attention to Jannat's outfits. In addition to the wedding outfit itself, it was customary to send girls to be married with a collection of salwar kameez – both formal and casual – that would last several years. When Jannat offered her opinions on how her mother could design some of the embroidery, she refused to take directions. 'Sit with me and learn to do it yourself, if you have so many ideas,' her mother said. Like all the girls in the village, Jannat already knew the basics of embroidery, but now she joined the older women in earnest. When Jannat sat there, embroidering her anxieties into physical designs, she felt initiated into a secret society of grown-up women, and for those moments, her future didn't seem so daunting.

Weddings were always a big deal in Lal Baksh. When the day came, the familiar contours of Jannat's village were transformed into a festival of colour, with bright tinsel and garlands strung up, and huge pots of food ready to serve to the guests – mutton *salan* and chicken biryani. The clouds of flies that proliferated in the village swarmed loudly over the food, to be batted away by the women at regular intervals. It took hours for Jannat to get ready. With the help of her mother and sister, she was adorned with gold – rows of bangles on her wrists purchased on a trip to one of the big markets in Karachi, ring upon ring running through her multiple ear piercings, a bejewelled stud in her nose. Her salwar kameez was heavy and ornate, carefully embroidered with gold thread by her mother. When they stepped out to join the festivities, it looked to Jannat as if there were thousands of people there. They had come to show their respect for Jannat's father-in-law, Shafi Muhammad, who was well liked in the area, and was often called on when people needed advice or help settling disputes over land, money or marriage. Among the guests were a few of Jannat's classmates from Kathore, attending with their parents. There had been no fanfare when Jannat left school, no farewell party; as the wedding approached, she had simply stopped going.

The wedding day passed in a haze. There was music and dancing, although not for Jannat. A bride couldn't dance at her own wedding, or even laugh or smile much. It was immodest to look as if she was too happy at the thought of getting married and ending her innocence. Jannat was respectful of propriety, so she stayed as still as she could, watching the festivities unfold around her. She was still young, but she was tall like her mother. When she stood next to her husband, she realized that she was taller than him.

After the wedding, she went to the home that Ghulam had built for them. Like the others in Lal Baksh, it comprised a single room.

The white corrugated-iron roof was adorned with wedding tinsel that dangled from the beams. Across the long back wall were built-in shelves. The pillows from her mother were stacked up all the way to the ceiling, a comforting backdrop to her new life.

Ghulam worked long hours at the business he ran with his brothers, selling chicken meat from the many poultry farms in the area to restaurants and wedding caterers. Their small shop was far away from Lal Baksh, past Kathore, just off Super Highway. The shop was behind one of the big chai hotels that catered to long-distance truckers and commuters with vats of oily dhal and sweet milky chai. Much of their business was done at night: the caterers drove out from the city to pick up chicken to prepare for their restaurants the following day. All three brothers would come home exhausted, covered in dust from the bumpy motorbike ride, soaked in sweat, the smell of meat clinging to their clothes. Chicken was the currency that kept Lal Baksh afloat, now that agriculture was practically impossible.

When Jannat had travelled out of the village – to school in Kathore or to a wedding – she had occasionally seen lush green fields, a striking visual contrast to the monochrome sand and thorns that covered the rest of the area. These fields, Ghulam told her, were owned by wealthy villagers who had the means to irrigate the land. Those who could not afford to cultivate crops in this costly way were forced to find other work. Some built poultry farms, rearing chickens to sell to market traders in Karachi. Some, like Ghulam and his brothers, slaughtered the birds and sold the meat directly. The Kachehlos had been on this land for hundreds of years and in that time it had changed to the point it was barely recognizable. But they clung to it and to Shafi Muhammad's words: 'This land is all we have. We are free on this land. The land will sustain us.'

Jannat had moved only a few metres away from the house she had grown up in, but her centre of gravity shifted. Now she was part of

Ghulam's broader household. Unlike her own home, where *Amma* had borne the pressure alone, here there were many women to share the load. Ghulam's sister was still a child, but both of his brothers were married and all three wives divided most of the tasks between them. At first, the two older women left Jannat to her embroidery and cooking while they cleaned and tended to the cattle and goats.

Soon after the wedding, Ghulam sat Jannat down and told her that although he couldn't take her to school in Kathore every day, her education was important to him. 'I'm going to get you all the textbooks and materials you need, and enrol you for the tenth-grade exams next year,' he told her. 'You can sit the exams as a private candidate. I'll drive you there myself.' Ghulam was true to his word. He brought Jannat the textbooks and encouraged her to study. 'Your *dada* wanted you to be the first girl from Lal Baksh to finish tenth grade, and I want that for you too.' But without the structure of school, the words in the textbooks washed over her. She had never struggled with concentration before, but now she would read the same page repeatedly without absorbing a thing. She was also getting used to the new demands on her time. Some of these were enjoyable, like the daily walk to get firewood, a leisurely stroll with the other women. Even the laundry, which was hard work – filling up the low metal basin from the manual pump that supplied water to the village, rinsing clothes by hand under the blazing sun – was tolerable, because all the women did it together. She often sat with her mother, squatting by one of their houses, chatting as they used a stone to scrape the soap suds out of the clothes, before hanging them to dry on one of the gnarly trees that stood between their homes, trying to find a spot where they wouldn't immediately be covered in dust again. Other tasks had fewer redeeming features. She now had responsibility for Ghulam's goats, taking them out to pasture each morning and bringing them back to the village in the evening.

Sometimes as she was sitting propped up on one of the beautiful pillows her mother had stitched for her, trying to read her Urdu or maths textbook, one of the goats would amble into the house and have to be shooed away.

By this time, electricity had come to the village. For years, pylons had stood, unused and unconnected, spaced at regular intervals from Lal Baksh out into the distance. No one in the village could say exactly when it happened, but at some point around the time of Jannat's marriage they had wires connected to them, loose loops strung across the sky. Now they had power for a few hours a day, enough to light their homes in the evenings. The single bulb newly attached to most houses provided far more light than the lanterns had done previously. Electricity was useful in other ways too. Some years earlier, the government had sunk a borehole for a well in the middle of the village. It was wide and square, surrounded by a low brick wall, the earth beside it turned to a muddy sludge by the overflow of water. It had run on an expensive diesel generator that everyone chipped in for, but now it was connected to the mains supply. It didn't work all the time – only for the few hours a day that the power was switched on – but it was less laborious to get water here than at the hand pump. Each of these small changes made life so much easier. Jannat had only a loose understanding of the forces that decided which services would come to their village and when, but she knew from listening to the men speak that everything good that happened was because of the PPP and the Bhuttos. They were powerful people, far away in grand houses in the city, but they were Sindhis too, and that meant they cared about Lal Baksh. Villagers across their region shared this conviction, despite the fact that decades of PPP provincial government control had not led to gas lines, running water or hospitals. The celebration of Jannat's wedding had coincided with the happy news that the 2008 election had returned the PPP to national government, even though it was tinged with sadness that their great heroine, Benazir Bhutto, had been assassinated. Jannat didn't pay close attention to politics, but after the electricity came her cousin Ataullah got a TV and sometimes she watched snippets of the news. As the men talked in glowing terms about the changing times, she daydreamed about a hospital, or a secondary school in Lal Baksh, so that other girls could finish their education. If a few hours per day of power could change so much, it was dizzying to imagine how much easier life would be with better facilities.

A year into her marriage, the day of the exams arrived. Jannat got on the back of Ghulam's motorbike and they drove to Kathore. Each bend in the road was at once familiar and alien, like scenes from a past life. Instead of *Dada*, she clung to her husband's back. She was full of a low rumbling anxiety that reminded her of her very first day at the school. Although she had ramped up her efforts in the weeks before, she knew that she had not been able to study effectively for the exams. When the results were ready a few months later, Ghulam drove her back along the same track to pick up the envelope. She had passed, with a D. 'My wife is the first girl in Lal Baksh to finish her intermediate study!' Ghulam whooped. When they went to her family house to tell *Dada*, his age-cracked face softened into a beaming smile. Jannat was happy to have graduated, she really was. It seemed churlish to mention to anyone that this was the first time in her life she had got a D in an exam instead of an A. Everyone in the village was celebrating her achievement. 'We didn't think a girl could finish school but she's done it,' people said. Ghulam began to talk about Jannat continuing her studies into the eleventh and twelfth grades. She nodded and smiled when he said this, but they both knew it wasn't on the agenda for now. They were expecting their first child.

Jannat watched her body change. Her belly swelled out of all recognition and she found herself fatigued by the simplest tasks. The goats exhausted her, the laundry even more so. Many women never went for a single doctor's appointment during their pregnancy, but Jannat was relieved that Ghulam did not want to take any risks. He took her on the back of his motorbike for regular check-ups with the doctor in Kathore. As Jannat waited anxiously for her baby to come, she began to question her life in Lal Baksh. Why didn't they have a doctor here? Why was it so far to get to the nearest hospital, so far in fact that her own father had dropped dead before getting the treatment he needed? What if she had a baby girl who wanted to study as much as she had? Jannat loved the land, just as the elders had always told her to, but she found herself wondering quietly if it was enough. They were free here, but they needed other things too: schools, hospitals, roads.

The baby came abruptly. There was no time to call a doctor. Jannat's mother and some other women from the village rushed over and they delivered the little girl – fair-skinned like Jannat and her mother – at home. She was named Aziza.

5

ZILLE

When I met Zille in 2015, he had been working as a crime reporter for over a decade and dissembling had become second nature. The job required it: he had to maintain good relationships with the police, with gangsters, with his own TV channel. His was dangerous work that involved angering powerful people. When he was reporting on screen, the truth was ostensibly the point. But Zille had also learned to self-censor, to hedge around the subject, to avoid mentioning a specific party name. And off screen, where risks lurked at every corner, he took this further: holding back, contradicting himself, leaving some mystery about his family, his past or even his whereabouts. Perhaps it was a rational response to a high-risk job.

We met after nightfall, on a pleasant Karachi evening in springtime. I had just arrived from London to research a story on the city's crime reporters and was groggy from the flight. Knowing that shadowing a crime reporter might be dangerous, I had opted not to stay with relatives, who would have concerns about my safety. Zille met me at my guest house, an unassuming building on a run-down side street off a main road in the affluent district of Clifton. The guest house was unmarked and from the outside looked like another rich person's house, protected by a low metal gate and a sleepy-looking guard. Men sat outside on stools, chatting and spitting out rust-coloured paan that resembled blood splatters on the unpaved street. After we had exchanged greetings, Zille darkly told me that I should move hotel. 'This place is full of criminals,' he said, and didn't elaborate further. I didn't sleep well that night.

Zille is a small man, very thin, with hooded eyes and a sharp gaze, constantly reaching for one of his two phones, lighting a cigarette, surveying his surroundings, or leaning sideways as if to avoid being seen. Over the next few days as I researched my story, I saw him only in the dark, on late-night drives to meet police contacts, snatching meals at anonymous roadside stalls. I asked his age three times and received three different answers. He told me thirty-two, thirty-three and thirty-eight, but when he gave me his birth year, it would have made him forty-one.

On other points, he was more consistent. Zille said that he had become a crime reporter by accident. It was the early 2000s and he was drifting. He had studied engineering at Karachi University, a subject chosen on his father's advice; his parents insisted that it would provide solid career prospects. He had four sisters but no brothers, so, as the only son, there was extra pressure on him to do well and get a respectable job. But he was an unfocused student with no interest in engineering. In lectures, the words swam over him, and the diagrams and numbers made him dizzy. He was more interested in going to parties and playing cricket than studying. He loved everything about cricket. When he was a child, whenever the violence wasn't too bad, he and the other boys from his street would gather after school to play impromptu games outside their houses. As a university student, he had access to proper playing fields and carried this childhood passion into a new phase. More than anything, he liked to win. He loved watching the sport too. When others – such as Safdar, the Edhi ambulance driver – were glued to the surreal TV footage of army tanks rolling into Karachi in 1992, Zille was much more interested in the Pakistan cricket team's glorious World Cup victory that year. Seeing these men who looked just like him travelling the world and emerging victorious opened a window into a different life. He dreamed of travelling outside Karachi, beyond Pakistan, to see everything the world had to offer. He scraped through his degree with a low pass.

Zille had even less interest in becoming an engineer than he'd had in studying engineering. The problem was that he didn't know what else to do. He wanted excitement, to be admired, to do something great. But that wasn't exactly a career plan he could pitch to his father. Zille had a vague idea that he could set up a small business instead. This was a respectable line of work for a middle-class boy and his parents were keen. He took steps towards this goal, even opening a hairdressing salon with a friend, but it floundered and he realized that he wasn't that interested in managing a business either. Around the same time, one of his friends told him that he should think about working in TV. It was 2003 and television was booming. A couple of years earlier, Musharraf had loosened the censorship laws and private media companies were opening up all over the place.

Like everyone else in the country, Zille had grown up watching PTV, the national state broadcaster and one of the few TV channels, with its staid studio discussions that closely toed the government line. Now, suddenly, there were scores of private media groups producing independent news, drama and political shows. It seemed that a new channel was starting up every week. Money was flying around and commissioners were experimenting with different formats in a dizzying whirl of opportunity. Zille's friend worked for one of these start-up channels and promised to get him an interview.

Even though, like all the rest, it was a new channel, Geo had a degree of prestige as it was owned by the Jang Group, a media conglomerate that published some of the country's most popular newspapers. This didn't mean much to Zille because he rarely read the papers, but even so it was impossible to grow up in Karachi and be unaware of politics. He was from Landhi, the same district as Safdar, but while Safdar resided in a poor, predominantly Pashtun neighbourhood, Zille's area was mostly populated by Urdu-speaking Mohajirs, who were educated if not affluent. Landhi was overpopulated and sharply divided. Throughout the 1990s and beyond, it was the centre of the Mohajir–Pashtun conflict, with all the political activity and violence that brought. In Zille's area, either you were with the Muttahida Qaumi Movement or you were apolitical; there were no other options. The MQM easily won every election in his part of Landhi and their distinctive green and red logo was everywhere – on lampposts, bollards and people's exterior gates. The consensus was that, for all its flaws, this was the only party looking out for Mohajir interests, and the only hope of ending the unjust quota system that kept well-educated people like them out of secure and lucrative government jobs. But at the end of the block was a Pashtun enclave. Sometimes this meant nothing more than noticing a different complexion or accent when you went to the shops there, but when Mohajir–Pashtun violence flared up, Zille and his family avoided even driving through the area. Occasionally you might hear that one of the Pashtun shopkeepers had been shot dead in a targeted killing. But for the most part, the violence remained in the background.

His first job with Geo was in the entertainment division. The office was situated in the heart of Karachi's business district, on Chundrigar Road, close to the stock exchange and the headquarters of various banks. They towered over the hectic thoroughfare, glass and concrete slicing into the pollution-clouded sky. The Geo office was set back from Chundrigar Road by a series of roadblocks, the entrance obstructed by armed security guards and metal detectors. The interior was decked out in the channel's signature colours of orange and blue, giving an impression of newness and excitement that was only slightly offset by the battered, wood-panelled lift. Zille worked as a producer across drama and factual entertainment, and from the outset, he loved not only the work but the whole world of TV. For someone who had always enjoyed parties, it was a dream. He was constantly invited to events, and got a rush when he gave people his card bearing the words 'Producer – Geo TV' and saw how impressed they were. He met interesting and creative people, both men and women, although he had grown up in a culturally con-servative environment where the genders were often segregated. He had lunch appointments most days and the disposable cash to spend on nice meals out. The work was stimulating too. One month he might be working on a drama series, another on a cultural discussion show. That was how he ended up on *National Investigation Cell*, a new programme that reconstructed lurid crimes using actors.

One of his first tasks was to go to Sohrab Goth, a sprawling, mostly Pashtun slum notorious for its links to the drugs trade and the violence that went with that. He had to visit a police station to scout for stories, and interview police officers and victims to turn their testimonies into material for the scriptwriters. The programme was interested in the most salacious stuff – family disputes, broken engagements, violent robberies – and that brief was at the forefront of Zille's mind as he hopped into the car. 'You're sure you don't mind going?' his boss had asked him doubtfully. Zille shrugged. He'd never been to Sohrab Goth, but he didn't mind giving it a go.

He and the office driver pulled up outside the area's police station, a small cement building set back from the road and protected by sandbags. When he saw the high security and the men in Pashtun dress loitering on the street outside, Zille began to feel nervous. He had grown up absorbing the casual anti-Pashtun sentiment that flew around his community every time there was an outbreak of violence, and here he was in an area often described as a no-go zone. His slightly oversized shirt tucked into his chinos formed a stark contrast to the salwar kameez-clad men outside. But he was determined to get the job done. He concentrated on the task at hand and interviewed the police officers. His bosses were pleased with his work and over the next few months Zille went to other no-go zones: Lyari, Kiamari, Orangi. Each time, he got in and out quickly and focused on collecting the weirdest details for the scripts. As far as the audiences were concerned, the more sensational the better. The show was a hit.

A few months into the season, Zille's boss called him to a meeting. He said that they'd noticed how resourceful he was in researching these crimes and how relaxed he was about working in no-go areas, then added, 'We think you should move to the news desk.'

Zille was surprised. 'I've never done any reporting,' he said. 'I've never found a news story. I've never spoken on camera.'

His boss insisted that he'd be able to do it and, as soon as it was suggested, Zille found that he liked the idea. There was the obvious allure of being on TV himself, his face beamed into hundreds of thousands of living rooms around the country. And then there was something else, something harder to define. The crime reporters he saw in the office and on his trips to Karachi's danger zones were impressive figures. Zille had noticed the way so many police and criminals mimicked the gangster style of Bollywood movies: aviator sunglasses at all times of the day, leather jackets and thick handle-bar moustaches. Something of this same macho glamour clung to the crime reporters too, with their sharp clothes and nice cars. He took the job.

The phone calls started the same week that Zille's first story as a crime reporter was broadcast. He immediately wondered if he had made a mistake in accepting the role. The story that they'd set off in pursuit of had seemed fairly straightforward at the time: it was about a clash at Karachi's Malir jail between prisoners from different political parties. The men packed inside were low-ranking activists, the foot soldiers considered unimportant enough to actually be convicted for the violence they carried out at the behest of their organizations. More senior figures tended to have the political clout and bribe money to avoid imprisonment. When Zille arrived at the jail to report on the story, his main concern was to avoid making any blunders that might reveal his inexperience. He pulled up with the office driver and a cameraman, as was standard for any assignment. The cameraman filmed Zille standing outside the main gate, holding his microphone and speaking down the lens, and shot some background scenes of the jail's exterior. But as soon as they tried to go inside, the guards stopped them and said that no cameras were allowed. Zille thought fast. He knew they needed shots of the jail's interior. This was his first assignment and he did not want to go back to the office with nothing.

At that moment, an Edhi ambulance drove up towards the gate. Zille ran over, tapped on the window and asked if the driver would mind taking him in as a passenger. The driver looked at him for a moment, then agreed. They drove into the compound. Once they had cleared the gates, Zille got out and walked in. The sharp smell of sweat hit him as he entered the jail. It was dark and hectic, housing many times more people than it was designed for. Men in stained clothes stared at him. Surreptitiously, he took out his phone and started filming.

Although he had visited police stations for his work on *National Investigation Cell*, Zille had never been inside such a large jail before and he was acutely self-conscious. Once he was sure he had enough shots, he went to talk to the supervising officer as if nothing was amiss. Aware of the risks of making a mistake, Zille checked carefully which prisoners were affiliated to which parties. The supervising officer showed him the relevant prisoner records and he noted everything down. It all seemed simple enough and the package went out on *Geo News*. When he watched the report, Zille was flooded with exhilaration seeing his shots and seeing himself standing outside the jail explaining the situation. He thought he looked authoritative – a real crime reporter.

The man on the other end of the phone felt differently. 'We don't know that person you reported on in Malir jail. Why are you associating our party's name with common criminals?' Zille tried to explain that he'd seen the jail records, but he was cut off. 'Don't run our party's name on air again,' said the disembodied voice, then hung up. Zille's new colleagues in the crime department told him not to worry about it. More calls followed, always from unknown numbers, at random times of day. Outwardly he brushed it off, but for a few weeks, every time his phone rang, he felt uneasy.

The calls stopped after a week or two, but they were Zille's first sign that being a crime reporter was somewhat more complicated than producing entertainment shows. The second sign came two months later, when he was reporting on an 'exam mafia' who had been stealing exam papers and sharing the answers with students for a fee. Exam mafias were widespread in Karachi, usually associated with whichever political party was in power in a particular area. Zille and his cameraman went to the exam centre that had been investigated and set up the camera tripod on the dusty street outside, Zille gripping his Geo-branded microphone and speaking over the background clamour of traffic. He was mid-sentence when someone walked out of the low-rise building behind him and punched him in the face, knocking the microphone to the ground and leaving him speechless.

The next few moments passed in a blur: a violent tussle, a bloodied nose, a rush to get the camera equipment back into the van. The man who had punched Zille was affiliated to the local governing party, so there was no point in going to the police. Back in the office, Zille gingerly washed his split lip and cleaned up as best he could. When he arrived home, his parents looked stricken.

'Please find a different job,' his mother pleaded. 'It's too dangerous.'

'You have to think about the family. You don't have any brothers,' said his father.

Zille brushed them off. Several years of a steady, generous TV salary meant that he had been able to move his entire family – parents, sisters – out of Landhi and into a house in the solidly middle-class area of Gulshan. Now they were hardly ever kept awake by gunfire. In the months since becoming a crime reporter, he had finally been able to buy his first car and he still felt a rush of satisfaction driving around in it. But he was rattled and wondered again if he had made a mistake. After all, it was his face on the news most days, reporting on these stories; his voice saying things that could upset dangerous people. He didn't want to get his parents' hopes up, but privately he started asking around about other work opportunities.

The thing was, none of the options he could think of seemed that appealing: work in a bank, like his father; use his degree to start from scratch in engineering. When Zille tried to picture himself in any of these other, safer jobs, he saw a dull image in tones of grey, not the blaze of technicolour he was living in right now. Geo was one of the most popular channels in the country and it didn't take long for people to get to know his face. The news was a national fixation and in Karachi, where violent clashes regularly shut down whole areas of the city, everyone was obsessed with the crime news in particular. Zille used to get a thrill from handing out his business card. Now people recognized him on the street or at parties. Sometimes he felt as if he was living a double life. He knew how much his parents worried, so he didn't tell them about the most extreme incidents: getting roughed up on a shoot, the persistent threatening phone calls, the increasingly common occurrence of seeing dead bodies as the violence ramped up across the city. But it wasn't always possible to keep a clear division, not least because his work was so public. His family congratulated him when he reported on a big story. They'd get phone calls from relatives who had seen him on Geo and everyone enjoyed the reflected glory. But at other times, when they saw him in his bulletproof vest, ducking for cover as gunfire sounded in the background, he would get back into the car to find twenty-five missed calls from his parents. Sometimes he came home to find his mother praying for his safe return. His parents reminded him constantly that he shouldn't take such risks. It was not simply that he was their only son; they were Shia Muslims and they worried that the very fact of being part of this religious minority made Zille more vulnerable now that he had such a public role. Shias made up a fifth of Pakistan's population, but they were routinely discriminated against, passed over for jobs and were sometimes even the target of sectarian violence. He would appease his parents with promises, but by now he was addicted to the rush of reporting, the dash to the shootings, the scrabble for the best story and the best interview at the scene, the constant split-second decisions to keep himself out of the firing line.

Before long Zille began to recognize the same faces at crime scenes. The moment he got a tip that something had happened – a shooting, a robbery, a political clash – he'd race across the city with his team, navigating gridlocked traffic and flyovers to get there fast. The aim was always to be the first on the scene, but that was easier said than done when everyone else was working with the same information and was equally keen to get the scoop. The dream was to forge such a good relationship with a police officer or gangster that they called you first. Zille pressed his card into the hands of anyone who would take it, telling police officers and gangsters alike to call him if they ever had a tip. The contacts were there for the taking, but every other journalist was hustling for them too. The media was a useful tool for police who wanted to show they were doing something, and for political parties who wanted to score points off their rivals. When Lyari was shut down by the turf wars between different gangsters, the top players – Rehman Dakait, Arshad Pappu – would call different TV stations to let them know when they'd bumped off an opponent. Keen for ratings, the channels broadcast it all.

Zille sometimes surprised himself with how untroubled he was by the residual violence of the stories he covered. When his car screeched up to a crime scene, the sulphurous smell of gunfire often hung in the air, or the cloying scent of blood. Victims of violence might be lying twisted on the floor, their faces frozen in anguish, until the Edhi ambulance drivers swooped in to take them away. The media industry had developed far too quickly to retrospectively impose ethical standards, and reporters did not recognize the necessity of giving space or privacy to injured people. The cameramen had the most arduous job, sometimes performing semi-acrobatic movements to shove their camera into the back of an ambulance to grab a shot of the face of a prominent person who had been injured or killed.

These scenes were frenetic and adrenalin pumped around Zille's body as he tried to make sure he was talking to the right people and getting the whole story. There was never time to dwell on how horrifying it was. Besides, there was almost always a throng of reporters crowded at the site of any explosion or shooting, a familiar crew that lent it the atmosphere of a staff room rather than a gruesome crime scene. The satellite vans bearing different channels' logos would be queued up, the ones that had got there quickest parked right behind the police cars and Edhi ambulances that were always closest to the action. The reporters would hustle for the best spot, their cameramen jostling for the optimum lighting and view of the scene. Between live pieces to camera, the reporters and police officers swapped cigarettes and tips, the younger journalists listening out eagerly in case there was a lead they could pick up from someone more experienced.

As the months turned into years, Zille noticed more and more new vans lining up on the street and an increasing number of unfamiliar reporters. The proliferation of TV channels that had felt so exciting and full of opportunity when he started began to seem like a threat. Geo was the top-rated news channel in Pakistan but, as the editors were constantly reminding reporters, that position could slip at any point. Zille enjoyed the feeling of superiority he got from no longer being one of the newbies, but he also felt a deep anxiety about being displaced. He was not yet one of the old guard, the really well-established reporters who counted police officers among their best friends and were on first-name terms with Lyari's gang lords. In fact, he had never even been sent to cover Lyari – the story was judged too complicated, the area too dangerous for someone who didn't have years of experience and contacts there. But he was no longer fresh blood. He was desperate to distinguish himself. He needed a break.

Given the anxiety his work caused them, the least Zille could do for his parents was agree to get married. They chose the girl. I don't know anything about the details of the wedding because Zille is particularly guarded about his family life. But he did tell me that afterwards, his brother-in-law politely asked, 'Is it possible that you could look for another job? You could run a business. I can help you with money if that's the issue.'

'No,' Zille replied. 'I have a good job already.'

'It's not good,' he said, more insistent this time. 'You're famous in Karachi and it's dangerous. Now you are not one person, you are two, and you need to think about your wife.'

By this time, Zille had become an expert in deflection and he managed to end the conversation. Soon after starting as a crime reporter, he had acquired the skill of melting into the background, an essential weapon in the crime reporter's arsenal. If you could make yourself invisible, you could stick around longer than the other reporters, hang about with the police after the cameramen had left, try to build up connections. In this way, Zille witnessed many instances of casual corruption. He saw police releasing suspects after a bulging envelope of cash was pressed into their hands. He heard talk of illegal gambling dens or brothels that they had no intention of raiding, unless it was to collect extortion money. He had never had a particularly strong moralizing impulse and was unfazed by this. He saw the circumstances in which police were forced to operate. There were just 30,000 of them to serve this city of over 20 million. They were underfunded and poorly equipped, putting themselves in danger every day, only to be overridden by the army authorities whenever it suited them. The whole system was corrupt – from the most junior officers to the judges sitting in courts of law – so who was he to think badly of a police officer who made his life a bit easier by taking a wad of cash? There were rumours that some crime reporters went a step further, taking bribes themselves, and that this was how they afforded the fancy cars, the designer sunglasses. But Zille didn't want money. All he cared about was contacts.

By the time of Benazir Bhutto's assassination and the 2008 election, Zille had found his feet as a reporter. Apart from Lyari, he had contacts in most of the key trouble spots, sufficient to gain access and secure interviews at short notice. Benazir was assassinated in northern Pakistan, after a massive bomb attack targeted her as she campaigned in Rawalpindi, next to the capital, Islamabad. But Karachi was her hometown, and after her death, people there poured out onto the streets in protest and mourning. Whenever such a big event took place, it was all hands on deck and every reporter pitched in. Zille and his cameraman filmed the unrest that engulfed parts of Karachi, occasionally getting roughed up by rioters who did not want their faces on screen. He was particularly intrigued by a photograph that appeared in a British newspaper, showing Benazir a year earlier, sitting in a car next to Rehman Dakait, the kingpin of Lyari. He had been coordinating her security. Zille was no longer shocked by the way in which crime and politics were tightly knotted together in Karachi. Every street criminal had a political affiliation; every political party had its fingerprints all over multiple criminal enterprises. If you pulled at the thread of a crime story, it was never long before the whole fabric unravelled to reveal the political forces that loomed behind it.

The general election went ahead despite Benazir's death, in a blaze of national grief that restored her party, the Pakistan People's Party, to power and installed her widower, Asif Ali Zardari, as prime minister. This shift in politics brought a change of personnel. Some police officers who had been actively involved in the brutal anti-MQM operation of the 1990s had quietly removed themselves from the city while the Party was in the ascendant under Musharraf. Now some of them returned and Zille had to recalibrate his contacts. One new face was Rao Anwar, a tall police officer with a trigger-happy reputation who was said to be close to Zardari. He was appointed inspector in Kiamari, a coastal area past Lyari that was thick with mangrove forests and drug traders. Within the space of a few months, he was promoted to deputy superintendent, then superintendent of the sprawling area of Gadap, over to the east of the city. This rapid promotion marked him out as someone to watch. Zille first met him at a press conference and went through his usual routine, hanging around as long as possible, giving him his business card and asking him to call if he ever had something to discuss.

With each month that passed, Zille's contacts with the police and different powerbrokers around the city improved, but he was frustrated. Lyari was a big story that he knew was only going to get bigger, but he didn't have an in or a fresh angle. After the violent ruptures that had forced Parveen, the young teacher, and her family to move from Lyari to Kiamari in 2004, Rehman had re-established his control of most of the area. Now, with his political connections to the PPP, he was distancing himself from his criminal past. 'These bastards are even running anti-street crime campaigns,' a police contact muttered to Zille, over chai and cigarettes one evening. When Zille called around his contacts, he found it was true. Despite the obvious irony, Rehman was discouraging crime in Lyari. Soon after the election, he had set up the People's Aman Committee (PAC), a respectable face for the gang. The PAC banned the open selling of narcotics and threatened drug pedlars with death, forbade aerial firing during weddings and imposed fines. The residents loved it. The police officers – who had made a healthy extra income by taking kickbacks from the drug dealers and pimps in the area – did not. Zille heard other whispers too, that the MQM leadership were concerned by Rehman's escalating political ambitions. Though the gangsters of Karachi commanded such respect that Rehman might appear invincible, there were rumours that he didn't have long left, that the MQM would get him if the police didn't first. Zille listened, and watched, and tried to work out how he could make this his story.

One sweltering day in August 2009, with monsoon clouds contributing to the oppressive humidity, Zille's phone rang. It was one of the police contacts he had been carefully cultivating, someone so senior that he wouldn't tell me who it was even years after the event.

'Zille, I can give you a big story. Do you want it?' the police officer said. Zille eagerly told him that he did. 'OK,' the officer replied. 'You know Rehman Dakait?' he said.

'Yes, of course,' said Zille. 'Everyone knows him.'

'We've got him. There's going to be a big encounter. It's going to start soon. We're just finding the right place. Wait for an update.'

Everyone knew what an 'encounter' was: an extrajudicial killing. Usually, police officers would claim that they had been fired on and forced to kill the suspect in self-defence. More often than not, this was untrue and they had actually embarked on the operation with the express intention of killing. Zille had some sympathy with this. After all, when criminals could bribe their way out of court and continue to run their drug-smuggling rings from prison, many senior officers argued that they did not have a choice. Excitedly, Zille told his boss the news about the apparently exclusive scoop. His boss was dubious; there was no evidence yet. But Zille had a hunch that this was his moment, that for whatever reason the police contact had deliberately selected him to report on this story. He waited by the phone, pacing up and down. It was five hours before the officer called again.

'It's happened. He's been killed with some friends. Get here with your cameraman.'

Zille immediately alerted the team at Geo, who ran a ticker along the bottom of the screen saying that there were reports that Rehman Dakait had been killed by police. The next hour passed in a blur as Zille rushed over there. Rehman had not been killed in Lyari, but in an industrial area called Bin Qasim. Zille pulled up and saw that a group of police and other people were gathered. It took a moment for him to notice the dead body on the ground, the pool of congealing blood. It was Rehman, already turning grey but otherwise a normal-looking guy with an oval face and a bulbous nose; the same face that had been caught by a photographer's flash, with a harried expression, in a car next to Benazir Bhutto less than two years earlier. Zille knew he didn't have long before the other reporters descended. Quickly, he began to talk into the microphone down the lens. It was his first big story. His break. He had arrived.

The days that followed were a hectic whirl of live broadcasts and hustling. It was a huge story, ratings gold – a gangster movie played out in real time on TV screens across the country. On this occasion Zille's lack of experience in Lyari didn't matter, because he had been there first. He went to Lyari every day, covering Rehman's funeral and the reaction in the area. He interviewed relatives of Rehman and another gangster who had been killed in the same encounter. His phone rang again and again with requests from the Geo office. Now that Rehman was dead and buried, people wanted to know who would be the next kingpin of Lyari. Zille introduced himself to everyone – local police officers, high- and low-ranking gangsters and their families, residents who came to loiter on the street and stare at the television cameras that had descended. It was the same approach he had honed over several years on the job. Hand out your card indiscriminately, ask people to give you their phone number and get them to take yours. 'Contact me if anything is happening, if there's any firing, if you hear a protest,' he said, to one after the other. 'You call me and I will give you full media coverage.' He made promises with no idea if he could or would keep them. The only thing that mattered was the contacts – you never knew who was going to end up being useful to you. Sitting in the Geo office after the funeral, he looked through his phone at the numbers he had acquired the day before and called every gang member to ask if they knew who would be the next boss. Most stonewalled or were vague. It was hard to know whether they were being evasive because they had something to hide or because they simply didn't know the answer. But Zille did not want to lose the story now.

Eventually someone had some information. 'It's not decided. Try again in two or three days,' the gangster said, readying himself to hang up.

'Give me some names,' said Zille quickly, trying to keep him on the phone. 'Just one or two names, anyone who is in the running.'

The gangster sounded impatient, but said, 'Baba Ladla. Uzair Baloch.' Then he hung up.

Zille alerted the news desk and they ran a ticker along the bottom of the screen on Geo straight away, keen to get the scoop out before someone else got hold of the same information: 'The next *sardar* [leader] of Lyari will be Baba Ladla or Uzair Baloch.'

Of course, this wasn't enough. 'Go to Lyari,' said Zille's boss, the news editor. 'Interview both these people.'

Zille got into his car and made his way through the clogged traffic of Chundrigar Road, the hectic throng of people and street hawkers that lined the streets of Saddar, towards the highway and Lyari's yellow arches, its tangled web of alleys. On the way he called every new contact he could think of who might be able to orchestrate these interviews. Someone told him he should come to a particular house, deep inside Lyari, to meet Uzair Baloch, who was a cousin of Rehman's. Zille drove straight there. When he arrived, he was ushered through to meet Uzair. He was surprised at how cultivated this supposed gangster was. He was sharply dressed and spoke Urdu well, with the polite manner and easy authority of someone well educated. Thinking of Rehman's political ambitions, Zille had a gut feeling that the man in front of him was going to be the next leader. As they carried out the interview, another man arrived. He was short, with a flat, round face and a rough manner. It was Baba Ladla, the other man in the running.

Zille greeted him and asked, 'Are you going to be the next *sardar* of Lyari?'

Baba Ladla shook his head. 'No. Uzair *bhai* [brother] will be the next *sardar*.'

Zille called the office right away. The news went out that there was a new leader in Lyari. It was an unbelievable buzz. There was no way Zille was going to give up being a crime reporter now.

6

ASHURA

Safdar the ambulance driver saw the news of Rehman Dakait's death and Uzair Baloch's ascendancy reported on the TV. He didn't much care about the machinations at the top of Karachi's conflicts. Rehman's was just another name on the long list of lives lost. When the gang violence was bad, Safdar had to go into Lyari several times a week to collect the bullet-pocked bodies of young men felled in battle. But at least they were gangsters who had deliberately courted danger. The casualties that left him queasy and despondent at the end of the day were the children, old men or women who had been caught in the crossfire. They were blameless victims of a city at war with itself. Sometimes reporters clustered at the scene of a death would refer to the dead person as a 'political worker', but Safdar knew that often they had just been in the wrong place at the wrong time. He frequently arrived too late to help, and could only collect the body and try to restore some dignity in death. The horror he had felt on his first day, picking up that rotting corpse from Lyari, had left him completely. Now he trained drivers himself. When Kamran, a new recruit under Safdar's supervision, panicked at the sight of a dead body, Safdar thought back to his own training from Chiri Babu. He slapped Kamran in the face and told him to pull himself together.

Safdar was posted all around the city. Sometimes, he was based at the main Tower office in central Karachi, where the bosses Edhi and Kazmi usually worked. At other times, he was posted to one of the makeshift depots that the Edhi Foundation had set up so that drivers could be closer to different parts of the city's sprawl. These usually consisted of a single kiosk, with space for one or two ambulances to park under a canvas awning held up by bamboo poles so that drivers could sit in the shade while they waited for calls to come in. The shifts were so long and frenetic that sometimes there didn't seem to be much point going home to Landhi afterwards, so instead Safdar hung around the office until he was back on duty. He had never needed much rest. This meant he could go for days without seeing his family, which had one major benefit: it allowed him to avoid his parents' constant pressure about marriage.

'I'm not going to get married, *Amma*,' he frequently told his mother. 'The work I do is too dangerous. I'm not employed at some fancy private company. I could get shot at any point. I don't want to make a woman into a widow.'

It had worked so far, but he could tell that his parents weren't happy and he didn't like to displease them. Still, there was so much happening in the city that it was easy to bury himself in work and ignore his nagging guilt about family responsibilities.

Safdar hadn't been home in over a week when, one evening in October 2009, he got a phone call from his grandmother, thousands of miles away in the mountains of Khyber Pakhtunkhwa. He was driving a patient home from hospital, but he answered the phone

Dadi was coughing and her voice sounded weak. 'I'm sick,' she said. 'You need to come to the village.'

After hanging up, Safdar immediately called his parents. They confirmed that *Dadi* was seriously ill and that many of their relatives were already making their way from Karachi to the village to pay their last respects. There was no time to waste. After dropping off his ambulance, Safdar went straight to the bus depot in Sohrab Goth. It was a twenty-four-hour bus ride, a long, bumpy journey on motorways and dirt tracks, across scrubland like the area where Jannat and her family lived, through agricultural fields and mountains. As he retraced the journey he and his family had made from the village to Karachi all those years ago, Safdar phoned his siblings, his aunts and uncles. All were either in the village or on their way.

The crisp mountain air hit Safdar as soon as he stepped out of the bus, a blast of childhood. He walked to *Dadi*'s house, where he found her sitting on a stool, in the middle of taking a huge pinch of *naswar* – a powerful green powdered tobacco popular in the region. She snorted it up her left nostril and blinked at the impact before looking at Safdar.

'How are you?' he said, embracing her.

'I was well all along,' said *Dadi*, sniffing deeply to pull in the remnants of *naswar*.

'OK,' said Safdar, confused. 'So what's going on?'

'It's your wedding,' said *Dadi*.

Safdar felt the colour drain from his face and he staggered to a seat. 'That can't be true. I'm not getting married. How can I? I've told everyone I can't marry. Think of the kind of work I do.'

Dadi shrugged. 'You are here now. You have to get married.'

Safdar mentally replayed the previous few days, all the conversations he'd had with his relatives. Everyone had said that *Dadi* was ill. They must have all been in on it. Had they hatched these plans in the ten days that he hadn't been home? Was this his punishment? Safdar felt like a sacrificial goat brought to the slaughter. Several of his aunts arrived and began washing rice in preparation for the wedding feast. Soon relatives were appearing every hour. It would be a huge dishonour to walk out on the arrangement now. His wife-to-be was his uncle's daughter, a member of the same family, and it would cause a rift if Safdar jilted her.

Safdar's cousins joined them in *Dadi*'s room. 'What music do you want at the party?' one asked. 'What do you need?' 'Do you have appropriate clothes?' 'What entertainment do you want?'

Safdar, who usually had a sharp comment for every occasion, was speechless. 'Why don't you ask the real planners of the wedding?' he muttered.

The *nikah* (religious ceremony) took place the next day, the wedding reception the day after. Safdar's new wife was pretty and good-natured; she was so fair-skinned that he thought she looked pink. She had finished school and could read and write far better than he could. But as his relatives danced and celebrated, Safdar was reeling from this seismic and unexpected change. He looked at his new wife, who was blushing and avoiding his eyes, and imagined her dressed in the pale colours of mourning, weeping at the news that he had been killed. On the third day of celebrations, Safdar told his grandmother that he was going to run some errands. He went to the bus depot and got a bus back to Karachi. He knew that his new life as a married man had started, but he had an urge to be at home.

The familiar mesh of Landhi's streets, the queues of brightly painted trucks and cylindrical oil tankers, the unpaved alleyways dotted with makeshift stores, the scent of fresh naan rising from tandoor ovens filled Safdar with relief. Even the acrid smell of exhaust fumes made him feel he was on firm ground. He spoke to his mother, who was still in the village. He told her he'd had to go to work. She was so elated that the trick had worked that she wasn't even angry he'd skipped out on the weeks of social engagements with extended family and neighbours that usually followed a wedding. 'I'll stay here with your wife and make the arrangements to come back to the city,' she said.

It was a month before they returned, a month in which Safdar had a growing sense of unease about the dangers he faced every day. He was not one person any more. He was responsible for two, and, if they were lucky, soon there would be children. But his work was not just a job. When there was so much need, it was the only thing he could possibly do.

Safdar had not spent a religious holiday at home since being hired as an ambulance driver. Even on Eid, the most significant holiday, he usually got up, put on his festive salwar kameez and said prayers with the family, then rushed off to work. Religious holidays often meant that crowds gathered, either at a procession or at the mosque. And crowds meant greater likelihood of a shooting or an explosion. The Edhi Foundation provided medical backup at every religious procession in Karachi, stationing their small red and white ambulances at regular intervals along the planned route.

The Islamic calendar is lunar, so the precise date of the holy days – Eid, Ramzan – changes each year. In 2009, the year Safdar got married, Ashura fell in December, around two months after his wedding and a month after his wife had relocated to the city. No one in Safdar's household minded too much that he would have to work; they were Sunni, and Ashura is particularly holy for Shias. It marks the death of Imam Hussein, the grandson of the Prophet Muhammad and the son of Ali, who founded Shia Islam. It is a day of mourning, and every year on Ashura Shias hold a procession through the streets of Karachi, ululating, praying and grieving. Some of the most devout worshippers self-flagellate, whipping their own backs with leather or metal-tipped tassels until they draw blood. People often needed rapid medical assistance. Some got caught up in the heady atmosphere and scourged themselves too hard, causing injury or excessive blood loss, or else the harsh metal-edged whips would hit the wrong person. Injury was not the only worry. The Shia community was often targeted by terrorist groups, so extra caution was needed at their events. The Pakistani army was fighting the Taliban and other Sunni extremist groups in the regions bordering Afghanistan, not far from Safdar's village. Increasing numbers of ordinary Pashtuns were fleeing to Karachi to escape the fallout of the warfare between militants and military. Hidden among the people displaced by the fighting were some of the militants themselves, escaping the army incursion to set up new bases in this lawless city. Safdar knew there was the risk of an attack, but that was always a risk in Karachi. He had no reason to believe today would be any worse than any other day.

Safdar woke up early and rode his motorbike from Landhi to the Edhi office. The streets were almost deserted. Most people were off work and the usual commuting crowd was significantly thinned out. He changed into his Edhi T-shirt and got into the ambulance. Edhi drivers usually parked two ambulances close together, so that if something did go badly wrong more than one person was on hand immediately to help. A bonus was that if nothing happened the drivers could chat to pass the time. Safdar was teamed up with Fazlur, a good friend with whom he had worked for several years. They drove their ambulances together, in convoy, to the spot they had been assigned on Muhammad Ali Jinnah Road. They went past the makeshift barricades that had been set up to stop traffic from interrupting the parade routes and the police search points that had been established overnight. Safdar was not thinking about his own safety. He was more preoccupied by his irritation with the Chhipa ambulances he saw as he drove to his designated spot. This new ambulance service had been set up just two years before by another charitable foundation. Safdar saw them as incompetent rivals, trying to muscle in on Edhi's rightful turf. 'As far as ambulances go, these guys are just kids and we are the dons,' he liked to say disdainfully.

Across town, Zille was also making preparations to attend the Ashura procession. Zille was Shia, so his bosses thought he would be well placed to cover the event – but Ashura was significant for his family. In the end, his wife, brother-in-law and a few other relatives decided that they would come along as well, to keep Zille company for at least the first part of the day. They walked together in prayer, Zille helping to hold up one of the banners, flanked by his brother-in-law. There were other families in attendance too, although men made up the majority of the crowd. After a while, Zille's relatives waved goodbye and headed in the direction of home, while he wove his way through the crowd to meet his cameraman and take up his allotted position along the route. He saw his bureau chief, Fahim, who was also Shia, at the procession with his seven-year-old son and niece. Fahim greeted Zille but was soon distracted, attending to the kids. Zille slipped through the crowd and made it to the blood donation station, where he had arranged to interview people. This was a big event and lots of reporters were working. Zille was stationed near the back, with his colleague Talha at the front.

Not far from where Talha was set up with his cameraman, giving live updates on the progress of the procession, Safdar and Fazlur spotted a stall over the road selling cold drinks. They inched their way through the thronged street to buy refreshments. Most of the shops that lined the streets were shuttered. People had gathered on rooftops and balconies above the stores to watch the procession. A group of officers from the Rangers, the paramilitary force, were standing guard nearby in their sand-coloured camouflage uniforms.

The cold can was in Safdar's hand when he noticed a scuffle nearby. The way Safdar remembers it, a man in a heavy, bulky jacket was trying to join the procession. The Rangers rushed towards him. Fazlur, who had spotted the disturbance before Safdar did, dropped his cold drink on the floor as he ran towards the scene, looking for a way to help the Rangers. Later, there would be some debate about whether it was a suicide bomber, as Safdar recalls, or a remotely detonated bomb. Whichever it was, the force threw Safdar to the ground. Dust clouds plumed around him. People started running, their feet close to his head on the pavement. The air was filled with the smell of blood.

Safdar wrenched himself up from the ground and tried to steady his gaze. The ambulances stood across the road, so damaged by the blast that he could tell immediately that they were unusable. He knew that forty ambulances were stationed along the route, and that backup would arrive, but in the chaos and panic he wasn't sure how long it would take. Smoke rose higher than the buildings. Flags and banners collapsed over the crowd in a claustrophobic canopy as the people carrying them sagged and fell to the ground.

Until backup arrived, Safdar and Fazlur needed to get as many seriously injured people as possible out of the scrum so they would not be trampled. Safdar began to push his way towards the scene, keeping his eyes out for Fazlur. The explosion had been so close that he could barely hear, lending the whole experience a nightmarish quality, as if he was in a vacuum. People didn't know where to go and were running in all directions. When Safdar looked at the people on the ground, it was difficult to see who was injured and who was dead. Dismembered body parts littered the street. He saw a groaning man prostrate on the street and ducked down to help him. Hauling the man up by his armpits, he looked around and finally saw Fazlur. His torso was right there on the side of the street, legs ripped off, face lifeless. Safdar stared, frozen for a moment. But there was nothing he could do. He channelled his strength into moving the prone man away from the stampede. He had to breathe. Help was coming soon.

At the other end of the procession, Zille heard the blast from a distance. Everyone began to scream and run, but there was nowhere to run to. People watching Geo at home would have seen Talha giving a routine update on the progress of the procession, then visibly jumping as the bomb went off in the background, turning around, his voice rising as he told viewers, 'There has been a blast.' Instinctively, Zille reached for his phone. He needed to call his wife, his brother-in-law, any one of the relatives who were at the procession. He did not know where they were, if they'd got home yet or if they'd been caught up in the explosion. But there was no point. Mobile phone towers were always switched off for big events like this. Zille did not have time to panic, because a voice was coming through his walkie-talkie. 'Please go to the hospital,' his colleague back at the news desk shouted. 'You can cover the story from there.'

Pushing all thoughts of his own family's safety out of his mind, Zille and his cameraman decided to walk to Civil Hospital, making their way through the screaming crowds. It wasn't until he arrived that the horror hit him. Ambulances were screeching into the car park. Harried drivers covered in dust and blood unloaded stretchers of people howling in agony, limbs torn apart, clothing ripped and flesh ruptured. Bodies were piled up in the corridors, some frighteningly contorted. There was blood everywhere. People were forced to share beds; some were on the floor. Somehow the people who weren't screaming were more frightening than those who were. Zille couldn't tell who was dead or alive. As he walked into the corridor, his entire sense of purpose left him. He had never covered an explosion before and he felt as if the ground had dropped away from beneath him. He saw bodies, large and small, their faces covered with sheets or tattered dupattas. He walked over to one bed, where a small body lay, and lifted the cloth covering the face. A child stared back at him, face smeared with blood and grime, life gone. Suddenly desperate for some air, Zille walked back out of the hospital, legs shaking, and called the office. A colleague told him that the bureau chief, Fahim, had been injured, and that his children were missing. Fahim's femur bone had shattered in the blast; it would take years of surgery to fix. They found out later that his seven-year-old son and his niece had been killed instantly.

Back at the site of the bombing, Safdar was still hauling people's bodies out of the carnage, unable to stop his eyes from darting back to the lifeless Fazlur. Through his ringing ears, he heard the sound of an Edhi ambulance siren. Help was here.

It must have been just a few minutes since the explosion, though it felt like hours. Through the haze of debris he saw the red T-shirts of his colleagues, felt their arms reach out to help him carry bodies, identify and treat survivors. Faisal Edhi, the son of the old man, was there too, coordinating the response. The sight of his colleagues snapping into action gave Safdar a boost, though his head was pounding and he kept catching glimpses of Fazlur's face looking up at him from the street. They worked for hours. Since Safdar's ambulance was too badly damaged to drive, he stayed on the scene, administering first aid and identifying the injured, as his colleagues ferried people back and forth to the government hospitals nearby. The need was greater than the resources, so they packed people into the back of each tiny ambulance, trying not to compound their injuries as they did so. Safdar could not think about his family at home, or about what a near miss it had been. When he told me about it six years later, he said it was the worst day of his life.

Meanwhile, outside the hospital, Zille was taking deep breaths to calm himself as he and the cameraman made preparations for their live broadcast to report on the numbers of dead and injured. When he checked his phone between pieces to camera, he saw that the signal had come back. His wife and brother-in-law had made it home before the explosion went off. His entire family had broken down in relief when they saw him appear on their screen and realized that he was safe. Throughout the broadcast, his phone beeped with frantic messages from his Shia friends and neighbours, begging him to look for their loved ones among the dead. Zille tried to respond to some, but he was overwhelmed. He put his phone away. There was too much to do. This was the biggest attack in Karachi in years and it was a huge story.

The government quickly came out with a statement that it had been a suicide bomb. The Tehreek-e-Taliban Pakistan claimed responsibility. Within hours of the attack, people were angry, throwing stones and torching cars as riots erupted along the route. Zille drove back to the area where the procession had been and found it in flames. Massive arson attacks claimed over 3,000 businesses. Flames licked the sky as TV cameras broadcast live; the smoke from burning buildings mingled with the plaster dust and debris of the bombing.

Although he was still shaking with the shock, Zille worked for twenty-four hours straight, covering the difficulties of identifying some of the bodies and interviewing many Shias, who expressed anger that the state had failed to protect them. The funerals for the thirty people killed in the attack began the next day. There was no chance for Zille to process the horror of what he had seen in the hospital, or to go home and embrace his loved ones. The story demanded everyone's attention.

When Safdar eventually made it back home to Landhi late that night, he was too exhausted to speak. His ears were still ringing, as they would for three days afterwards. His mother and wife begged him to go to a doctor to make sure he had not sustained an injury himself, but he ignored their pleas. He slept a heavy, dreamless sleep, then went back to work the next morning. The hundreds of injured people who had survived the blast needed to be transported home, and there were injuries from the fires and riots to deal with. In the office a few weeks later, Safdar noticed a small photograph, a head-shot against a blue background that looked as if it could be a school picture. It was of Fazlur. When he saw it on the wall, Blu-tacked alongside the other Edhi ambulance drivers who had been killed on duty, grief hit him right in the gut.

As the dead were buried, conspiracy theories whirled about the real cause of the fires that had engulfed Muhammad Ali Jinnah Road after the explosion. Zille and his colleagues tried to pick through the rumours for their reports. Was it the Muttahida Qaumi Movement? The Pakistan People's Party? Some land mafia spying an opportunity to move in on this valuable commercial land and buy it up cheaply? Or Sunni extremist groups trying to exacerbate sectarian tensions? Conspiracy theories are the background music to life in Pakistan and their chords overlapped until the real events were almost completely obscured. Goaded by rumours and inflammatory rhetoric, the supporters of opposing political parties entered into gun battles in different parts of the city. Grief and mourning were pushed aside. Zille practically lived in his car, driving between locations with a cameraman, speaking to contacts in the police force and city government in search of an elusive inside scoop. The centre of Karachi stank of burnt rubber and plaster dust, but the blood splatters on the streets were soon covered by the daily grime of pollution and footfall. Zille was so busy that he did not have time to worry about the anonymous faxes which had been coming through to the office. They warned the station to get Zille and other Shia reporters off air. But Zille reminded himself that he was a reporter, not a victim.

Sunni extremist groups had had a foothold in Pakistan for decades. One of the most prominent, Sipah-e-Sahaba, was founded in 1985. But militancy had ramped up after the war on terror began in 2001. The US-led invasion of Afghanistan had pushed many Afghan Taliban and Al-Qaeda members out of the country. Afghan fighters and foreign militants alike fled US troops, travelling over the porous border into Pakistan to take refuge in the mountainous tribal areas, where the state had little jurisdiction. They set up new strongholds there, and a subsequent Pakistani military incursion aimed at rooting out foreign militants was mishandled. It alienated local tribesmen, some of whom sympathized with the extremists. Different radical Islamist groups established themselves in the area and, in 2007, they coalesced into a single movement: the TTP. It had close ties to Al-Qaeda, but was distinct from the Afghan Taliban. Headed by Beitullah Mehsud, a Pakistani militant, its stated aims were opposition to Pakistani military action in the tribal areas and the destruction of the Pakistani state. The movement had quickly grown in power, staging attacks around the country. But until 2009, the Taliban and other terror groups had mainly used Karachi as a fundraising base. To do this, they mimicked the MQM and the Lyari gang lords, using kidnapping, extortion and bank robberies to raise funds. This meant they were embroiled in Karachi's street politics, clashing with the Awami National Party, which controlled the mostly Pashtun areas where the Taliban wanted to assert itself, and targeting other political parties and their workers too. But although this presence had been steadily growing, the Ashura attack was different – a major terror attack on the city itself.

On 5 February, forty days after Ashura, another Shia procession was held to mark the end of the ritual period of mourning for Imam Hussein, an important figure in Shia Islam. Once again, Shias gathered from around the city, carrying banners. Karachi was on high alert. Police and Rangers issued warnings that there could be trouble. But the worshippers were undeterred; in fact, if anything they were more determined than ever to demonstrate their faith. Despite their near miss, many of Zille's relatives decided to go. Safdar's wife begged him to stay home for the day, but all the Edhi drivers were on duty, standing by in case something happened. Minibuses packed full of Shias from different parts of Karachi drove towards the procession route. The buses were mostly small, and people were packed into the seats and aisles, sometimes even clinging to the exterior.

The blast came in the afternoon, from a bomb strapped to a motorbike which detonated next to one of these buses, when it was close to Jinnah Hospital. The passengers had been families: men, women, children. At least a dozen people died immediately. The mangled bus stood in the middle of the road, the ground streaked with blood. Safdar heard the explosion and leapt into an ambulance from the depot, careering in and out of traffic to get to the scene. He worked quickly and methodically, pushing his way through crowds of people and putting as many of the injured as possible into the back of his ambulance. He drove the short distance to the hospital and pulled up onto the small strip of tarmac in front of the building. He unloaded the people from the back, wheeling the stretcher as fast as he could to the emergency room on the ground floor. It was packed. Multiple ambulances were unloading scores of seriously injured people. Those who were wounded but walking had made their own way since the bomb had detonated so nearby. The corridors were full, and relatives of the injured crowded into the car park. Inside it was hot and claustrophobic. Edhi himself was there, helping to coordinate the relief work with his son Faisal.

Safdar rushed back outside with his empty stretcher, planning to drive back to the scene of the attack. That was when the second explosion ripped through the crowd at the hospital. The impact sent Safdar flying backwards. When he looked up he saw that the glass of his ambulance's windscreen had shattered. In a daze, he noticed several Edhi colleagues had rushed to his side and were inspecting him for injuries. He looked down and saw blood pouring down his body and what looked like wounded flesh hanging from rips in his clothes. 'You're OK, you're not hurt,' one of his colleagues yelled. Safdar looked again and realized that it was not his blood. Pieces of someone else's flesh were stuck to him. He tried to respond, but he couldn't hear his own voice. Somehow, with the help of his colleagues, Safdar got to his feet, his legs unsteady. 'I'm all right,' he tried to say. 'I can help.' But his ambulance was one of three that had been rendered unusable. Everything was filthy, with blood and body parts, dust and grime, together with the guttural sounds of agony and fear. The front of the hospital had been badly damaged. Edhi ordered the drivers to get as many people as possible to other government hospitals nearby. As Safdar worked, he kept Edhi in his line of vision. The old man's flowing white beard and his air of authority were comforting amid this chaos.

Safdar wasn't sure exactly when the motorbike came into view, but it was immediately noticeable, because it was so clean, and because of the TV set strapped to the back. Safdar pointed it out to a colleague, who shrugged. The police were already on the scene, with sniffer dogs checking for more explosives, and they hadn't flagged it. The bike sat right in front of the Edhi ambulance kiosk, where the old man was sitting and surveying the scene. Safdar kept his eyes on both – the bike and his boss – as he worked through the dirt and horror and the pounding in his own head. He ran over to Edhi and pointed out the bike. 'Faisal is worried too,' Edhi said. Faisal walked over to the bike and gingerly opened the top of the TV monitor. Inside was a canister packed with hundreds of metal nuts. It was a third bomb. They yelled for the police. Safdar watched, frozen, as they defused it, unable to think of anything except how close to Edhi the bomb had been. Images of his colleague Fazlur's lifeless body flashed through his mind. He did not remember how he made it home that night, but when he later gave in to his family's pleas to get checked out by a doctor he was told that he had suffered internal injuries – a head wound, damage to his eardrum. He did not take time off to recover.

In July 2010, a few months after the attack on Jinnah Hospital, the monsoon burst over Pakistan, a heavy rain that saturated the land and filled the Indus River until its banks collapsed and thousands of kilometres of land were flooded. It swamped the villages of Sindh outside Karachi, in Punjab, all the way up to Khyber Pakhtunkhwa. Karachi saw just a few days of rain. At first the monsoon breaking was a relief, but then the lack of drainage turned the streets to a sludgy soup of rubbish and sewage. Electricity pylons and the wires that spread like vines through the sky and across the sides of buildings sparked and ruptured. Then, just like that, the rain stopped. The heavy clouds passed over Karachi and dumped torrential rain over other parts of Pakistan. The map-maker Siraj left the stultifying heat and drenched alleys of the city for ten or fifteen days at a time, travelling to some of the worst-affected areas around Sindh and Punjab to map the damage and work on reconstruction.

By now, Siraj's regular work in Karachi had expanded into all sorts of community programmes. In one project, the Technical and Training Resource Centre helped groups of women band together into collectives to pool their resources and save money. In another, they worked with the small, low-cost private schools that filled the gaping holes left by poor state provision. The TTRC helped these schools to budget more efficiently so that money could be channelled back into study materials or extracurricular activities like sports days. Siraj had started a huge mapping project too. He wanted to locate every school in the district, with the aim of seeing what was there, which services were missing and which were being duplicated. He did not see areas in terms of their political affiliation or ethnic make-up, but of what amenities they lacked and the improvements that could be made. Many parts of Orangi were still without proper sewage lines; most did not have easy access to running water. In some of the worst areas, people lived in unplastered houses, with dust from the local factories floating in the air and giving people serious lung problems. He worked in the Mohajir areas close to his own home, as well as in the neighbouring Pashtun districts in Orangi and beyond, in Baldia Town, an industrial area called SITE Town. But like everyone else in Orangi, he learned to fit his life around the ethnic violence. When Siraj was going to a Pashtun area, the person he was visiting would send someone to collect him at a specified meeting point. Siraj was clearly Mohajir – his clothes gave him away, even before he started speaking – but if he was accompanied by a local, he would not be perceived as a target. He extended the same welcome if a Pashtun person needed to enter a Mohajir area. Siraj was almost always greeted with generous hospitality, regardless of the area's ethnic make-up, but he never knew where political thugs might be lurking. It was frustrating, to have to rethink and reshape around this confected battle that was beyond his control.

As the summer months wore on, heavy heat blanketed the city and the political tension rose. In August, it finally tipped over into violence. An MQM politician, a member of the Sindh Assembly – the provincial government – was gunned down as he attended a funeral in Nazimabad, a sprawling middle-class area not far from Orangi. MQM leaders blamed their enemies in the ANP, the dominant political force in Pashtun areas – a secular, leftist party that advocated for a separate Pashtun state. Founded in the 1980s in Pakistan's north-west, it had significant support in Pashtun areas of Karachi. After the shooting, riots erupted across Karachi, centred in Orangi Town. Shots were fired across Mohajir–Pashtun lines. (Later, it emerged that this was misplaced and the ANP were not to blame – two men from the Sunni militant group Lashkar-e-Jhangvi carried out the assassination.) More than eighty people were killed over the course of the fighting. Siraj was away from town working on the flood relief during the worst of it, but every time he came back he saw shops burned out, heard of more deaths, saw bullet casings littering the streets. The by-election to replace the murdered politician was held in October and riots broke out again. Boys from the MQM with guns slung round their shoulders patrolled Siraj's area, asking residents if they could count on their votes. 'What's the point in voting?' people joked darkly among themselves. 'Our votes are already cast for the MQM.' Ethnic divisions deepened as more displaced Pashtuns, fleeing the devastating warfare between the military and Taliban extremists in northern Pakistan, crowded into Pashtun neighbourhoods.

Perhaps it was inevitable that among the new arrivals from northern Pakistan would be some of the very militants that the refugees were fleeing. On his visits to Pashtun schools in Orangi and Baldia Town, Siraj noticed a claustrophobic atmosphere that reminded him of his own area, held in the iron grip of the Party. Although this was not entirely new, something had markedly changed. Most political parties in Karachi operated on two levels, seeking not just votes but also tight territorial control. While the MQM ran the most organized state-within-a-state of any of Karachi's parties, the ANP also ran extortion rackets and controlled voter banks in the areas which it dominated. The ANP often clashed violently with their MQM rivals. When the Taliban established itself in Karachi, it was in the Pashtun neighbourhoods run by the ANP. This was not a happy coexistence. The Taliban wanted territorial control of these areas and launched an astonishingly brutal campaign against the ANP, attacking its workers, its offices, its gatherings.

The new presence of the Taliban and other extremist groups had tipped the balance of power in Pashtun neighbourhoods, but to Siraj this stranglehold felt like a fresh iteration of the same criminal control he had seen for years. When he spoke on the phone to the teachers he had known for years, most were tight-lipped about what was going on, but some confided that they had been threatened or issued with demands for extortion by the Taliban. Some were resisting, but others had capitulated and were decimating already scant school budgets to pay off extorters, afraid of what might happen if they didn't.

Meeting people in person was a crucial part of Siraj's work. All of it – the maps, the savings groups, the schools programmes – was founded on personal relationships and helping people to work for themselves. Siraj spoke regularly on the phone to the different head teachers he was working with around Orangi and Baldia Town, but sometimes face-to-face contact was necessary. There were contracts that needed to be signed, cash loans distributed. Speaking on the phone to a Pashtun head teacher he had known for years one evening, Siraj's worst fears were confirmed. Things were too tense for the usual tactic – going to an area with a local chaperone – to work. 'Siraj *sahib*, it is completely impossible for you to come here as an Urdu-speaking person,' the teacher said.

Siraj remembered his mentor, Sahiba's advice: 'Think flexibly.' If they couldn't cross into each other's areas, perhaps they could meet on the border that divided them. Halfway down Manghopir Road, a main thoroughfare in Orangi, was a roundabout. On one side was a Pashtun neighbourhood and on the other an Urdu-speaking area. Siraj asked the Pashtun head teacher to meet him at the roundabout. They nodded greetings and walked together to a footpath that ran alongside the road a few metres away. They sat on the large, dusty slabs that formed a rudimentary kerbstone, faces illuminated by the lights from cars whizzing by, shouting over the noise of traffic about the school's annual budget. People paused and stared. Occasionally someone would mutter, 'What are these people doing sitting on the footpath?' But it worked. From that day, whenever Siraj could not carry out his business on the phone and had to meet someone in person, he asked them to meet him at the roundabout.

It wasn't a perfect solution. You never knew who was watching. MQM and ANP informants were everywhere, and Siraj knew that he was taking a risk by making himself conspicuous. He always kept the meetings short. They would discuss contracts for stationery or textbooks, exchange cash loans or signed documents. Then they would stand up and say their goodbyes, disappearing back into starkly divided territories.

7

LYARI

When Rehman Dakait was killed and Uzair Baloch was installed as the new *sardar* of Lyari in 2009, Parveen and her immediate family had been living in Kiamari for five years. Parveen and her mother had been the first to move. The other siblings followed, one by one, until only the youngest, Faheem, was left. He was fifteen years old and still at school, and for several months he stayed with *Mamoo*, their maternal uncle. But soon he began experiencing headaches and a pounding heart and the doctor diagnosed high blood pressure, most likely caused by the stress of living in such violent surroundings. So eventually all seven of them, plus spouses and children, were in Kiamari, packed into the government housing granted to Parveen's sister Nasreen because of her job as a nurse.

Kiamari is wrapped around a long coastline of sandy beaches interspersed with mangrove forests. Right outside the house was a huge tree – unthinkable in Lyari, where every spare patch of earth was built on. In the early morning, birds sang. The house was separated from the neighbours' place by a low wall covered in jasmine flowers, their sweet fragrance filling the air. They had a direct view of the sea, a shimmering grey-green expanse that stretched out beyond the port and its piles of stacked shipping containers bearing the names of international companies. Kiamari had problems of its own: it was a low-income area that, like Lyari, formed a centre of the drugs trade, with shipments of heroin and cocaine passing through the port from Afghanistan and onwards to Western countries. But it was not an active battlefield. The greenery, the water, the fresh air, all of it gave Parveen a sense of peace she had not felt in years.

After her initial reluctance to leave Lyari, Parveen's mother, *Amma*, now said she never wanted to go back: 'I want to live out the rest of my days in Kiamari. I am done with listening to the sound of gunfire.' The family felt settled there, but their lives were inextricably tied to Lyari. Most of their relatives were still there and two of Parveen's sisters moved back after they married, so the Kiamari contingent visited often. Each time Parveen returned, the intensity of the violence struck her afresh. It was not unusual to see a dead body lying in the street as she made her way to a family member's house, and there was always news of a friend, relative or acquaintance who had been killed. Sometimes, when clashes between different gangs tore through Lyari, relatives took refuge in Kiamari, squeezing into the living room on roll-out mattresses for a few nights.

The extremity of their circumstances did not mean that normal family pressures disappeared. Parveen's mother and siblings did not push her on the subject of marriage, but every time someone from the extended family passed through, it was the first thing they asked. All her sisters, even the youngest, were now married. But Parveen had no intention of following suit. In the 1980s, Pakistan's military leader Zia al-Huq had popularized the slogan *Chador aur char diwari*, which translates as 'A veil and four walls' – the proper place for a woman. Parveen liked to joke that she wore a chador but would never be trapped within four walls. She had watched friends marry and lose their freedom. She had too much work to do, too many injustices to tackle, to take that risk. After moving to Kiamari, she had started working in development, taking on research projects and field coordination with Pakistani and international NGOs. This often took her to Balochistan, her family's ancestral home, a place that made her feel rooted and complete.

When *Nani*, their maternal grandmother, got sick, Parveen offered to stay with her for a few months. Things had altered in Lyari since the change in leadership. Uzair was more explicitly political than his predecessor. Rehman Dakait's name had been famous, but many people had no idea what he looked like. By contrast, Uzair's face adorned posters all over Lyari, often daubed with the colours of the Pakistan People's Party flag. It was said that his gang acted as the street enforcers for the PPP, ready to fight the Muttahida Qaumi Movement when necessary. The two parties were in coalition together in the national government, but at street level they were involved in an aggressive turf war. This association with the governing party made Uzair untouchable. When Rehman had been in charge, he was known for trying to keep the worst of the street crime out of Lyari; it was only when he split with other gangsters that violence engulfed the area. Uzair was different from the start. He seemed to have taken some inspiration from the way the MQM ran Orangi Town and his men patrolled the streets. There were drug dealers everywhere and stories of torture cells circulated. Arshad Pappu ran the main rival gang and fighting between the groups broke out often. Uzair was originally from the Singu Lane area of Lyari, but he was constructing a house right by Rehman's old place in Kalakot – just across the street from Parveen's cousins, Aisha and Sayed. They had grown up together and Parveen considered them to be more like siblings than cousins. Aisha was animated and gossipy, and always had juicy stories. She told Parveen that Uzair was generous with his money. While Rehman had often quietly footed the bill for weddings or funerals for poorer residents, Uzair was more flashy, handing out stacks of money at local events in front of everyone.

A few months into her stay with *Nani*, Parveen had an early-morning flight to catch. She travelled around Pakistan frequently, flying to the capital, Islamabad, for meetings or to Balochistan for relief work. Her employer wouldn't send their office drivers to Lyari because it was too dangerous, so she usually had to make her own way to the airport. This was easy enough when there was no fighting. But the weeks leading up to this flight saw the streets around *Nani*'s house caught up in gun battles. Parveen stayed at her sister's apartment in another part of Lyari, thinking the journey to the airport might be easier from there. However, as they ate dinner localized fighting broke out and the streets around the apartment shut down. Everyone told Parveen to cancel the trip, but she was reluctant to do so at such short notice. She hated the idea of allowing gang violence to dictate what she did or didn't do.

That night, while everyone slept, Parveen kept watch from a window, hoping for a cessation in the firing. Gunpowder filled the night air. Men ran onto the street, fired shots down it and then fled. There would be yelling, a pause – sometimes ten minutes, sometimes twenty or thirty – but then the pattern would be repeated from the other direction, a battle dance that looked almost choreographed. Parveen watched in growing agitation. As the clock inched towards her flight time, she made a split-second decision to risk it. All she had to do was get out of the immediate vicinity, where the fighting had blocked off the streets, and reach Leigh Market, a busy area where she could hail a rickshaw. Before anyone could stop her, she quietly left the apartment, clicking the door shut behind her, and walked down the stone steps of the building. It was that time when late night meets early morning, and apart from the echo of gunfire, it was oppressively silent. Parveen stood at the entrance of the apartment block. She was suddenly aware of how easy it would be to get caught by a bullet.

'Listen, *Bhai* [brother],' she shouted, unsure what response she'd get. 'Can someone hear me?'

Eventually, a young man from the group gathered at one end of the street walked over to Parveen. He was tightly gripping a gun. His clothes were drenched in sweat.

'What do you want?' he said.

'*Bhai*,' she said, the words tumbling out, 'I really need to get to the airport. I really want to go. I know all these streets will be blocked and it's not safe for me to walk down them. Please help me, *Bhai*. I can't go there by myself. I need to get to Leigh Market.'

He nodded and walked off. The silence descended again. Parveen's heart beat quickly. She waited, wondering if she should go back inside, but then another man emerged. Wordlessly, he gestured for her to follow him. As they walked, Parveen's thoughts swung back to the day she had left her job at the street school after she was forced to walk escorted by a gangster. Now she was doing the same thing. The gangs had become so ubiquitous that to avoid them entirely would be accepting a life within *char diwari* (four walls). She wondered if she was being led to her death. Then Leigh Market emerged, a full stop to her thoughts. The man walked off, leaving her there. Hands shaking, Parveen hailed a rickshaw. She made it in time for her flight. When she returned a few days later, the family shouted at her for being so imprudent. Usually, Parveen did not back down from this kind of fight, but this time she was shaken by her own risk-taking.

Lyari was part of Parveen, but when she spent prolonged periods of time there, it felt as if the streets were constricting around her. She told *Nani*, with profuse apologies, that she couldn't stay with her any more. The reason she gave was that movement was too difficult, but there was something else too, something harder to articulate. Lyari was a geographically contained trauma. It was never far from her thoughts, but its violence was overwhelming.

Living away from Lyari meant that Parveen didn't see her old friends so frequently. She worried constantly about Nasir, her body-building friend from the street school. Every time she spoke to him, he had lost another relative either to death or to gang membership. Nasir remained as good-humoured as ever, but his sweet face was often clouded with a dark, anxious expression. Parveen often wondered if Nasir's fierce protection of her family after her sister Samreen was attacked had provoked the gangsters, but she could not bring herself to voice her concerns.

One day, Nasir turned up at the house in Kiamari with Akeel and two other boys from the street school. Parveen squealed with delight as she said hello and ushered them inside. Nasir was quiet. He tried to smile but his usually open and cheerful face looked almost frozen. Parveen noticed he was sweating profusely.

'What's your problem?' she teased. He didn't reply. She turned to Akeel, laughing. 'What's happened to him? He never used to sweat so much.'

The boys looked at each other. 'Oh, nothing,' Akeel said quickly. 'We've made him walk a long way. That's why he's sweating.'

There wasn't a chance to push further, because *Amma* came into the room and the boys were distracted by greeting her. *Amma* embraced Nasir. Parveen noticed the embrace lasting longer than usual. Then she saw that Nasir's shoulders were shaking. He was crying.

'Nasir?' said Parveen. 'What's going on?'

'It's nothing,' said *Amma*. 'He's getting emotional because we're meeting after such a long time.'

It was strange, but lots of people had unexpected emotional reactions these days – it was the effect of living with so much violence, day in, day out. Parveen let it go. The evening passed in a blaze of laughter and chatter. But Nasir was quiet, sitting at the edge of the room, beads of sweat on his forehead. Parveen worried that he might be ill. When they got up to leave, she noticed he was limping.

'What's going on with Nasir?' she said, as soon as they had left.

'Nasir has joined Uzair's gang,' her brother Faheem blurted. 'He was shot in the leg protecting Uzair.'

The limping and the sweating suddenly made sense: he had been in pain. Everyone knew. *Amma* had known when she covered up for Nasir's tears. Akeel knew when he pretended Nasir was sweating from the long walk. They had kept it from Parveen because they were aware of how harshly she judged the gangs and anyone who became a member.

As Faheem spoke, a white-hot panic swept over Parveen. This was Nasir, the friend who had coaxed her back to health when her father had died, who had walked her home from the street school every single day to make sure she got back safely. It was hard to imagine him taking a bullet for Uzair.

Many people in Lyari had a more flexible attitude to their loved ones joining gangs. The pressures were immense, and for young men with no social status or employment prospects, it was a simple route to making money and – in theory – protecting your family. But Parveen had no sympathy with this view. Everyone was under pressure. It still required an active decision to join forces with the criminals ripping Lyari apart. Even if everyone else was willing to continue to love Nasir despite his decision, Parveen knew that she could not. She texted him to tell him she never wanted to see him again.

Cutting off contact was not easy, because Nasir was close to the whole family. Knowing that Parveen did not want to see him, he visited on days when she was out of town on business. But occasionally she crossed over with him in the house. 'You are a bastard dog,' she shouted, the first time she saw him again. 'If you keep taking bullets for that son of a bitch, you are responsible for what is happening in Lyari.'

Nasir looked exhausted. He did not defend himself. 'Tell me more about what I am, *Baji* [older sister].'

'You are the son of such a beautiful, loving mother, and this is what you have become, a no-good bastard like the rest of them.'

'How am I a bastard if I have such a loving mother?' Nasir said. He was smiling now, gently teasing Parveen as if nothing had changed.

Parveen knew Nasir valued her opinion; she also knew that her words were unlikely to achieve much. It was very difficult for young men to extricate themselves once they were involved. Becoming a gang member meant you were no longer neutral, but leaving meant you lost protection while still remaining a target for the other side. Losing Nasir to the gang was like a bereavement.

It wasn't just people who were vulnerable to the gangs; property was a target too. Although the family had moved to Kiamari, they still owned the big family home in Kalri that Parveen's father had built. After getting married, Parveen's younger sister Samreen and her husband, Rashid, decided to move back there to have more space. Two years later, in 2011, Samreen gave birth to identical twin boys. They were born prematurely and Samreen was drained by the experience. Rashid worked long hours and she did not want to be alone as she recovered, so when she was discharged she returned to Kiamari to stay with her mother and sisters. This meant the house in Kalri was empty during the days.

Kalri was a strategic spot for Uzair's gang. It was dominated by Ghafar Zikri, a gangster allied with Arshad Pappu, Uzair's main opponent. The gangsters saw the opportunity. One day, while everyone was out, Baba Ladla, Uzair's right-hand man, sent his men to smash through the front door. Word came to Samreen from her neighbours: the house had been occupied. Ever since Parveen was a teenager, she'd heard stories of gangsters taking over homes – sometimes just for an evening, sometimes for months on end – and using them for torture and executions or as a base from which to stage attacks. People in Lyari had no real recourse to the authorities. The gangsters were politically connected and better armed than the police. Besides, most police saw everyone in the area as brutes and criminals, so they weren't much help. When somebody's house was occupied, they had little choice but to find another place to stay and wait it out. Rashid joined Samreen in Kiamari.

They strategized in a frenzy. People living in Kalri were considered to be under the protection of Ghafar Zikri, so they had to be careful how they proceeded. They decided to try to appeal to the gangsters' humanity. Everyone knew someone who had gang links. Each of the sisters and brothers asked their friends and neighbours to get a message to Baba Ladla or his associates, to tell them that this was a house where a young couple lived, that they had newborn babies and were now homeless. Parveen was not optimistic about this approach and she was proved right. Messages came back to the family, from contact after contact: 'Nothing can be done. Get used to it.' *Amma* took the occupation very hard, weeping when she thought of the home her husband had built, where she had raised her children, defiled by crime.

Samreen and Rashid stayed in Kiamari. Caring for the two new babies took up a huge amount of energy; their screams filled the already overcrowded apartment. But then, five months after the gangsters took over the house, word came that they had left. Before the family had a chance to survey the damage, friends from the neighbourhood went in and sent an update. There were dead bodies in the house, strewn on the floors that Parveen's father had tiled. No one knew who they were or why they had been brought there. When the family arrived, they found that someone had removed the bodies. That was one small mercy. But there was blood everywhere, dried in spatters on the walls, congealed in pools on the floor, streaks of it where bodies had been dragged. The inside and outside walls were pocked with bullets to the point that they looked like they might crumble at the touch. Parveen wondered what they had been doing inside the house to put so many bullet holes in the walls. It was obvious they had been executing people here, but had they also been firing from one end of the house to the other, just to practise? The clothes and jewellery that the family had assembled for Samreen's dowry were gone; the storage room had been ransacked. Parveen set about finding workmen to repair the battered walls and install extra metal grilles and padlocks over every door and window. The women from the neighbourhood gathered at the house with sponges and buckets. Grimly, silently, they got to work. They washed the house from top to bottom, until the soapy water in their buckets turned a deep murky brown from blood and gunpowder. Soon afterwards, Samreen and her family moved back in, but she was afraid. Every time Parveen spoke to her, Samreen said the same thing: 'I can still smell the blood.'

In late 2018, some seven or eight years after the occupation, I asked Parveen to take me to Kalri. The house featured so heavily in her memories that I wanted to see it for myself, and because her sister still lived there, I assumed she was a regular visitor. She agreed immediately, casually: 'Just tell me when you want to go.' A few days later, we walked along the narrow alleys of Kalri, a carpet of trash shimmering in the sunlight. The city was calmer then and the old women had resumed the habit of gathering outside their houses, carpets spread out, sucking deeply on bubbling hookah pipes and chopping fresh herbs and vegetables. One by one, they stood up to greet Parveen, flocking to her and smiling widely, introducing themselves to me. Usually a warm and effusive person, Parveen was noticeably tense. Samreen was away for a few days, so the house was empty. Parveen undid multiple locks and gates, then we sat in an upstairs bedroom that was lit by the sun coming through the metal grilles on the window. Parveen tells stories so vividly that you feel like you were there. On other occasions, she had relayed the story of the house occupation as if it was a scene in a movie. But as we sat in the house and Parveen talked about what had happened, her voice got smaller and she stared at her hands, as if trying to avoid taking in her surroundings.

'I came back here for ten minutes in 2014 and the entire area sent chills down my spine. Samreen was making tea but I left without drinking it,' she said. 'The next time I came was in 2017. And now I am here with you. Even if you paid me, I would not live here again.'

Trying to steer the conversation to a more positive place, I asked if she had any happy memories of the house. She shook her head. 'They snatched all the happiness from us.'

While the quicksand of Lyari's gang war sucked in more people and places, Parveen focused even harder on her work. The devastation wrought by the 2010 monsoon was long-lasting. When new floods struck Balochistan in early 2011, more than 100,000 people were still homeless. It was strange that such harrowing work could be an escape, but at least in the wide-open expanses of rural Balochistan Parveen could do something to help, while in Lyari she was powerless. The 2011 floods saw heavy rainfall particularly in Jaffarabad, an area of Balochistan nestled next to Sindh, the province in which Karachi sits. Parveen channelled her energies into raising money and purchasing supplies for the racked region, and had some early success with a fundraising rally that brought in thousands of rupees. She was closely connected to Lyari's community work scene because of her history at the street school and her ongoing activism. But the gangs had infiltrated even this sphere. Just before Rehman Dakait died, he had launched the People's Aman Committee. This was intended as a bridge between the PPP and Rehman's gang. Uzair had taken it up with gusto. The PAC gave the gang an acceptable face and a more formalized way to carry out the social work that the top gangsters had always engaged in as a way to keep the locals onside. Uzair, as head of the PAC, co-founded an organization called the Lyari Resource Centre, which invested in local parks and other public spaces, and gave money to new street school intiatives and other charity projects. It had just enough distance from the gang to have a veneer of respectability, but everyone knew where most of the funding came from. A lot of people supported the PAC and the Lyari Resource Centre. Parveen even had arguments with her own family about it. Her elder sister Nasreen's husband was adamant that this was a positive change for Lyari. *Nani* also defended the PAC, pointing out that they were making the streets cleaner. Every time Parveen went back to Lyari, it seemed that more of her former colleagues were working with them. Some justified their actions, saying that if the end goal was to bring literacy to people, did it really matter where the money originated? Street schools like the one Parveen had helped to run were at the mercy of the forces in the area and had to shut down when violence worsened. Wasn't it better to cooperate and keep the services going, since the gangs weren't going to be dismantled any time soon? Parveen couldn't wrap her head around it. How could these good-hearted people go into partnership with those who perpetrated the violence, essentially enabling the destruction of Lyari and sacrificing their ability to speak out? To Parveen, it looked as if people were being bought off, taking money for their projects in return for silence.

When she came back from visiting Jaffarabad, determined to raise funds, Parveen asked around for advice about who to approach for her flood relief effort. One name came up repeatedly: Uzair Baloch. Whoever she spoke to pointed out that he was the richest person in the area and he was often generous with his cash. Parveen's friend Sohail sat her down. 'Look, Parveen,' he said. 'The real power lies with Uzair, and if you are raising funds, I think we should get monetary support from him.' Sohail had a meeting with Uzair planned already and offered to take Parveen with him. These days, every new social intiative had to go through Uzair, and Sohail and a friend needed permission for an idea they'd had: launching a youth cafe where young people could gather to talk. Parveen didn't want to go. But then she remembered the desperation of the people in Jaffarabad and what a difference a big cheque could make. They wouldn't care about the source. People were always telling her that she was too rigid in her beliefs. She agreed to go with Sohail to the meeting and ask for a donation. She was apprehensive, but at least one of Uzair's houses was pretty much next door to where her cousins, Aisha and Sayed, lived. It was reassuring to know that your own people were around if something went wrong.

Parveen had seen the exterior of Uzair's place when visiting her cousins, but nothing prepared her for the scale of the grandeur inside. The space she and Sohail entered was so large that it could barely be described as a room. One area had a traditional Balochi seating arrangement, with the cylindrical pillows and low tables familiar from Parveen's own home. On the other side was a huge ornate wooden swing. The middle of the room was taken up by a swimming pool and there was a waterfall against one wall. The scale of the house and its luxuries was terrifying; it spoke of riches beyond Parveen's imagination and a frightening level of power. Parveen and Sohail were led to the area where Uzair was sitting on a huge chair, almost a throne, next to an associate who managed the gang's social work. Behind them was a bodyguard pointing his gun at Parveen and Sohail. When Parveen looked at the bodyguard, she felt as if the ground beneath her had dropped away. The man pointing a gun at her was her cousin, Sayed. They made eye contact for a second before he averted his gaze. As far as Parveen was aware, Sayed had a low-level government job which he had got through contacts in the PPP government. The party had close ties with Uzair, but she was still shocked to see her civil servant cousin here, wielding a gun. Parveen was so disoriented that she couldn't see clearly. As she tried to focus, she realized that she could hear screaming from beyond the waterfall. A torture cell. It was a stark contrast to the garish luxury.

'Parveen, we have heard a lot about you,' said Uzair, as Parveen remembers it. 'You do a lot of work for Balochistan and Sindh.'

She nodded, unsettled that they already knew about her. She explained that she was here to raise funds for the flood victims in Jaffarabad.

'I'm not saying that I am not going to help you,' said Uzair. 'I could give you a blank cheque and you can write any amount. But I'd rather have you help the people of your own area instead of looking elsewhere. I'm the *sardar* of Lyari and I care about Lyari, not about Balochistan.'

'You really do like the people of Balochistan, don't you?' said his associate. 'I don't like those Baloch separatists, all the people who say, "*Balochistan zindabad*" [long live Balochistan].'

The screams from another part of the compound continued to echo out, rising over the gurgling of the waterfall. Parveen's eyes kept darting back to Sayed, who was still standing silently, gun pointed at her, avoiding her gaze. The dismissal of Balochistan's struggles was too much to bear. Parveen could feel the words bubbling up.

'Do you know what the army is doing to Balochistan, to its own people?' she said, getting angrier as she spoke. 'You call yourself a *sardar* and you have no idea what is happening to people everywhere.'

Sohail put a hand on her arm. 'Calm down, Parveen,' he muttered. She could see her cousin's eyes widening. She stopped talking and the pounding of her heart was so loud it filled her ears. She was suddenly absolutely certain that they were going to kill her.

'Please calm down,' said the associate. '*Beta* [child], our people should help our own people. There is an opportunity at the Lyari Resource Centre. You can work on whatever problems you want – women's issues, children's issues. You can stay behind the scenes if you don't want to be publicly associated with us. How much do you really earn now anyway? We're here to stay. Work with us.'

So this was how it happened. But she would not give in. 'I have not come here to negotiate my salary,' she said firmly. 'Please tell me if you would like to give me money for the floods or not.'

Uzair shook his head.

'And I just want to tell you that if someone does not value education, I do not consider them human,' said Parveen. She could hear her voice sounding more agitated. 'And you – all of you – have caused so many schools in the area to shut down.'

They stared at her. Sayed kept the gun pointing at her steadily. A servant arrived with a tray of chai. 'I am not going to have anything here,' said Parveen.

'Please, Parveen, show some respect for these guys,' said Sohail, his tone sharp.

His voice snapped Parveen back into her surroundings and she realized she did not have a choice. She sat in silence and drank the chai while Sohail pitched the idea of his youth cafe. Uzair agreed that he would allow it to go ahead. When they stood up, Parveen's legs were trembling so much that she thought they might buckle underneath her.

Later that day, Sayed came to their house in Kiamari. He was furious. 'Why the fuck were you speaking to that guy like that? Do you know how powerful he is?' he shouted. 'You shouldn't have said all those things.'

'Just look at you! You were flaunting that gun to scare me! I'm your cousin and you were working for *them* to threaten *me*,' Parveen screamed back at him. 'On top of it all, you're a government employee.'

'You know what? The PPP has told me to be a bodyguard for this guy. I was doing my government job.'

'You have no shame. You're my aunt's son but you were pointing a gun at me.'

Amma came in to see what the commotion was.

'Ask Parveen what is going on,' Sayed yelled. 'You need to deal with your daughter. She is going to get herself killed.'

When *Amma* heard the full story, she was so worried that she didn't get out of bed for several days. Parveen, in the meantime, was raging. How dare Sayed tell her how to behave when he was now a criminal too? As far as she was concerned, their relationship was over. But as the days inched on and the anger receded she was also worried. She had never been afraid of speaking her mind, but making an enemy of the most powerful gangster in Lyari was reckless. She cursed her inability to stay silent. Friends advised her to lie low for a while. But even without a donation from Uzair, she had raised a significant amount of money and was gathering supplies to take to Jaffarabad. Everything was stored in Lyari and had to be collected from there. As the supplies mounted up and the date approached, Parveen couldn't sleep for worry that the trucks would be intercepted. You needed Uzair's permission to do anything in Lyari. What if the trucks were robbed and the goods never reached Jaffarabad? What if the road was blocked? 'It'll be fine,' her brother Faheem reassured her. 'We'll find a way.' He was right. Parveen did not know how it happened, but one by one each truck made it safely out of Lyari, onto the highway and across to Jaffarabad. The final hurdle was for her to leave and then follow the last truck to Balochistan so that she could oversee the distribution of aid.

The night before she was due to go, her phone rang. It was Nasir. Parveen thought about not answering, but she did because it was so unusual for him to ring her. He knew by now that she had no desire to talk to him.

Nasir spoke quickly, blurting out the words as if worried that Parveen would hang up. 'You have stopped me from being present in any way, but I told everyone, this is *Baji*'s work and I have to take care of it. I have looked after all the supplies, they've all reached their destination safely. But now it is a question of your protection. I am going to make sure that you are safe, and I can't make sure of that unless I am there, so please don't say no to me, *Baji*.'

Parveen hesitated for a moment, but she knew that she needed to get to Balochistan. Just as she had made the split-second decision to go to the airport in the midst of a gunfight, she agreed to let Nasir escort her to Balochistan. He would drop her off in Quetta and she could make her own way to the rural areas from there.

The next day, Nasir collected her, along with another gangster. Parveen got into the car. She looked at Nasir and was flooded with emotion. She wanted to say something, to hug him tightly one more time, to tell him that although she would never forgive him for joining the gang, she still cared about him. But she couldn't say any of that with the other gangster in the car. They barely spoke for the entire twelve-hour drive to Quetta. The tight knot of Lyari's alleys turned to smooth highway and the mountains of Balochistan loomed along the sides of the road. As they pulled up at where she was staying in Quetta, she invited the two men in for chai. Nasir shook his head sadly. Parveen looked at the other gangster, knowing that she couldn't insist. She stood at the gate and watched the car turn around. She stood there watching for a long time, until the car was just a speck in the distance.

8

ANARCHY

Uzair and his brother Zafar frequently called journalists to their mansion. In front of gathered reporters, Uzair would hold forth about issues in Lyari such as water shortages, with no apparent sense of irony about his own swimming pool and elaborate water feature. One frequent visitor to the house was Zille, who prided himself on being on first-name terms with the leaders of all the main gangs – not just Uzair Baloch and the different factions affiliated to him, but also rivals like Arshad Pappu and Ghafar Zikri. Gangsters liked to be in touch with crime reporters. They used the TV news to boost their image and curry favour with local residents in the areas they controlled, as well as to score points against rival gangs by blaming them for outbreaks of violence.

Some crime reporters, including a number of Zille's colleagues, refused to have direct contact with criminals. They argued that it was morally wrong to have any part in their self-promotion, and that although these contacts might be useful in the short term, they could ultimately end up being dangerous when the tide turned. Zille had no such concerns. In fact, he barely gave any thought to such ethical considerations. His priority was to get the story: to be the first and the best. With so many rival TV news stations, the pressure was relentless.

It came from the newsroom and now, after a decade on the job, from inside Zille's own head. The Lyari gang war was a big ratings winner. Besides, in a context where the party of government, the Pakistan People's Party, was working with Uzair in Lyari, what was the point in a crime reporter drawing lines about who to talk to? On his visits to Uzair's place, Zille witnessed meetings between Uzair and Zulfiqar Mirza, a PPP minister in the provincial government, as well as other senior party members. Mirza's involvement with the gang was no secret. He said proudly in a 2011 interview that he had given out hundreds of weapons licences in Lyari so that people could protect themselves against the Muttahida Qaumi Movement, though he was at pains to deny any involvement in Uzair's gang activity.

Zille privately suspected that most journalists who made these arguments were either afraid or incapable of balancing contacts on different sides of the law. He found himself walking a tightrope often enough himself. Frequently, after covering a story in Lyari, he would receive an outraged phone call from one of his police contacts, who would demand, 'Why are you making Uzair Baloch look like a hero? The man is a gangster!'

'It's my job,' Zille always replied. This was his mantra, a standard response to everyone.

Many of the gangsters in Lyari were rough-mannered and it was obvious they came from the criminal underworld. Uzair was different. He was educated and spoke with a relaxed confidence. Zille actually liked him. Although Uzair was deeply enmeshed in the drugs trade, he didn't use drugs himself. Everyone knew about the money laundering, the extortion, the torture and killings, but as far as Zille could see, Uzair was more interested in nice clothes and expensive watches. Zille observed Uzair's manner with the many people who came to the house to ask for help. He was very still and quiet, listening carefully until they finished talking. He would think for a while before delivering his verdict: permission to start a football club here, a cheque for a community centre there. Spending time at Uzair's house made Zille feel right in the thick of things. It also helped him demonstrate to the gangsters that he was a reliable journalist, so that he was well placed to get access at short notice.

Crime was Zille's beat, not politics. But the hushed conversations held between politicians in the parliament buildings of Karachi or Islamabad had a ripple effect, spilling out of staid wood-panelled meeting rooms and onto the streets of Karachi, often leaving destruction in their wake. In 2011, the MQM ramped up the pressure on the PPP to end their alliance with Uzair and his gang, threatening to withdraw from coalitions in both the Sindh Assembly and the national government if they did not. Bowing to this pressure, the PPP officially banned the People's Aman Committee, Uzair's political wing. Random police raids in Lyari increased; innocent and gang-affiliated people alike had their houses ransacked. Zille sometimes went along with one of his police contacts to film the aftermath. He also stayed in touch with Uzair and other gang members, who appeared unfazed by the change in their status and continued to talk up their social work projects.

In 2012, the situation shifted. A local PPP leader was shot by gunmen suspected of working for Uzair. When Zille spoke to police contacts afterwards, he detected a change in energy, particularly among the high command. Chaudhry Aslam, Karachi's police superintendent, was notorious for his rough-and-ready tactics. He hated the Lyari gangsters. Liberated by the PPP's break with Uzair, Aslam was ready to do something big.

On 27 April 2012, 3,000 policemen gathered around Lyari in armoured personnel vehicles, which people in Karachi commonly describe as tanks. Masked men guided them through the web of streets to strategic points – members of Arshad Pappu's gang, people said, helping the police to target their rivals in Uzair Baloch's collective. The police were heavily armed and prepared for a long battle. But so were Uzair's men. The police were met with heavy fire. Gangsters emerged with sub-machine guns, spraying bullets across the narrow alleys in an ear-splitting assault. Others fired rocket-propelled grenades from their shoulders, shooting balls of fire and sound that ripped vehicles apart and blasted holes in the sides of buildings.

Lyari's streets had been a battlefield many times before, but this was different; the police armoured cars and gangsters' heavy weaponry made it look like a war zone. Parveen's relatives in Lyari told her, 'It's like Afghanistan.' Everything shut down: electricity, gas, water. Parveen talked frantically to her sisters, her aunts, her grandmother, urging them to get out of Lyari; many women were trying to leave while the men stayed behind to protect their houses. But getting out was not a simple proposition. The police had blocked off streets, ostensibly so that the gangsters couldn't escape. The machine-gun and rocket fire was so intense that it was dangerous to step outside. No food supplies were allowed in or out of Lyari, lest they contain ammunition for the gangsters. No one could get to work. Many people worked shifts for daily wages and they quickly ran out of money. Shops emptied of supplies, then closed altogether. Water was in scarce supply. The sound of gunfire and grenades rocked their houses night and day. Parveen's sister Samreen, afraid to leave the house, ran out of powdered milk and nappies for the babies.

This was supposedly an operation to arrest the kingpins, but the fight-back was so intense that sometimes the police could barely leave their bulletproof vehicles. They kept Lyari in lockdown, hoping to starve the gangsters of supplies and force them into submission.

Safdar, in the Edhi office, itched to get in his ambulance and go to Lyari to help. Calls came into the office every day from the area, and not just regarding people injured by gunfire. Women were still going into labour; the elderly were still suffering strokes and heart attacks; diabetics had complications due to food shortages. Some old people died of natural causes, but their families were unable to take them to a cold-storage unit or graveyard, so they had to keep the bodies at home. Throughout all this ambulances were not allowed through the police blockades. In desperation, some families used donkey carts to push sick relatives to the local hospital. If they made it without being caught in the hail of bullets, they found the hospital understaffed and low on supplies. Safdar was relieved when, a few days into the siege, Abdul Sattar Edhi made a statement at the Karachi Press Club. Dressed in a brown salwar kameez, his long white beard flowing, he said that police had cut off supplies to Lyari and had even prevented him personally from entering. He asserted that regardless of the continued siege, he would send his ambulances in on humanitarian grounds to deliver life-saving drugs, food and water. Safdar volunteered immediately.

On his first day of duty, he hauled large hessian sacks of rice, flour and powdered milk into the back of his ambulance, where injured people normally lay, and drove along the main road that led to Lyari. The dense knot of streets that sprawled out behind the yellow arches, usually so crowded with people, rickshaws and motorbikes, was deadly quiet. The tyres of the ambulance crunched over a blanket of bullet casings. Many of the residential alleys were too narrow to drive down, and people were too afraid to come out of their houses to collection points, so Safdar and the other drivers had to go door-to-door on foot. They knocked, shouting out that they were from the Edhi Foundation. Safdar was nervous. Rumours were swirling in the city – not least among the police – that Edhi drivers were being paid by the gangsters to distribute arms along with the food. But seeing the relief on people's faces when he knocked on the door and handed them their supplies made everything worthwhile.

A few days later, Safdar was unloading his ambulance when an imposing figure in a starched white salwar kameez walked over to him. The face was familiar from news bulletins. It was Chaudhry Aslam, the police superintendent, cigarette hanging from his lips, pistol loosely held in one hand.

As Safdar remembers it, Aslam spoke roughly to him: 'What are you doing? Let me search your goods. There could be arms and ammunitions in there.'

'It's just groceries,' Safdar said.

Aslam slashed holes in the sides of each sack, the white rice and dusty powdered milk spilling out onto the filthy alley, where it mingled with sewage water and bullet casings.

Despite finding nothing in the sacks, Aslam handcuffed Safdar and his colleague, and forced them into a police car. Safdar watched his ambulance getting further and further away as they were driven to a police station. He couldn't think who to call, how long he was going to be held, or how he would retrieve the discarded vehicle. When they got to the police station, he was pulled out of the car. Inside the building, Aslam and another police officer beat him badly. After a few hours, Safdar was released, lip split and body bruised. He still reported for duty the next day. It later transpired that four Edhi workers had been arrested that day, in an apparent tit for tat for the organization flouting the police blockade to deliver aid. When he told me about this incident, a few years later, Aslam was dead, murdered by the Taliban in 2014 in a massive explosion that targeted his car. But this had not tempered Safdar's rage. 'The only regret I have,' he told me, 'is that I was not able to slap Chaudhry Aslam in the face as he arrested us.'

Just over a week after storming into Lyari, the police retreated. The mission, which became known as the eight-day operation, was an unmitigated disaster. Five policemen were dead. The official figure for civilian casualties was twenty, but most local residents believed many more died. Some days after it ended, Parveen received a call from a colleague at a human rights group she often worked with. Given her close personal connection to Lyari, they asked her to take part in a project gathering testimony from civilians about their experience. Although Parveen wanted to make a contribution, her initial response was one of dread. The operation had changed nothing and Uzair was still in charge. If anything, he was even more popular, as people had seen him fight off a brutal police incursion. She told them it was impossible. But the colleague was insistent: it was vital to record the wrongs that had been committed and they needed the testimony of people from Lyari to do so.

Parveen went into the area with three local journalists. Although the operation had ended, many people were still suffering the after-effects. The loss of daily income during the blockade meant that families had borrowed money to survive and were now struggling to get the funds together to pay back their debts. Hospitality was so culturally embedded in Pakistan that it was second nature, but Parveen noticed that in many houses people did not even offer her water. She wondered if they couldn't afford to share the water they had, or if they were so traumatized that they couldn't think about basic hospitality.

She and the rest of the team went all over Lyari to gather evidence, but one particular appointment loomed large. When the day came to interview Uzair about the operation, Parveen was full of trepidation. She had questions for him, but she was so angry that she was not sure she would be able to ask them politely.

As they approached the house, one of her colleagues hesitated.

'I don't think it's a good idea for you to come inside, Parveen,' he said. 'It's too risky.'

The others in their delegation agreed and Parveen did not argue. Walking up to the house had made her legs begin to shake, as if the memory was in her body as well as her mind. She waited outside. When her colleagues returned, they told her that Uzair had been dismissive about the operation, saying, 'Why should I worry about Chaudhry Aslam? We have better weaponry than he does.' Parveen was reminded afresh of how much power Uzair wielded and felt queasy at the thought. But the police, with their harsh tactics, seemed scarcely more law-abiding than the gangsters.

At home, Safdar recovered from the shock of his arrest. Although he would never have admitted it, he had begun to think his parents had made the right decision in tricking him into marriage. He had always been closely anchored to his family, but something had changed since the wedding. He no longer stayed away from home for days on end; he had a wife and a child to think about. His soft, pink-faced baby was like a thread pulling him back from the violence and brutality he saw every day, keeping him tethered to normality. Umaima was her name, born a year before the Lyari operation. Sometimes, Safdar felt the bombings, gunfights and accidents were coming so fast he could barely take a breath. But then he came home and, miraculously, life continued. His youngest siblings, Fatima and Nadir, were now at school. They had gone past the fifth grade, the year that Safdar had stopped studying. He watched them reading and writing with more confidence than he had now as a fully grown man and was so proud that tears pricked at his eyes. He did not think of his work in terms of the money – the pay was low, sometimes augmented by tips from patients – but seeing his contribution to his younger siblings' education bolstered his sense of mission.

He was not the only one focusing on work. The family had always assumed that Safdar's brother Adil would never earn much because of the polio that limited his use of his right leg. When he started work at a mobile phone stall in the local market, he earned just a hundred rupees a day, and Safdar and his father told him to keep the money for himself. Over the years, without fuss or fanfare, Adil had continued to step out each day, wooden crutches under his arms. He had always been good at fixing things and learned quickly how to repair phones and computers. Soon the owner of the shop allowed Adil to manage it for days at a time. Freed from the obligation of contributing his small daily earnings to the family pot, he had quietly saved the money, getting involved in several informal community savings groups where everyone pitched in a modest sum to a common pool and then each had their turn to use the money. One day, after Safdar's marriage, Adil sat the family down.

'The savings groups have paid off. I am in a position to start my own shop,' he said, smiling. 'Let's find a place I can rent.'

Safdar took a day off work and walked around Landhi with his brother, scouring the hectic maze of hole-in-the-wall shops and makeshift stalls for the right location. They found somewhere the same day. The owner of the lot said that because of Adil's disability, he wouldn't charge a deposit on top of the first rent payment. 'I hope you thrive here,' he said. The landlord's words made Safdar happy. He liked to think of his city as a place where people helped each other. Within a few years, Adil got married too. They decked out his room in the family house with tinsel strung across the ceiling in a criss-cross pattern and prayers in glittery lettering stuck to the walls. His wife's parents provided furniture for the room as a dowry. Their mother propped up some faded photos on the cabinet. One showed Safdar and Adil as children in the village, grinning naughtily at the camera. Another showed Adil as a teenager, during the year of his surgery, his leg painfully stretched out in front of him, encased in a metal cage. Safdar looked at that picture, sitting against the backdrop of his brother's new marital space. In a sense, Adil's polio had defined Safdar's life by leading him to the Edhi ambulance service. But Adil had refused to let it define his own.

There were still times when Safdar was away from home for long stretches. In September 2012, around six months after the eight-day operation consumed Lyari and Safdar was battered by the police, a fire broke out in the industrial area of Baldia Town at a textile factory by the side of a busy road. In the early morning, flames spread fast across the compound, ripping through the four-storey factory where workers stitched cheap clothes for Western brands. Some tried to escape, but for most the effort was futile; all but one exit had been locked by bosses who did not want the workers to take breaks or steal the products. Those who could threw themselves out of windows to escape the flames and the suffocating smoke, but many of the windows were blocked by metal bars. Anyone who made it to the front gate of the compound found that locked too.

Safdar was part of a convoy of Edhi ambulances dispatched to the factory. As he drove to the scene, he saw thick swirls of black smoke from some distance away. Relatives of workers had gathered in droves outside the gates of the compound, screaming, crying, clamouring for information. Firefighters worked to battle back the flames. The smell of burnt plastic and chemical smoke was overwhelming. Safdar surveyed the scene. Dead bodies were strewn all over the site. Some people had managed to jump out of a window, breaking a limb on the way down; others were half-unconscious from smoke inhalation. The priority was to see who could be saved. Safdar had done some basic training on fire safety, so he wrapped a dampened cotton scarf over his nose and mouth to keep out the fumes, then he and his colleagues got to work, hunting for survivors who needed urgent care. His arms broke out in painful white-hot blisters from proximity to the flames. That same day, the factory owner – who was personally worth millions of dollars – went into hiding. He and his son were barred from leaving Pakistan.

The MQM announced three days of mourning across Karachi. But Safdar could not observe it because, for the next four days, he was working at the factory, pulling the dead out of the building. By this time, he was expert at handling bodies, but the corpses from the fire presented an entirely new challenge. In the lower storeys of the building, where the fire had first spread, bodies were piled up near the exits where workers had tried to escape. Some were so badly burned that when Safdar started to pick them up, the bones crumbled, flesh falling away. Safdar had seen bodies in all states of decay, but he did not know until the fire that even human bones could melt. In the basement, the boiler had burst, filling the entire floor with water. Safdar half waded, half swam through blackened water to retrieve floating body parts. They improvised solutions, using plastic sheeting and metal hooks to pull the most damaged remains out of the site. Though the official death toll was 289, making the Baldia Town fire Pakistan's worst-ever industrial accident, Safdar was sure that the real number was far higher; he could not reconcile that figure with the piles of dead bodies he had retrieved. Many of the bodies were so badly damaged that they couldn't be identified. On the fourth day, Safdar was sure that he could hear screaming in the building, even though it was impossible that anyone there was still alive. His whole body ached. When he went home to sleep, he dreamed of the factory, tormented by visions of howling children who had lost their parents in the blaze, spectres haunting the building.

The official cause of the fire was an electrical fault. The media highlighted the horrific impact of lax regulations and said that the

fire showed how ruthless business owners put profit over humanity.
There was no doubt this was true. But rumours whirled. Was it
really an electrical fire? Or was it an arson attack? Some alleged that
the factory owner had refused a demand for $100,000 in extortion
from none other than the MQM. Safdar heard the rumours too. In
the aftermath of the fire, he took the bodies to the Edhi mortuary,
where his colleagues had the task of trying to identify the remains
and return them to the correct family. It was slow, difficult work.
Ghulam, who worked at the Edhi mortuary, was a serious man
who took pride in systems. In the days after the fire, he said MQM
workers came by and demanded that he release the bodies in order
to placate grieving families. He explained that they followed a strict
procedure because it was important not to send bodies to the wrong
people. One party worker pinned him to the wall and told him that
families were waiting to bury their dead and that they should not
be kept waiting. The MQM workers were armed. They left with
the bodies.

When Safdar recounted the story of the Baldia Town fire to me, he
was characteristically animated, his face contorting in horror, leaping
around to demonstrate how difficult it had been to drag the bodies
out. I believed him. I had seen the factory and, even three years later,
it remained a burnt-out husk, a hulking black charcoal monument to
death looming at the side of the highway. We talked about the causes
of the fire and the allegation that it had been set by the MQM after
the factory owner had failed to pay extortion money.

Safdar's whole demeanour changed. Like many Karachiites, he
instinctively self-censored, particularly when it came to the MQM,
the city's most powerful political force. 'I don't want to get into the
details,' he said, brushing the question away. 'It's not good for me to
talk about it. My focus is only on rescue work.'

In the autumn of 2012, while Safdar was wading through the wreckage of the Baldia Town fire, I was adjusting to life in Karachi. Earlier that year, I had quit my job at a London-based politics magazine and flown halfway across the world to make a go of freelance journalism. I was insulated from the worst of the violence and infrastructure issues because I was living with relatives who could afford a private supply of electricity and water. The TV news channels were always switched on in the house. The scenes of violence they played all day sometimes seemed like they could be from another world. Everything was escalating – the gang war, the fighting between political parties and ethnic groups, the terror threat. People were desensitized; an attack that killed just two or three people barely seemed significant. Long-term residents were used to changing plans because of street violence, avoiding going out on Fridays when the risk of attack was higher and having no phone signal on religious holidays – a government measure to reduce the chances of a bomb being detonated using a mobile phone. Cousins who had lived in Karachi all their lives told me that in these few short months working as a journalist I had seen more of their city than they had. Yet I felt intensely restricted.

A few months after my move, I was sitting in the back seat of the car, being taken home from dinner by the family's driver, absently looking at my phone. It was dark and we were driving fast. When I looked up from my phone, I noticed something strange. The roads were empty. The throngs of street hawkers and market stalls that stayed open all through the evening selling fried snacks and paan were shuttered. The honking horns and puttering exhaust pipes had been replaced by an eerie silence. Then, suddenly, I heard the familiar revving of motorbike engines. Two, maybe three, or maybe four bikes sped past either side of the car. As they streaked into the distance I heard the sharp, blistering sound of gunfire, saw smoke rise. I instinctively ducked, although they were firing into the air and were long gone by the time I looked up.

When we got back, I found my aunt and uncle waiting for me, tensely watching the news. The MQM had called a citywide strike for twenty-four hours, in protest at the arrest of their leader, Altaf Hussain, in London, where he lived in self-imposed exile. Even as I waited for my heart to stop racing, I was sceptical about the strike. I couldn't imagine anything bringing this manic, sprawling city to a standstill. The next day, I went for a drive to see for myself. Sure enough, everything was closed, from the local vegetable shop to the major marketplaces. Just as Parveen had seen Uzair's wealth and been afraid of what it meant, I looked at this cavernous ghost town and suddenly understood what power looked like.

Zille learned this lesson early on. From his very first assignment and the anonymous phone calls that followed, he'd been warned not to name a particular party when reporting on crimes by their workers. For the most part, coverage of the MQM was the work of political reporters, but the close links between politics and crime sometimes brought it onto Zille's beat. In his eyes, the MQM operated at two levels. One was a slick, media-friendly political operation, where the Party positioned itself as a modern, secular force that opposed the rising tide of terrorism. The other was a mafia enterprise deeply enmeshed in organized crime and street wars. The political section denied all existence of the street wing; it was something everyone knew but no one could comment on. As with stories about the military and intelligence apparatus, reporters and editors learned to self-censor. It was second nature to know when it was better to use vague language, or avoid a story altogether.

Sometimes, Zille thought of himself as an addict, hooked on the rush of danger, afraid of what emptiness might be there when the firing stopped – though he rarely had time to really reflect on this. Everything came together in such a frenetic rush of violence that it was easy to get the hit of adrenalin and even easier to ignore the suggestion that he find another, safer thrill. On top of the political violence, Karachi's lawlessness made it an attractive place for the Taliban and other extremist groups, whose presence had been steadily growing in the years since the Ashura attack. They operated with near-impunity around the country and there were terror attacks in Karachi every few weeks. Often Zille covered the aftermath, one of the hordes of reporters who rushed to the scene when an explosion went off. Gunfights had long ceased to shock him. Now the once-unimaginable destruction of a bombing – the screams of despair and the twisted bodies – was normal too.

Although many people saw terrorism as an existential threat, Zille viewed it as more of a technical challenge. Terrorism was a big story, but covering it made you visible to terror groups. A euphemistic lexicon developed. Some reporters never referred to the Taliban by name, others called them 'activists' rather than 'terrorists'. While it was broadly acceptable to consort with gangsters, it was too risky to maintain contacts within terrorist organizations. Terror groups often sent in video and audio statements about their attacks, but government regulations forbade showing anything that made terror groups look heroic. The only way to report on these stories was by cultivating relationships with residents or police in areas known to be terrorist hotspots. These local contacts were just as useful as the most senior superintendents – sometimes more so, since they were there, on the ground. Zille spent an increasing amount of time in Sohrab Goth, a sprawling slum of dull brown concrete houses that stretched out past the airport, not far from his house. He had first visited the police station there during his work as an entertainment producer on the crime reconstruction show. Back then, the area had been dominated by the drugs trade, but that had been gradually displaced by militancy and the problems it brought – bank robberies and kidnappings to raise funds for operations elsewhere in the country, bomb and gun attacks. Sometimes the streets broke out into miniature wars between different militant groups, shutting down whole areas. The police station had a Wild West feel to it. It was a basic concrete structure protected by a maze of sandbags after a series of attempted bombings. The police openly talked about shooting militants dead whenever they could.

One night in November 2012, a police contact in Sohrab Goth called Zille to tell him about a gunfight between Sunni and Shia militants. Zille moved fast, jumping straight into his car and calling the office on the way to ask them to send a cameraman. This was such a familiar routine by now that he was barely even nervous. He often experienced the physical adrenalin of a dangerous situation – the quickening breath, fast-beating heart – without the accompanying mental anxiety.

Sohrab Goth was a poor area with shoddy infrastructure; the electricity was off for hours each day. As Zille drove down the motorway past the airport, the lights went down, plunging the area into darkness. He parked and reached into the back seat. The bulletproof vest provided by the TV station that he kept in the car was old, heavy and probably of limited use, but he put it on anyway, along with a helmet, which he balanced loosely on his head, barely fastened. He met up with the cameraman from Geo. They planned that Zille would do a live piece to camera as the fighting continued in the background. They quickly set up the camera, sticking masking tape over its red light so they would not be mistaken for snipers. Zille adjusted the helmet, holding a microphone in one hand. As the camera started to roll, he spoke quickly down the lens, his voice raised so that it was audible over the gunfire that ricocheted in the background.

The sound of shooting was getting closer, but Zille kept talking, his natural fight or flight responses numb. They had been filming for a few minutes when the bullets struck his arm. Zille heard his own voice yell out, saw the microphone drop to the ground. Blood swelled through his shirt. He had not felt any pain, only a powerful force hitting his body, like a truck. Time slowed down, or sped up – it was difficult to say. In his memory, it was a sequence of disconnected scenes. Seeing his own blood. Being bundled into a car. Driving out of the darkness of Sohrab Goth's alleyways and onto the highway that went past the airport and back into town. The relief of the familiar sounds of traffic. The strip lighting of the hospital. Through it all, the overwhelming fear that he would lose the use of his hand forever. Flashes of himself unable to drive or write or hold his microphone. In the hospital, he was rushed through. He heard himself ask about his hand. 'Don't worry,' said the surgeon. 'I'm going to operate and I will try my best.'

When Zille emerged from surgery, his family was there to greet him – parents, sisters, wife – ashen-faced and tear-streaked. His arm had been hit by four bullets. The surgeon had removed three but one was too risky to remove and remained lodged beneath the skin, a hard bulge where his right forearm met his wrist. The doctors assured him that he would be able to use his arm. Other journalists arrived and gathered round his hospital bed. Someone filmed him lying there and someone else took a photograph; suddenly the story of the crime reporter caught in the crossfire was being reported in all the major news outlets.

As soon as they felt reassured that Zille was out of danger, everyone in his family pleaded with him to quit the job. 'Isn't it enough now?' his wife said. His mother's face was frozen in tears. The Geo office was concerned too. A few days into his hospital stay, a psychologist arrived to assess Zille's mental state. He asked whether

Zille was worried about continuing his job. In fact, what frightened Zille most was the idea that his work might be taken away from him. He shook his head in response to the questions. He was fine to continue, he insisted. The psychologist told him that he would write a report saying that Zille did not need to be signed off on psychiatric grounds. Calls came from friends overseas, in the UK, America, Canada. They offered him a place to stay, suggested that he claim asylum based on the direct threats he faced as a media worker. Zille considered the offers. He loved to travel; he had been on many trips to Europe both alone and with his wife. He particularly liked London, where he was free to walk wherever he wanted without fear of being recognized. He tried to imagine himself living there, on those chilly anonymous streets. But what would he do there? Take a job in a corner shop? Karachi was dangerous, but he had a role here. He had a good salary and everyone knew who he was.

Geo took the photo of Zille lying in his hospital bed, dazed and bloodied, and printed it onto a huge poster, emblazoned with a slogan about the dangers journalists faced. For days, it was displayed outside the Karachi Press Club, where everyone could see it. People sent Zille photographs of it. He swelled with pride and tried to appease his family. He understood their worries, but he was a real journalist, and now everyone knew it.

9

SAHIBA

Just as the Taliban presence in the city had raised the stakes for Zille, so Siraj was having to adjust his work to the new political and criminal landscape. The various areas he worked in were controlled by different groups: the Muttahida Qaumi Movement held the parts of Orangi Town around his house and office in an iron grip, while the Taliban had displaced the Awami National Party to dominate some of the neighbouring areas where he ran women's savings groups and schools programmes. Just as the MQM workers patrolling the streets with heavy weaponry had long ago blended into the background, now the added threat of Taliban thugs lurking around the periphery of Orangi became a feature of daily life.

Siraj retained a close working relationship with his mentor Perween Rahman, whom he still called Sahiba (madam), even after all these years. He always trusted her assessment of the lie of the land and deferred to her on many operational matters too. A few years after opening the Technical and Training Resource Centre, he spent some of their annual budget on a motorbike for his employees to use for far-flung fieldwork. It was the middle of summer, when the harsh heat of the sun beat relentlessly through the misty haze of pollution. Siraj was the director of the organization and it was his job to manage the finances, but Sahiba often looked over the documentation and he often referred big decisions to her. The motorbike cost 4,200 rupees. He did not consult her before buying it, instead informing her afterwards, as they sat in her office poring over the budgets for that month.

'What's the point of this?' she snapped.

Siraj bristled. 'What, do you think I'm just spending our users' money?'

'Well, why get a bike?'

'Do you see this heat?' Siraj said, gesturing at the sun-bleached yard outside. 'I can give bus fares to my workers and make them go to places, but it takes hours and they'll be exhausted. With this bike they can get work done in a few hours that would otherwise take an entire day. It's not a bad investment. It's not as if I've bought an air-conditioned car.'

Sahiba nodded but didn't respond. A week later, she called Siraj and apologized. 'Look,' she said, 'I think I was needlessly upset with you. You made a good decision.'

Siraj laughed to himself as he hung up the phone. She did not say it, but he was absolutely sure that Sahiba's change of heart was because she had spent the last week monitoring him to make sure that he wasn't using the bike for his own personal purposes.

Over the years, Siraj had seen her use that same attention to detail to investigate the real sources of the city's multiple conflicts, the common threads that tied together the different political parties, the street criminals and the terrorists. Siraj loved listening to her talk. Sahiba's clarity on these unseen forces behind their daily lives – from sewage lines to the illegal water industry – was like a map of its own. Beneath the party posturing, the government alliances being made and broken, the thugs patrolling the streets and the hateful ethnic rhetoric was an altogether more bureaucratic battle for water and land. These commodities became only more valuable as the city's population grew.

After I moved to Karachi, I got used to hearing people talk in a casual way about 'mafias': the water tanker mafia, the real estate mafia, the transport mafia. As a newcomer, it was difficult to unpack what this meant, although it was clear that these basic utilities had extremely high stakes attached to them. One of the first stories I reported on was a short-lived government project to install desalination plants in low-income areas of Karachi to address the water scarcity. The scheme had the potential to undercut the water mafia's income stream: if people had access to drinkable water for free, they would not need to buy from overpriced tankers. In an armoured vehicle provided by the company contracted to implement the project, I visited a desalination plant in Lyari. The front gate was locked and heavily padlocked, guarded by multiple men with large guns. The desalination equipment itself looked small and insignificant compared with the security around it. I asked a few questions, but within minutes I was bundled back into the car by the armed guards the company had sent and driven out of the area. Clearly, those running the plant worried about the possibility of a violent attack. Water was as valuable a commodity as heroin and the unregulated way it was bought, controlled and distributed affected everyone. In the affluent areas of Clifton and Defence, where I spent much of my time, people tended to have water delivered to their homes periodically in large tankers. A few months after I moved, in late 2012, I stayed with a family friend for a few days. During my visit, phone networks across the city were switched off for twenty-four hours because of a terror threat. My host's water tanker was due that day, but the driver didn't turn up and she was unable to get hold of him because they communicated only by mobile phone. She spent an entire day in a panic, trying to get hold of another water provider, lest her family run out altogether.

That water in Karachi was scarce was repeated so often as a fact that people rarely stopped to question why. Several years earlier, Sahiba had embarked on a research project with a simple question in mind: if water was available through tankers, then why wasn't it available through the pipes? Over the course of months, Orangi Pilot Project workers travelled around different districts of Karachi to track information about the flow of water. They spoke to everyone they could: local elders who could facilitate access to particular areas, water board employees, hydrant operators, the men who drove tankers of water around the city to sell on at extortionate rates. They sat for hours watching the locations of hydrants to see who was filling up tankers and where the water was being transferred to. When the report was published it was uncompromising, explaining in detail how criminal interests were siphoning away water in bulk, setting up illegal hydrants near key water distribution sources to fill up tankers they could sell on for a premium, leaving low-income areas without any mains water supply. It was a thriving racket, involving corrupt officials at the water board, tanker owners and political parties. Siraj was impressed at how detailed the report was, proving beyond doubt what everyone intuitively knew: that water had become a valuable criminal commodity and that officials up to the highest echelons were implicated. Physically mapping the nature of such a significant crime was risky. But nothing happened after the report's publication in 2008. Besides, Sahiba had received many threats over the years and she usually brushed them off with a joke: 'What are they going to do, kill me?'

It was not just the water that people drank and washed in that was a criminal currency, but the very land on which they had built their homes. The OPP launched a project to map all the *kachi abadis* (unregularized settlements) around Karachi. These were areas that, like Orangi Town, had sprung up without formal planning. The residents lacked amenities and documentation, even if they had lived there for generations. This meant that if a property developer spied an opportunity for a lucrative housing complex, it was relatively easy to force these people out of their homes for little or no money. Developers often had links to political parties, who offered a level of protection, and to street gangs, who could help them forcibly displace and intimidate people.

Siraj's brother Shamsu's primary skill was as a mobilizer – he was good at connecting with people. Sahiba had launched the *kachi abadi* project back in 2006 and from the outset Shamsu had been closely involved. He forged links in the villages at the periphery of Karachi so that OPP mappers could go in without facing pushback from the local community. Once he'd made contact, Sahiba frequently went out to these areas herself, further convincing people with her straightforward, passionate manner. Siraj provided manpower for the actual mapping. Sometimes he went to make the maps himself and sometimes he sent eager trainees or young TTRC employees to the areas where Shamsu and Sahiba had made connections. Over the course of weeks and months, they would painstakingly document every alleyway, every house and makeshift shop, every business and school, drawing them into a map that would prove that these people and their homes existed. The OPP then took those diagrams to the city government so that the areas could be included on their maps of Karachi and legal leases granted to the residents. Once the areas were legally recognized, they were protected to some extent from being forced off their land – either because property developers decided to stay away or because, armed with official leases, locals could command much higher rates if they decided to sell. The maps had other uses too. People could use them to lay down sewage lines or demand electricity connections, as Shamsu once had in his part of Orangi Town, decades earlier. The project slowly inched along the chaotic periphery of Karachi, getting recognition for more than a thousand *kachi abadis*. Shamsu continued to press ahead, going further and further afield to make links with local elders. The further they went, the more apparent the magnitude of the problem became.

Siraj did not dwell on how dangerous it might be to map the physical reality of crimes in the city, though the murder rate had sky-rocketed and by 2012 was one of the highest in the world. Alongside the *kachi abadi* project, OPP staff were working on an update to the 2008 water report, sending staff out to locate illegal water hydrants in different areas. At Sahiba's instruction, they scoped out the hydrants, but with the situation in the city so febrile, it was even more dangerous than it had been a few years earlier. Siraj, Shamsu and Sahiba all shared the same view of the so-called 'mafias': they didn't really exist, but were instead a convenient cover for state collusion. The updated water report was never published; Sahiba told friends that she worried she'd be killed if it was made public. But when she gave talks or media interviews, she didn't hold back. 'Influential people are stealing 41 per cent of Karachi's water and pocketing 50 billion rupees annually,' she said in one interview, referring to her unpublished research. 'At least control the theft!' In another, she said, 'Some say there's a land mafia in Karachi. There's no land mafia. The land mafia is the government itself.'

In early 2013, Shamsu told Siraj he had received a threatening text message. He handed his phone to Siraj so he could read it for himself. 'You're going too much into the *goths* [villages],' it said. 'You should leave the OPP. Otherwise . . .' Siraj stared at the screen, his stomach dropping. A lot was contained in those ellipses. Shamsu told Siraj that he had already spoken to Sahiba about the message, having taken her aside after a meeting and shown it to her. She'd read it and nodded, replying softly, 'Me too.' Sahiba and her co-director Anwar Rashid had both received calls from unknown numbers; if they answered, a rasping voice told them to stop their work. They agreed not to answer calls from numbers they didn't know.

Sahiba decided the safest option was for Shamsu to leave Karachi for a while, and for her to temporarily stop taking trips to the *kachi abadis* they were mapping. Shamsu didn't like the idea of sitting idle, so he suggested that he work on some of the OPP's projects in Punjab, Pakistan's most populous province, for a month. Before he left, the brothers agreed not to mention anything about the threats to the rest of the family. Siraj couldn't work out how worried he should be. Threats were part of life in Karachi; even the head teachers Siraj worked with were constantly fielding death threats from extremists. He found it difficult to imagine that his brother or Sahiba could be seriously at risk.

A few weeks later, Siraj finished work and went to meet some friends on a busy street in Orangi Town, not far from his house. It was March 2013, a pleasant springtime evening. He watched the traffic go by, as he chatted with his friends over chai. Around 8 p.m. his phone rang. It was an OPP employee called Irfan. It was strange for him to be calling Siraj, especially so late. As soon as Siraj answered, Irfan blurted it out: 'Sahiba has been shot. She might have passed away. Her body is at the hospital.'

Siraj felt everything disappearing – the busy street, the traffic noises, the faces of his friends. He put the phone blindly back in his pocket and didn't say anything as he stood up and stumbled towards his motorbike. He sat astride the seat, but found that he could not start the bike. His hands shook. As he fumbled over the ignition, the friends he had been sitting with ran over and gathered around, asking what had happened, placing hands on his back as if to steady him.

'Sit for a while and drink some water,' he heard his friends say. 'Calm down a bit before you drive.'

'No,' Siraj said. 'No, this is not a time to sit down. I have to go.'

Hands still shaking, he managed to turn the key in the ignition and, in a daze, drove the short distance to his house. He burst in through the front door. His family were already sitting in front of the TV, stricken. A ticker ran along the bottom of the screen: 'Social activist and architect Perween Rahman has been shot near the Orangi Pilot Project office.'

Siraj is usually calm and collected; he recounts stories in detail, generally focusing on the impersonal, the quantifiable. But when he described this evening to me, six years after it had happened, the distress was visible on his face. He stopped retelling it to pull up his shirtsleeve to show me his arm. It was covered in goose pimples, the hairs standing up on end.

As soon as he saw the ticker confirming what Irfan had told him, Siraj went back to his bike and drove to the hospital. He entered the room where Sahiba had been taken and found Anwar there already, his face telling Siraj all he needed to know. Sahiba's clothes were stained with blood. Her face, usually so quick with a smile, was lifeless.

That evening, Sahiba had been working late in the office, as she often did. When she left, Orangi was dark. She waved goodbye to Anwar, who was also working late, and got into the back seat of her car, heading home to spend the evening with her mother. The driver navigated his way out of the OPP compound and onto the narrow street outside it. They turned onto the main road and went over a speed bump. At the next speed bump, a man on a motorbike pulled up beside the car. He fired at her four times, the gunshots shattering the glass of the passenger window. The bullets struck her in the neck. She died almost instantly.

By the time Siraj arrived at the hospital, others who had heard the news were already gathering – OPP staff and directors, Sahiba's relatives and friends, local politicians from the MQM. Siraj heard an MQM politician say, 'She is the daughter of the nation. Altaf *bhai* [the leader of the MQM] has requested that she be brought to our mortuary.' He was jolted from his fugue of grief into anger. These people turned the focus on Altaf Hussain when a gutter line was laid or a manhole lid was fixed, he thought, so it was no surprise that they would bring him up now as they tried to take ownership of Sahiba's dead body, but he was still shocked by the hypocrisy. On many occasions, the MQM had made it hard for them to do their work and now, suddenly, Sahiba was the daughter of the nation? He held his tongue, fearing what he might say if he allowed himself to speak. The senior OPP members who were there dealt with the demand politely, insisting that it would not be appropriate for the MQM officials to take her body because Sahiba's mother had requested that she be transferred to the Edhi mortuary. That settled things.

The night passed in a blur. Siraj woke up early the next morning, the rising sun still watery over the concrete landscape. He had agreed to go to the morgue and ensure that the body was transferred to the graveyard at the right time. He was so tense when he woke up that he went straight there, although it was only 7 a.m. and the burial was not taking place till after midday prayers, to allow time for her family and friends to reach Karachi. Sahiba's sister Aquila lived in Abu Dhabi and had taken a late-night flight as soon as she heard. When Siraj arrived with the body that afternoon, the graveyard was crowded. Some of the hundreds of thousands of people Sahiba had helped through her work were gathered to pay their respects. As Siraj watched the shroud going into the ground, he wept.

The murder of such a well-known activist and public figure made international headlines. As Sahiba was laid to rest, the police released a statement saying that they had caught and killed the man who had shot her. His name was Qari Bilal and they claimed he was a Taliban militant. The execution did not satisfy anyone who knew Sahiba. It was too convenient. Aquila, herself a formidable woman, was outraged. Where was the evidence? What was the motive?

Aquila and some senior members of the OPP filed a successful petition to the court for the investigation to continue. In the media, speculation began about why Perween Rahman had really been targeted. Some cited her work on documenting illegal water hydrants, though others felt this was unlikely, given that the OPP's last published report on the matter had been five years earlier. A few suggested that the land mafias wanted to get rid of her.

The day after she died, the guards at the OPP office reopened the compound. Most of the staff were busy with the funeral, but the guards believed that Sahiba, who had insisted that they keep working through all the violence and hardship outside, would not have wanted the office to sit closed. Within a few days, everyone was back at work.

The *kachi abadi* project had been temporarily suspended, but Siraj tried to cope as he always had, by focusing on the work. This was disorienting without Sahiba and her guidance. For years, he had given more time to his work than to anything else – his family, his friends – and her death left a gaping hole in his day-to-day life. It also sharpened his mind to the risks he ran. Three months after her death, an Orangi-based community worker was shot and killed. Soon after that, another OPP director, Saleem Aleemuddin, was targeted; he survived. As attacks continued on people who had been associated with Sahiba, Siraj began to vary his schedule, setting off for work earlier or later each day. He changed his route to the office every few days, going on circuitous loops around the familiar alleys. Although the grief and shock weighed heavily on him, he never thought of taking time off. He was the director of an organization and it was his responsibility to keep things running, setting an example as Sahiba had. He rebalanced the TTRC's workload, following the OPP in pulling back from mapping *kachi abadis* and *goths*, focusing instead on flood relief and schools. He did not talk about his fears, worried that if he expressed his anxiety, he would create panic for everyone else. Instead, he silently absorbed it.

The assassination took place in a febrile political climate. Pakistan was gearing up for a high-stakes general election. Despite the street violence, this was a democratic landmark. The same week that bullets sprayed into Perween Rahman's car and people took to the streets by the Karachi Press Club to protest against the killing, I had relocated to Islamabad for a few months to cover the run-up to the general election. I had never met Perween and didn't yet know Siraj, but I thought of all the human rights activists, women's advocates, charity workers and business people I had interviewed and socialized with in Karachi. Most of them felt that they were potential targets. This fear came out in different ways: some spoke about varying their routines, others about avoiding certain topics of conversation in front of guards or drivers. Since arriving in Karachi the previous autumn, I had covered attacks on many women seeking to improve society: the shooting of Malala Yousafzai in the north of Pakistan; a spate of killings of polio vaccinators in Karachi. Now here was 'Sahiba', Perween Rahman, a woman who was focused on simply trying to alleviate poverty. Perhaps that was why her killing attracted so much attention, despite the fact that in 2013 Karachi recorded 3,000 murders, more than any other city in the world. Adjusting to the cool mountain air and relative sleepiness of Islamabad, I read all the coverage of the murder in the English-language newspapers. One haunting line from an editorial in *Dawn*, the oldest of these papers, stuck in my mind: 'What will become of a society that, for the most part, sits quietly as its messiahs are systematically wiped out?'

The May election was big news. After decades of disruption by military dictatorships, it was a transition from one elected government to another. But the road to democracy was bumpy. As well as the violence between political parties that accompanied every election in Karachi, the Pakistani Taliban and its affiliates had the stated aim of destroying the state. They thwarted democratic participation at every opportunity. Each day brought news of a terror attack in some part of the country, and the spectre of violence made it difficult for certain parties or politicians to hold rallies. The incumbent PPP, along with the ANP, faced particularly violent opposition. By the end of the election campaign, 130 people had been killed, most of them while attending political events. On the day of the election, I drove around polling stations in Islamabad and Rawalpindi. Somehow, despite the bloodshed and threats, the overall mood was one of jubilation that Pakistan had reached this democratic milestone. Women queued around the block to cast their votes; young men in party bandanas danced in the streets. In Karachi, the election returned a majority for the MQM, as it always did. But overall in Pakistan, the balance had tipped. The left-leaning PPP was trounced; they handed over government to the centre-right Pakistan Muslim League (Nawaz), the main opposition. The PML–N advocated negotiating with the Taliban. The PPP retained power only in their heartlands of Sindh.

In Lal Baksh Kachehlo, out on the dusty scrubland at Karachi's eastern edge, a PPP candidate was, yet again, returned to power. Jannat wasn't overly concerned about the change in national government, but she was aware of it because these days she watched the news as often as she could. There was a sweet spot late in the afternoon, after the goats had been taken out to pasture, before she needed to gather the firewood and start cooking dinner, when – if those snatched minutes coincided with one of the intermittent hours when the village had electricity – Jannat and the other women from the village could crowd into one of the few houses with a TV. She had to fight with the others to put on one of the news channels; they were far more interested in watching soap operas with their salacious tales of city folk behaving badly. Jannat had a vested interest in the news. Her husband, Ghulam, had achieved the ultimate dream for a man from their district: he had got a government job – in a department overseeing wildlife policy – which meant a better salary and permanent, reliable employment. It also meant a daily motorbike commute to Karachi, to a small government office in Landhi, the sprawling area where Safdar and his family lived. On a good day, it took an hour and a half, on a bad day, more than two. The cost of petrol and maintaining the bike ate into Ghulam's already limited earnings, but they had faith that things would eventually improve for them. This was a government job – as good as it got. But for Jannat, it also brought a daily feeling of fear. When her husband had spent his days at the chicken shop off Super Highway, she could visualize the surroundings and know that he was safe. There was no such guarantee now that he spent every day in Karachi, where people were murdered and bombs went off. Ghulam insisted that she shouldn't worry, but she couldn't help it.

10

THE KARACHI OPERATION

It was the middle of June and still hot even at 11 p.m. Safdar was exhausted after a long shift. He parked his ambulance and went through his regular routine, taking the damp rag he kept in the vehicle and wiping off the remnants of the day – streaks of dirt, splash-back from the road. Safdar's colleagues teased him about his obsession with keeping his ambulance spotless. There was no escaping the filth of the city; as soon as he pressed the accelerator, it would be covered in dirt again. Above the drivers' stools, the electric ceiling fan hummed as it spun half-hearted circles through heavy air. There had been no rain for months. The blades of the fan cut through the dim electric light, making it flicker over the faces of the drivers as they chatted.

Suddenly, a colleague from the control centre burst through the adjoining door into the office, puncturing the sleepy atmosphere. 'The airport is under attack,' he shouted.

Safdar leapt up, knocking his stool over as he dashed to his ambulance. By the time he was in the vehicle, a colleague was putting out a radio message to the whole Edhi network, saying that security forces were going in and needed medical backup.

Siren blaring, Safdar pulled out into the swarming traffic and headed towards the airport. During the intense summer months,

Karachi's rhythms shift so that the streets fill as the temperature drops. The roads were frenetically busy with late-night commuters and families out for the evening. Fortunately, the ambulance was small enough to weave between the multiple lanes of cars and motorbikes, and Safdar was an expert navigator. As he sped towards the airport, he saw smoke billowing.

Karachi's Jinnah International Airport is Pakistan's busiest. It is a low, blocky, sandy-coloured building fronted by a neat green lawn, surrounded by a wide perimeter guarded by the camouflage-clad Airports Security Force. Shortly after 11 p.m. on 8 June 2014, ten men dressed in imitations of these military uniforms split into two groups outside the airport. Armed with automatic weapons, hand grenades and rocket launchers, they entered the complex. One group went over a perimeter wall and the other through a side entrance generally reserved for top government officials and foreign dignitaries. The assault was meticulously planned and the men were prepared for a long siege. Some wore suicide vests under their uniforms. Safdar was well accustomed to the aftermath of terror attacks by now. But usually the targets were Sufi shrines, markets, processions – places where the poor gathered in large numbers. This attack on the airport, with its manicured lawn and conspicuous security, struck at the point of transfer between the city and the world.

Zille was off work that evening and had invited a few friends over for dinner – two police officers and a businessman. The lines between his work and his social life were so blurred by now that he had stopped drawing a distinction. His house was around ten kilometres from the airport, in the comfortably middle-class district of Gulshan-e-Iqbal. They heard the explosion. 'The airport – it's terrorists,' one of the police officers said immediately, grabbing his phone. 'We had intelligence about this.' He rushed out of the house. When a second explosion went off soon afterwards, the other police officer jumped out of his seat and moved towards the door. 'Are you coming?' he asked Zille.

Zille nodded. The businessman friend looked appalled. 'Why are you going there?' he demanded. 'You're not at work now. Let's watch it on the TV.'

'I have to go,' said Zille, repeating his familiar mantra. 'It's my job.'

If he went inside the police officer's car, he might be able to get better access than if he turned up in his own vehicle along with the other journalists. Without stopping to listen to his wife's protestations, Zille followed his friend out of the door. The police officer's car was parked outside; he was off duty and had come with a driver. They got into the back seat and the driver started the car.

As they drove, Zille called the news desk to report the disturbance. His channel, Geo, was under pressure. It had been riding high as the most popular news station in the country, but two months earlier a top anchor, Hamid Mir, had been targeted in a bomb attack. Geo had taken the unprecedented step of publicly blaming the intelligence services. They were briefly taken off air. Now they were broadcasting again but had dropped in the rankings. They needed to reclaim their top spot. Speed was crucial to the mission. As soon as Zille dialled in the news, Geo ran a ticker on screen declaring a possible attack.

Within twenty minutes of first hearing the blast, the driver pulled up at the airport. The night sky was aglow with the blaze. Police were already on the scene but the significant backup needed to guard the perimeter had yet to arrive and the area hadn't been cordoned off. They drove into the airport compound and parked the car. The police officer Zille had arrived with quickly disappeared to report for duty. Zille saw several senior officers he knew outside the main entrance looking harried. One told him that the militants had made it inside the airport, that they were heavily armed and that planes had been grounded with passengers on board. Zille texted the information to his colleagues in the newsroom. As the officer turned away to take a phone call, he slipped inside the compound.

Over at the cargo entrance, Safdar's ambulance screeched to a halt. During any major disaster, the Edhi Foundation worked quickly and a group of around ten drivers had assembled, with more on the way. A small senior management team, including Faisal Edhi, stood to one side, working out a strategy while the sound of gunshots drummed from inside the compound, rippling over the distant sound of shouts and screams. The bosses briefed the drivers. This was no ordinary bombing: the militants were trying to seize control of the airport and members of the Airports Security Force were fighting them off. Faisal explained that whoever went in had to closely shadow the fight and provide medical backup. 'Who is ready?' Faisal asked. Safdar's hand shot up at once. He strapped himself into a heavily plated bulletproof vest and ran back to his ambulance to get the rudimentary metal stretcher. He and the other drivers sped towards the runway.

It was a battlefield. The Airports Security Force and the militants wearing imitations of their uniform were engaged in a running gun battle, their silhouettes illuminated by the stark fluorescent lights that dotted the warehouses of the cargo area. In the warehouses and inside the airport itself, staff and passengers hid anywhere they could, clambering under the seating at the gates and cramming into the small stores that sold handicrafts and fridge magnets. Hundreds of terrified people were trapped on grounded planes, listening to the piercing crack of gunshots directly outside their windows.

Safdar and the other ambulance drivers dispersed around the runway, placing stretchers at the sides of the field and finding places to duck and hide to avoid the bullets. Safdar's body was tense as he closely watched the security forces, trying to spot when anyone was shot or injured. He was not afraid, although when he saw how heavily the militants were armed, he thought momentarily of the faces of his young daughter and new baby son. Safdar saw an officer fall to the ground just behind a plane. He darted out to help, putting himself into the firing line. The ground was evenly paved and the wheels of his stretcher smoothly sailed over it. Praying that the plane was obscuring him from sight, Safdar checked the officer's air passages. He placed his arms under the unconscious man's shoulders and hauled his body onto the stretcher. The man's dead weight was compounded by the heaviness of the bulletproof vest. Standing up, Safdar felt as if the whole field was shaking around him. He heaved the stretcher back to the sidelines and dressed the bullet wound.

By now, hundreds of police officers and Rangers, the paramilitary force, had arrived at the scene. The airport complex was sealed off. Journalists had arrived in droves and were gathered outside, reporters in bulletproof vests and cameramen jostling for space. In the studios, anchors speculated about what might be going on, while behind the scenes, reporters scrambled for information, calling police contacts and the Edhi Foundation's central office. While this scrum was going on just beyond the perimeter walls, Zille alone was locked inside the airport. The gunshots and sounds of battle were uncomfortably close. He texted updates to the office about what he could see. Cameras were strictly forbidden at any kind of sensitive operation; his presence was tolerated only because he did not have a cameraman with him. Glancing around to check that no one was watching, he surreptitiously began to film clips and take pictures on his phone to send back to the newsroom.

Zille's updates from inside the compound went straight on air. Across Pakistan, viewers were glued to their TV sets. Reporters, desperate to hold viewer attention, shared whatever information they could glean about the precise positions of soldiers and police. Behind the gunfire and screams that echoed in from the runway was the sound of the urgent, raised voices of the reporters, blaring out from the multiple TV screens affixed to walls around the airport. The terrorists, patrolling the main airport building, were paying close attention to the news broadcasts. Every time a ticker ran along the bottom of the screen or a reporter shared a new piece of information about the security forces' strategy, the militants inside picked up their walkie-talkies and radioed the attackers outside so they could adjust their positions.

After an hour or so, Zille realized how isolated he was. He had long since lost sight of any of his friends in the police force. His phone was running low on battery and he didn't have his own means of transport. He was comfortable with the police, but less so with the Rangers and the army, and in the absence of the officers who had brought him, he suddenly worried that a soldier might spot him and demand to know what he was doing there. He walked hurriedly towards the entrance through the sound of ringing gunshots, his phone vibrating with calls and messages from the office. He scoured the line of vehicles, looking for the car he had arrived in. He spotted it and saw the driver sitting nearby. Zille ran over to him. 'Please take me out of here. It's really dangerous,' he said. The driver nodded. They got into the car and drove off. Once they were outside the compound, Zille jumped out and entered the familiar crowd of journalists, looking for his colleagues from Geo.

Back on the runway, Safdar's back was soaked in sweat under the heavy bulletproof plates as he ducked and dived to avoid the gunfire. He worked all night, running out to get injured officers, to administer first aid or to keep bodies safe the moment someone was hit. Though he was sickened by the violence, at a certain level he also felt a new thrill. He had always dreamed of joining the army and here he was, acting like a real commando, supporting his nation against those who sought to destroy it.

Around 4 a.m., an hour before dawn, the fighting finally stopped. Security forces had shot dead eight of the ten militants. The last two had killed themselves by detonating their suicide vests. The blasts shook the ground and lit up the night sky. Four airline employees had been killed too, as well as fourteen members of the security forces. It was some time before the people crammed into every crevice of the airport realized that it was safe to come out. The death toll rose a few days later when the corpses of seven people were found inside the airport's cold-storage facility, where they had attempted to seek refuge.

Orange sunlight streaked across the sky above the angular airport building. Zille, who had been dropped off among the scrum of reporters outside the airport complex, called the office – he was going home. In his rush to the airport, he hadn't thought to bring water and he was completely dehydrated. The Geo driver took him back, past the police cars and army trucks, past the rows of fellow news reporters still broadcasting live. He knew that he had done the wrong thing that evening. They all had. But at least he had been first one there.

The days after the attack were busy. Zille scouted out information about the identity of the terrorists, the police operation and the weapons retrieved from the airport. As he focused on the minutiae, hunting for a scrap of information no one else had uncovered, the Pakistani Taliban officially claimed responsibility. They said the airport attack was retaliation for army air strikes in northern Pakistan, the region bordering Afghanistan, where a military operation had been rumbling on for years. The 2013 election had brought the PML–N to power, and their policy had been to negotiate with the

Taliban. But after the airport attack, negotiations were shelved. A week later, a new military operation was launched, called Zarb-e-Azb (sharp strike). Planes dropped bombs over the rocky mountains and remote villages of northern Pakistan. This wasn't the first serious air strike the region had faced; it had been under sustained military pressure since 2001. This was what had pushed many of the militants thousands of kilometres south to Karachi, where they hid in plain sight in cramped slums and apartment blocks. But Zarb-e-Azb was different. At the same time as a bombing campaign in the north of Pakistan, the Rangers ramped up their operations in all Pakistan's major cities in a pincer movement designed to prevent militants from simply relocating to urban wastelands and staging attacks from there instead.

Their beige camouflage uniforms had been a familiar sight on Karachi's streets for decades – they had never completely withdrawn after the first army operation in 1992, which had aimed to stop ethnic violence and clamp down on the Muttahida Qaumi Movement and stop ethnic violence. In September 2013, the new government had announced the so-called Karachi Operation to get the city under control and tackle target killing, kidnapping, extortion and terrorism. The escalating violence in the city was a political issue and a financial one too, each gunfight and terror attack striking at Pakistan's economic heart. This meant that by the time of the airport attack, the Rangers were already there, ready to step into action. Armoured personnel vehicles patrolled hotspots like Lyari and Sohrab Goth and drove around the flyovers and highways that connected the different building blocks of Karachi. The Rangers set up makeshift checkpoints all over the city. They had carte blanche to arrest or shoot suspects at will. In Lyari, Orangi and the Pashtun areas where terrorists hid out, Rangers stormed in, detaining and shooting people. Not to be outdone, Karachi police also stepped up their raids.

Many of Zille's police officer contacts were offended that the Rangers were leading the Karachi Operation. Their dominance suggested that the police had failed to keep things under control and could not be trusted to do so now. In Sohrab Goth, the area where Zille had been shot, the station house officer Shoaib Shaikh, a surly man with a handlebar moustache, raged about shoddy resourcing. 'We are trying to fight rocket launchers with Kalashnikovs, and now the extra money is only going to the Rangers?'

Shoaib was a key contact for Zille. He was right at the frontline of the battle against militancy. Shoaib believed that the higher-ups – the people in government – forgot about police stations like his, nestled deep in an area where militants were operating. He was known as Shoaib Shooter because of his taste for extrajudicial killings, which were known as encounters. Most officers who chose to shoot a suspected militant instead of arresting them had the same rationale: the justice system was not fit for purpose and the terrorists would either bribe their way out of jail or continue operating from inside. Zille was broadly sympathetic to this position.

A few months before the operation began, Shoaib found out that he was on a Taliban hit list. Without fuss or fanfare, he moved into the back room at the station, which was already furnished with a bed. The first thing he saw when he woke up was a screen showing CCTV footage of the station's exterior. He kept a pistol under his pillow. Once a month, he left the station under cover of darkness to visit his wife and children. Other than that, he went out only on encounters, with an intensified determination to slaughter militants. Along with a cameraman, Zille often accompanied Shoaib on these trips, which typically took place at night. They would stand outside a building the police were targeting, the footage rendered eerie and green by the night-vision setting. Zille, in his bulletproof vest, talked quickly to camera to give the context, instinctively ducking and flinching as bullets rang out in the house behind. Films of these terrorist raids were mutually beneficial. The police wanted to show the public they were getting something done and the channels liked to air them because they were good for ratings. And beyond his habitual concern for his own place in the pecking order of reporters, Zille had a vested interest in bringing the ratings up. After Geo's run-in with the intelligence services, the station had been moved from their usual channel to a random spot that no one could find. Ratings were down and advertisers were slipping away. Reporters' salaries were not being paid.

As the crackdown escalated, Zille found he rarely spent a full night at home. He would get a call from a police contact to say something was happening and would rush to either the station or the location of the planned encounter. He and a cameraman would set up outside, sometimes filming the police beforehand, sometimes waiting outside the building. Afterwards, Zille would go in and photograph the faces of the men who had been killed, in case there was someone prominent whom he could identify later. His phone's photo gallery filled up with the dead faces of bearded men staring glassily into the lens. Zille was unfazed by these scenes. He believed that the police usually acted in good faith, even if it was inevitable that they occasionally got the wrong person. Every crime reporter covered encounters, but Zille thought that he covered more than most – the pay-off for years of cultivating contacts. He had lost count of the number he'd attended. There were whispers from other journalists that Zille was too close to police and too quick to laud their work, but he dismissed this as jealousy.

In November 2014, Zille was sitting at home with his family when he got a phone call from an unknown number. He was in the habit of leaving the room to take these calls. When he told me about this one, Zille wouldn't specify who it was from. 'Not police,' he said, typically vague. 'Sometimes calls come from Rangers, sometimes the ISI [the intelligence agency].' The person on the other end of the phone asked him to come for a meeting. Zille knew immediately that this was serious. He did not mention it to his family.

At the meeting, the official told Zille that his name was on a hit list of an extremist group, an offshoot of the Taliban. Hit lists were forced out of militants during interrogations, usually before they were killed. An interrogator had written down a list of names that Zille was now looking at. He was in third place. According to the official, his name was there for two reasons: first, because the terror group thought he was glorifying the police who killed militants, and second, because he was Shia.

'Tell me what to do,' said Zille, panicked.

'I'll try to catch the people who might be after you, but in the meantime, you have to be careful with your movements,' the official told him. 'Don't travel with anyone else in your car. Watch your surroundings.'

Zille left the meeting disturbed. He felt conspicuous, as if his forehead was marked with a target. He knew what it meant to be on a Taliban hit list. He had seen the blighted lives of his friends in the police force. Sitting in his car, he called a few police officer friends who were in the same situation. One after the other, they were blasé. 'You show the criminals' faces,' one said, his voice almost a shrug. 'It's natural. Be careful. Carry a weapon.' Other contacts were no more comforting: 'Change your routines', 'Don't move around the city unnecessarily.'

Over the following weeks, Zille made changes. He bought an extra car so that his wife, children and parents could get around without him. His family knew something was wrong but he never explained what was happening to them. Everyone knew that his work was dangerous, so he let this vague threat hang in the air without going into specifics. His parents were old and he feared that the anxiety might kill them. Sometimes he'd agree to go out with his wife and kids, but only if they travelled in a separate car. He would park his own vehicle far away from the destination and go the rest of the way on foot, lest the number plate be recognized. Occasionally, he called up an old friend, someone from outside the media or the police force, but they made excuses to avoid meeting him. The friends he used to play cricket with stopped inviting him to games. He never asked if they knew about the hit list, or if they were put off by the general aura of danger around his work. He soon stopped calling. But the most painful ostracism was yet to come. When Zille and his wife enrolled their three-year-old daughter at the local school, the headmistress looked at him intently. Later, she took his wife aside. 'We'll accept your daughter to this school,' she said. 'But only if your husband never drops her off or collects her. We have to think of the other children.'

He spent more time with his friends in the police, other marked men who understood what he was going through. Practically every night, Zille's phone lit up with an alert from one of these contacts telling him about another encounter. Under cover of darkness, he drove to the location to film the aftermath. Focusing on being there first and getting the facts was almost a refuge.

As the Rangers patrolled Lyari like an occupying force, Parveen's family home in Kiamari filled up with relatives. Just as they had sought relief from the outbreaks of gang violence there at different points over the last decade, now they were desperate to escape the perpetual, indiscriminate raids by the paramilitary. Every day when Parveen came home from work, it seemed there was a different aunt or uncle there, bringing updates about the Rangers operation. Countless people had disappeared without trace; others turned up lifeless and mangled on the streets. The house was so chaotic that Parveen thought it resembled a farm.

Within months of the Rangers operation starting in earnest, almost all the biggest hitters in the criminal world had quietly slipped out of the area. Some, like Uzair, went to Dubai, or Oman, or as far afield as South Africa and the UK – places where they had relatives and owned property. Others sought local hideaways, leaving the tangled alleys of Lyari for the wide, bougainvillea-lined avenues of Clifton and Defence, where the Rangers rarely strayed. Parveen heard of each escape with growing dread. If the top gangsters had simply relocated, they could come back whenever they wanted. And while it was good to see their stranglehold being broken after all these years, she wondered if a crackdown so steeped in violence itself could create positive change. It was difficult to have faith in the system, given that these institutions had facilitated the criminals for so long.

Parveen had not spoken to her cousin Sayed since her fight with Uzair. Her relationship with that whole side of the family was awkward, though she still spoke to his sister, Aisha. They lived right across the narrow street from Uzair and Rehman's now abandoned houses, which had Rangers stationed outside. Their proximity to the gangsters' former homes was enough to make the Rangers suspicious. They were constantly searched, even though the Rangers never found drugs or weapons. Aisha's young son was stopped on his way back from school, his bag roughly taken from him right outside the front door, the books in it chucked onto the filthy road as the Rangers searched – for what? Weapons? In an eight-year-old's backpack? Parveen heard these stories and felt a flash of the distress she had experienced during the eight-day operation, when punishment had been inflicted on the entire community. She heard from relatives that Sayed had left Lyari for another area nearby and was keeping his head down. She didn't care. She did not worry about Sayed, or Nasir, or anyone else she knew who had thrown in their lot with the gangs. They deserved to be brought to justice before a court of law. But the senior gang members had been allowed to get away scot-free, while the young men who had signed up with them were being illegally detained, tortured and murdered. Rather than peace and justice coming to Lyari, the gangs had been replaced with another equally violent force.

Not long before the crackdown began, Parveen's mother had been diagnosed with cancer. For a few months after the diagnosis, they temporarily moved back to Lyari. *Amma* had once said she would never go back there, that she was sick of the sound of gunfire, but when the end of her life was on the horizon, she wanted to be close to her family. They thought it might be easier to look after her in Lyari, but travel between different parts of the area was so often completely impossible that it was actually harder for Parveen's sisters to see their mother than it was when she was in Kiamari. When Nasir heard that Parveen's mother was ill he came to the apartment unannounced. Given his affiliation to Uzair, even visiting their place put him at risk, as it was on a rival gangster's territory. But he knocked on the door without taking the precaution of covering his face. Parveen was surprised to see him. In general, he visited her relatives when she wasn't around. Usually she felt a mix of fury and grief when she saw him, but this time she was grateful that he had come. He sat with them for a while. Before he left, Parveen wrapped her arms around him in a tight hug. He was still as ostentatiously muscular as he had been all those years ago when they both worked at the street school, when he was constantly lifting weights, dreaming of becoming a professional boxer.

'You were always showing off your body, but you never became a boxer,' she said, as she hugged her friend. 'It makes me so sad to see that you're now using your body to do wrong.'

Nasir didn't say anything.

'I never saw you get a job. I never got to choose the bridal clothes for your wife, because you never got married,' Parveen said tearfully. 'It has all gone to waste.'

Nasir hugged her back. His voice was small when it came out. 'I know, *Baji*. It's the truth.'

That was the last time Parveen ever saw Nasir. As the operation intensified, he was picked up and questioned by the Rangers. Some days after being detained, Nasir's body was found on a main road in Lyari. It was clear that he had been tortured. He was covered in bruises and cigarette burns. Parveen never found out exactly what had happened to him. Telling me about it a few years later, she was visibly distressed. She kept returning to her memories of that terrible day in 2004, when her sister had been attacked and Nasir had shouted at the gangsters that he would fuck up anyone who fucked with her family. Of course there were other factors that led to him joining a gang – his brothers becoming involved, his relatives getting killed, his difficulty in finding a job. But Parveen couldn't shake the conviction that the moment Nasir had turned down the wrong path was the day he shouted at the gangsters on her behalf. It was hard for her to believe that it wasn't her fault. Parveen's mother died of cancer soon afterwards. The grief was almost too much to bear.

As Parveen grappled with these personal tragedies, the net was closing all over Lyari. In December 2014, just over a year after the Rangers operation began, Zille got a call from Uzair Baloch, his long-cultivated contact, who was hiding in Dubai with an Interpol warrant out for his arrest. Uzair told Zille that he was planning to be arrested in Dubai. There, he said, he had a chance of staying alive, while in Pakistan he would be killed as soon as the police got their hands on him. A few days later, Uzair was arrested by Interpol. Zille covered the story for Geo: the images of Uzair Baloch, the formerly untouchable don of Lyari, being led away in handcuffs, showed how fast fortunes in Karachi could change.

The Karachi Operation targeted the whole city, but it played out differently in different areas. In Orangi Town, the threat from the MQM rapidly began to feel less acute.

Without Sahiba, Siraj's working life was more lonely, but work was his only way of coping with the loss. One day, as he was sitting in the Technical and Training Resource Centre office poring over some documents, he heard an unfamiliar voice and looked up to see a young man. Siraj recognized him as the son of a woman who headed up a local savings group. People from the various communities he worked with often stopped by, either to check in about their loans or other projects, or simply to say hello. Siraj smiled and told him to come in. But the man's demeanour was strange. He did not sit down. Instead, he threw a bunch of booklets onto Siraj's desk.

'Guess what?' he said. 'Each one of these booklets is worth 10,000 rupees. You have to pay.'

Siraj looked at the booklets and immediately recognized them as demands for extortion money. Each one was filled with receipt slips to give the veneer of respectability. In Orangi Town, there was only ever one extorter, the MQM, which had once again been voted into the local parliamentary seats. Looking at the desk, he counted ten booklets. If each was worth 10,000 rupees, that was a total of 100,000 rupees – a huge amount, the equivalent of £480 today.

Siraj kept his voice calm. 'How did the thought even cross your mind that I would be able to pay this money?'

'I know it, because you grant loans to people, so of course you have the money.'

'Do you understand whose money this is?' Siraj said. 'It doesn't belong to me. It belongs to people like your mother.'

The young man looked agitated. 'Whoever's money it is, you need to pay it to me.'

Siraj excused himself and stepped outside the room. Quietly, he asked a colleague to go and find the man's mother – the family lived very close to the TTRC office. Siraj went back into the office and tried to keep the man talking, avoiding the subject of the extortion demand. Around ten minutes later, the colleague returned, along with the man's mother.

'What's going on?' the mother asked, looking anxiously at Siraj.

'Well,' said Siraj, 'there's this person here who has come to ask me for 100,000 rupees. You are the head of the savings group, so I thought you might be the best person to explain how it works.'

The woman looked at the booklets still strewn on the table and then at her son. 'Who do you think you are?' she shouted. 'You're a dog, your party are dogs, and now you and the other dogs need our money? I'm going to give you a slap. I'll teach you a lesson.' She reached down and pulled off her sandal, wielding it in the air as if she was about to wallop him with it. 'How dare you come here? Don't you ever come here again to ask for money from this organization!'

The young man stared at the floor. He would not speak disrespectfully to his own mother, but when he looked up he stared directly at Siraj. 'You should not have done this,' he said, but he sounded more embarrassed than threatening.

After they left, Siraj laughed hard about the incident with his staff. He was not worried about repercussions. This was one time when he was confident that his work with the community would protect him. The young man was obviously low in the chain of command, new to the whole business of extorting. He was like so many others in the MQM – drawn in by the promise of power and reduced to committing petty crimes.

There were more Rangers visible on the streets. They had set up makeshift stations on the main roads and roundabouts. But it wasn't just their physical presence that had shifted the mood in Orangi; it was what they symbolized and the historical memories this triggered. During Operation Clean-up in 1992, the army had torn through Orangi Town like a marauding gang, killing countless people in their mission to destroy the MQM. The Urdu-speaking community had been indiscriminately targeted, with men rounded up regardless of their political affiliations. This had vastly increased support for the MQM, laying the groundwork for the vice-like grip they'd held Orangi in for decades. This time, the Rangers operation was different: there was no big spectacle, no tanks rolling in, no tortured bodies thrown onto the streets. Instead, there were whispers. People were picked up and not heard from again – but most had some connection to the Party. The MQM workers who used to patrol the streets around their ward and sector offices had vanished. On his rounds of the area, checking up on his projects, Siraj heard rumours that the Rangers had employed informers. They were often the most inconspicuous people – the chai seller on a busy corner, the old man who sat begging at a mosque close to a unit office. Their information had given the Rangers a list of important people to target. But the operation was not limited to the big guns of the MQM, particularly as time went on. So many families had some relative or other who was involved with the Party. They did not trust the Rangers to treat them fairly, nor did they believe the MQM leadership would protect its foot soldiers. The Party had always casually disowned their street enforcers when the law caught up with them.

It was hard to say that this was justice. People rarely stood trial. They simply disappeared into detention or death. But still, as the Rangers operation picked up pace across Orangi, there was a slackening of tension among people who did not have any connection to the MQM, and a general sense that power had shifted and it was OK to say what you meant. People spoke more freely than ever, from local gossip to national press reports. After the election, the leader of one of the opposition parties, Imran Khan, accused the MQM leader, Altaf Hussain, of being personally responsible for the murder of one of his political workers. As TV stations aired the speech and others began to be vocal in their criticism of the Party and its leader, Siraj noticed that the people around him were expressing criticisms too. These were things that friends and family had always said to each other behind closed doors, but would never have dreamed of saying in public.

Just over a year after the operation began, at the festival of Eid al-Adha, the goats were slaughtered and skinned as they always were. But for the first time in at least a decade, when Siraj and his family sat down to their meal, no one knocked on the door to take the goat skin. And no one ever came back to his office to demand extortion money.

I had moved back to London about a year before the attack on the airport and the subsequent crackdown. I watched the news of the Karachi Operation from afar, unable to imagine the city I had known being brought under control. Crime was so closely tied to political power that I couldn't see how the crackdown could be anything more than a superficial measure. When I thought of Karachi, I felt tense – muscle memory from the months I had spent there living in a constant state of high alert.

In early 2015, around eighteen months after the operation started, I returned to Karachi for a newspaper assignment. I was steeled for the difficulties in getting around, but when I landed I noticed a different atmosphere almost immediately. The same relatives who had warned me to take off my jewellery before going out and to carry a spare burner phone – so I could hand that over to an armed robber and hang on to my actual phone – were now happy to sit outside bustling restaurants, phones in hands, wearing gold earrings. Terror attacks and street crime were less frequent. Both murder and kidnapping were down. The Rangers were stationed on practically every main road in Karachi, their beige camouflage uniforms blending into the dusty surroundings, guns tucked into their holsters. Their armoured personnel vehicles were a common sight on the flyovers and highways that make up the centre of town. But no one I spoke to seemed to mind the heavy paramilitary presence. It was the price of security.

The day after I arrived in Karachi, my uncle signed me into a private members' club. I drank tea on the veranda and tapped away on my laptop, trying to push through the jet lag to prepare for the reporting project ahead. That was when I saw the news pop up online. Early that morning, Nine Zero, the MQM's head office, had been raided by the Rangers. They were still on the scene and supporters were protesting nearby. I wanted to get there, but I didn't yet have a car or a driver. I asked the front desk to order me a taxi, but when I said where I wanted to go, the otherwise extremely polite receptionist laughed: 'With respect, madam, no taxi driver is going to take you there.' I had to settle for watching developments on the news and social media, even though I was only a few kilometres away. The Rangers retrieved a stash of weapons and dozens of party officials were arrested, including the man accused of murdering a colleague of Zille's, Wali Khan Babur, in 2011. The Party had been under pressure for a while; as the Rangers operation raged in Karachi, Altaf Hussain was under investigation in London. But I was still shocked to see the headquarters stormed. As I watched the news, my mind wandered back to the strike I had witnessed just a few years earlier, when MQM workers on motorbikes had fired into the air at night and brought the entire city to a standstill. They had appeared unassailable.

Zille had no such problems getting to Nine Zero. As soon as he heard about the raid, he sped to the area. As he made his way through crowds of angry protesters, he noticed that the Rangers there were wearing black balaclavas pulled over their faces to conceal their identities. Even as they dismantled the MQM's headquarters, they were clearly aware of the organization's power and the potential for personal repercussions. It was a huge story and it did not cross Zille's mind to miss it, even though he was not actually reporting. A few weeks earlier, he had quit his job at Geo. He had not been paid for months and was tempted away by an offer from a new channel, Bol TV. There was serious money behind this new company, though no one seemed to know exactly where it came from. Still, it seemed like a safe bet. Vans, rickshaws and billboards all over Karachi bore the Bol logo, declaring it 'Pakistan's imminent number one media enterprise'. The channel was not yet on air and its launch date kept being pushed back. Zille spent his days at the Bol office, building up a team of cameramen, junior reporters and drivers. But he desperately missed reporting. After more than a decade on the job, it was disorienting not to be on TV every day. He worried that if he didn't keep up regular contact with the police, they'd start calling some other journalist. So although he had nowhere to broadcast what he found, he continued to keep two phones on him at all times, driving to encounters almost nightly. At Nine Zero, he took photos, filmed scenes on his camera, spoke to his contacts. Then he put his phone back in his pocket. He put some of his material on social media, to show that he was still in the game, but it was not the same as airing on TV to hundreds of thousands of people.

Zille was still adjusting to life as a marked man and felt safest circling Karachi's highways and flyovers in his car, hidden by the darkness. He covered his car windows with black panels designed to keep out the sun, so that a passing gunman on a motorcycle would not be able to identify who was inside. He did not like to stay for too long in restaurants and spent meals looking over his shoulder to see if anyone was watching. After years of reporting on crime, he knew that all it would take was for someone to spot him and make a single phone call. He was still alive, but he often felt that being on a hit list had killed his ability to actually live.

Two months later, Bol TV was embroiled in its own scandal: its parent company was found to be selling fake university degrees online. Because the company's CEO was facing criminal charges, the channel's broadcast licence was revoked. In some of the photos of the CEO being led away in handcuffs, Zille is standing by his side. He wrote to me: 'These are very difficult days in my life. My news is not going on air. I cannot send tickers. I am disturbed. I am mentally disturbed.'

As he searched for a new job, Zille continued to circle the city at night, witness to its horrors, cultivating his contacts, hooked on the thrill.

11

BAHRIA TOWN

The Karachi Operation might as well have been happening on a different planet to Lal Baksh Goth, but things were changing there too.

Sometimes, Ghulam took Jannat to Karachi on the back of his bike, so that she could shop for jewellery and plain salwar kameez to embroider. Just as her own mother had started stitching dowry pillows after Jannat was born, now Jannat embroidered pillows, thinking ahead to her daughter Aziza's marriage. Jannat didn't particularly like visiting Karachi – it was loud and hectic. But she still couldn't help but notice the hundreds of schools and colleges that clustered at the side of every road, or the signs advertising hospitals and pharmacies. The couple had two children now – their son, Gul, was a few years younger than Aziza – and they worried about their prospects. How was it possible that people who lived in the city had so much, while the people of Lal Baksh – who had nourished this land for generations – had so little?

The villages dotted around the arid earth that surrounded Kathore were poorly connected. Clusters of houses were surrounded by vast tracts of land owned by the respective villages. Once they had grown crops here, but now much of the land was barren. Despite these long distances, news travelled around the district, spread when the men from different villages met each other in Kathore. That was how the Kachehlos of Lal Baksh got to hear about Bahria Town, the new housing development being constructed on the land close to Super Highway, the motorway that ran all the way from Karachi to Hyderabad and along the outer edge of Kathore. Developers had been buying up land from the villages closest to the highway. Some people had sold their land easily; they couldn't use it to cultivate crops anyway and this was a means to make some immediate cash. They reinvested the money, buying property in Karachi or setting up businesses in Kathore. There were whispers that others had been pressured into selling, that the man behind the development, Malik Riaz, was friends not only with the former president Asif Ali Zardari but with the district police superintendent, Rao Anwar, and that they were conspiring to force people off their land. It quickly became a constant topic of conversation.

Jannat listened avidly to these conversations whenever she could, although she was exhausted by the adjustments needed to care for two children instead of one. When she and the other women gathered during the day, they exchanged what information they had overheard. Some of the women were anxious that they might come under pressure to sell their land, but others thought the new development would ultimately be good for their village. Jannat's uncle had recently married a woman named Saira who had grown up in the city. Saira was educated and urbane and had a tendency to be dismissive of everything, from the locals' hygiene habits to their manners. She insisted that the Bahria Town development could only be good news. Perhaps it would mean a gas line, she said, or proper electricity provision, or running water. Jannat found herself wondering, hopefully, if it would be beneficial for their village if Bahria Town did come just a little closer, even though the men seemed to agree unanimously that if this happened they would be in grave danger. More than anything Jannat wanted better facilities in their village, and if the city was coming towards them, perhaps tarmacked roads, a school or a hospital would be coming too.

Aziza had started going to the village primary school. She took to it immediately, just as her mother had. Jannat loved seeing her learn to read and count. She thought her daughter was even cleverer than she had been as a child and harboured private fantasies that Aziza would become not just the first girl to go to university from Lal Baksh, but the first person from their village to qualify as a doctor. Then she could come back here and set up a clinic to treat everyone in Lal Baksh. Jannat did not tell people about this dream, because she knew that realistically, when Aziza got too old for the village primary school, she would have no way of getting to and from the school in Kathore. Ghulam worked such long hours and left so early that he would not be able to take her, and as a woman Jannat could not travel beyond the village unaccompanied, given the risk of encountering unfamiliar men. It was restrictive, but Jannat had grown up with this as the norm. She sometimes asked me about the fact that I had travelled so far from my home in London to visit Lal Baksh; but her questions centred more on how expensive it was to take a plane, or whether I also had to scrub my clothes with a stone when I was at home. She never questioned the disparity in our circumstances as I travelled, unaccompanied by a man. 'You're a city person, it's different for you,' she would say.

After Saira had moved to Lal Baksh from the city, she had set up a small tuition centre where she helped the girls study past fifth grade. They were then driven to the Kathore school or another centre to sit the exams. But Saira was just one person, and Jannat knew from bitter experience how hard it was to do well outside a formal classroom.

One day when Aziza was at school, Ghulam took Jannat to see the new development. Piles of construction equipment and rubble stretched out as far as the eye could see. Already, apartment blocks and houses had begun to go up, their smoothly plastered pastel-coloured facades incongruous against this rebellious, barren landscape. But what Jannat noticed were the lights. There were lights everywhere: street lights along the semi-built roads, lights in the buildings which had already been constructed. She took everything in and was overwhelmed with relief and a vague tingling of excitement. It was so pristine here, so perfect, so modern. Suddenly she was sure of it. They would get a gas line. They would get a hospital. They would get schools. They would get a university.

'Why are you looking so happy?' Ghulam said, his voice faint against the billowing wind. 'This is not a good thing. It'll be so much better if they stop where they are now and don't expand. If they expand, we will be gone.'

But Jannat was in a daze, hypnotized by the lights in the distance.

There were already some tangible benefits to the new development. Jannat's sister, Bushra, had been betrothed ever since childhood, but ten years on, in her mid-twenties, she was still waiting. For a decade, Bushra had followed the village ritual of covering her face with her dupatta and running into the house whenever her husband-to-be was nearby. The marriage had stalled for so long because Luqman, Bushra's intended, did not have a job and lacked the means to build a house for them to live in, or to support a family. He helped run the poultry farms he and his six brothers owned, but this didn't generate much income. Luqman applied for job after job but was always passed over. When the Bahria Town construction started in earnest and the rest of the village debated whether it was a threat, Luqman immediately went to the construction site to ask about a job. He was hired on a casual contract as a watchman, working for daily wages to guard the equipment and materials strewn around different sites across the Kathore area. Sometimes he worked for two solid weeks, only to be told not to come the next day – but it was better than nothing. Luqman immediately started saving to build a house for Bushra. Jannat was delighted. She teased her sister, who was always loud and raucous, about the need to be reserved at the wedding. 'It will be hard for *this* bride to sit still,' Bushra admitted.

As she waited for the wedding date to be set, Jannat was absorbed by her children. She worried constantly about her son, Gul, who was now a toddler. He was small for his age, he got sick all the time and was fussy about food. Just a year before he was born, Jannat had given birth to a second daughter, Azra. The baby died when she was only a month old, a desperate tragedy which had been hard to recover from. Jannat and Ghulam now took their children to the doctor in Kathore or even in Karachi more often than most people did. This was expensive and time-consuming, and it was only possible because Ghulam had a stable income. The doctor told Jannat that Gul had allergies and should not play in the dust, but what was she supposed to do? Their whole village was built on dust. There was nothing for the children to do except play outside in it. Everyone in the village agreed that the dust had now taken on a different consistency and smell – something chemical and unnatural carried on the wind from the new development. Bahria Town was an invisible but constant presence in Lal Baksh. It had even begun to intrude on their dreams. By night the village was usually blanketed in a silence so thick it was almost tangible, punctured only by the wailing of jackals or the buzzing of mosquitoes. But now the Bahria Town construction team ran the heavy machinery at night, so that it wouldn't fail under the blaring sun. Jannat did not know what the machines did, but the distant chugging, beeping and whirring often kept her awake.

It was unsettling, but she held on to her hope that the new development would bring good things within their reach. Jannat's elderly aunt Amina had hepatitis, the same disease that had killed Jannat's father, and she struggled to get to the government hospital every month for her check-ups and low-cost medicines. It was not just the cost; Amina walked with a limp and the journey exhausted her. A hospital in Bahria Town would make such a difference. Jannat held this certainty deep in her gut, that things could improve, even if the process of change was difficult.

When Jannat realized that she was pregnant again, Ghulam decided to take her to Karachi for a check-up at one of the government hospitals. It was her first trip to the city for a while. As they passed through Kathore, Jannat noticed how busy it was, bustling with extra custom from Bahria Town's construction workers; new shops had been opened by the villagers who were flush after selling off part of their land. As they drove up onto Super Highway, Bahria Town loomed at the side of the road. It was huge, unrecognizable since her last visit. The roads and plastered houses she had been so impressed with when she first saw them had expanded and been replicated beyond belief. But this time, Jannat's eyes were drawn not to the sparkle of electric lights, but to the huge white gate and barrier wall that surrounded the front of the complex. The gate looked like a spaceship, with its gleaming white geometric arches standing out against the pollution haze. It was set back behind a security barricade, where uniformed guards with guns tucked into their belts stopped visiting cars and charged an entrance toll. Jannat took it all in. As she stared at the gate, her hopes collapsed. That gate was there for a reason: to keep people like them out. The hospital would come, the schools would come, but none of them would be for the people of Lal Baksh. They would be glossy buildings with shining glass windows and tiled floors and air conditioning and heavy doors, where people in fancy clothing carelessly paid extortionate sums. Jannat looked at the gate looming. It was so close, but it would always remain out of reach.

The rhythm of Jannat's days was the same as it had always been: cooking for the family, caring for the goats and cattle. When the blistering afternoon heat had passed, the women strolled from their village and into the open land that had belonged to the Kachehlos for generations to gather firewood. Because this was their land, it was assumed that they would encounter only men they knew, making a male chaperone unnecessary. The land stretched out under a sweeping expanse of darkening sky, the reddish sun-parched soil billowing clouds of dust over clustered thorny bushes. When they arrived, they set to work gathering twigs and branches, knotting them into small bundles. Shrieks of laughter filled the air as the girls teased each other, while the older women complained about their children. They sauntered back to the village as slowly as possible, holding bundles of wood on their heads, prolonging the moment before the hard work of cooking began.

Ever since construction on Bahria Town had started in earnest, the evening walks were different. Just beyond the area where the women gathered wood were unfamiliar machines and stacks of material covered with grimy tarpaulins. What worried Jannat was the group of men who were there to work with and guard the equipment. No one knew what tribe or village they were from, or who their families were. Being seen by other men without their own male chaperone present went against everything that the women of Lal Baksh Goth had been brought up with. The men kept their distance, never breaching the Kachehlo land. But they stared, sometimes putting down their tools and standing up straight, turning their heads to follow the women with their eyes as they moved around. As soon as the unfamiliar men came into view, silence fell on their group like an iron weight. Previously, they let their dupattas slip back over their heads as they worked, unconcerned about who might see a flash of exposed hair. But now they pulled them tightly over their faces to cover themselves, leaving only a small gap for their eyes. They worked as quickly as they could, eager to get back to safety.

The new development itself was still some distance away, not quite visible from Lal Baksh. But it was so large that much of the surrounding area was being used to store and prepare materials – tarmac, bricks, plaster, wood. It was difficult for Jannat to imagine how big the site was; she did not leave Lal Baksh often and the mental image she had of Bahria Town was a snapshot of her two brief visits – the beautiful, tidy houses, the rows of lights, the looming gate. The men brought back stories from other villages around the district. Jannat's husband, Ghulam, told her about elders who had sold part of their land to Bahria Town, only to find that the developers never paid up, or that Bahria Town had expanded over the land that the village had not sold, leaving local people with nowhere to pasture their cattle. He told her about other elders who had refused to sell, only to find bulldozers outside their doors. Jannat heard the stories with growing unease. But it all felt abstract until someone from her own village was targeted.

For most people in Lal Baksh and the surrounding villages, it was not feasible to go all the way to Kathore every time they needed groceries or other basic supplies. That was where Karim Baksh's shop came in. From the outside, it looked like any of the houses in Lal Baksh: a blocky single-room structure that sat by itself on a stretch of arid earth. The shop sold everything, from large sacks of flour and rice to plastic bottles of petrol, *naswar* (powdered tobacco) and syrupy sweet cartons of mango juice that the children fought over. The floor was cracked concrete, the walls a faded blue, the wooden shelves stacked with a disparate array of supplies. Amid the heaps of packaged food and cheap children's toys were two plastic chairs, where customers with time to pass could sit and chat with Karim, who was always stationed behind the counter or leaning on the battered chest freezer in the middle of the room. He was the uncle of Bushra's husband-to-be, but like everyone in Lal Baksh Goth, he was related to Jannat and the others in multiple ways. Karim was a large man, with sun-worn skin, a thick white beard and a dry sense of humour. He ran a poultry farm on a stretch of Kachehlo land, but his main business was the shop. When I visited, I told him how beautiful it was – colourful jars filled with knick-knacks, glass bottles stacked like ornaments – and he laughed: 'You only find it beautiful because it's in the middle of the jungle.' It was a place of nourishment, a place where people knew they could always get food or change their tyre, a place where stories were exchanged. Everyone held Karim in high regard. That made it all the more shocking when he was attacked.

One night in April 2016, Karim was asleep at home when his son shook him awake.

'What's happening?' Karim asked blearily.

His son spoke quickly. 'People have come here and destroyed our poultry farm. They have broken it down.'

The two men ran out of the house. When they got to the poultry farm, Karim saw police cars lined up, as well as a machine that he had never seen before. He described it to me: 'It had huge tyres and a long neck with a shovel at the end.' A bulldozer. Karim's poultry farm, a long, thin structure with a corrugated-iron roof, had already been turned into a heap of rubble. Feathers flew and half-dead chickens squawked in the debris. The bulldozer was getting to work on the other farms nearby.

Karim strode towards the police car to demand answers. A police officer pushed him roughly and frisked him, checking his pockets for a weapon. Karim was suddenly relieved that he did not have anything valuable in his pockets. As he was searched, he saw his son being forced into a police car. Karim tried to run after the car, but was restrained by the police, who ordered him to go back to his house.

He paced around at home, waiting desperately for dawn. After a few hours, his son came back, dishevelled but unharmed. He said that police had taken his phone and the 250 rupees he had in his pocket. The village woke up to the news that the same thing was happening to other poultry farms situated near Karim's. Bahria Town vehicles, accompanied by the police, had stormed in and mowed down the farms. People were panicking. If the police were involved, they said, there was nothing they could do. But Karim was not afraid. He was furious. This was his land. Unlike some people in the area, the Kachehlos had paperwork and legal leases going back to the late 1800s. He was damned if he was going to let a bunch of thugs seize his property. If the police were in cahoots with Malik Riaz, the owner of Bahria Town, he would go above their heads.

It took him some time to compose the letters. He had been to school and could read and write in Urdu, but he did not have cause to do it often. Karim sat down in his shop, where he also stocked cheap notepaper, envelopes and pens, and wrote to the National Accountability Bureau, a court that deals specifically with corruption cases. Karim was sure that if he could let the right people know what was going on out here, they would step in. He read it, and reread it, crossed words out and wrote it again more neatly. After a few days, he decided it was as good as it would get, and posted it.

'Malik Riaz and other employees of Bahria Town created fear and threatened us and tried to kill us,' the letter to the National Accountability Bureau said. 'In the middle of the night, with the help of their pet criminals, they tried to illegally grab land in

Kathore, District Malir. This is our ancestral and personal land, which Bahria Town's criminals and thugs are trying to occupy. All this work is done in the darkness of night. My name is Karim Baksh Kachehlo. In a collective with three other people, I am the owner of sixteen acres of land. These people are trying to grab our land and they use the local police and district administration to help them achieve their goal. They are doing this in return for bribes. We are extremely poor people and we are very scared. There is God above us and on this earth there is only one institution that we poor people can trust: the National Accountability Bureau. We have lost faith in other law enforcement agencies, especially the police, who choose to cooperate with the oppressor. I respectfully request you and your top hierarchy and the Rangers to help us, and to listen to us.'

It took more than two months for a reply to come. When it did, it was crushingly brief: 'Your complaint has been examined. It does not disclose any offence under the National Accountability Ordinance 1999 and therefore cannot be processed any further.'

Everyone in Lal Baksh Goth heard about what had happened to Karim's land. Jannat had only the flimsiest understanding of what it meant; just like Karim, she had never seen a bulldozer before. But now when she stayed awake at night listening to the metallic sounds of machinery carried on the dry winds, she imagined the whirring coming closer and destroying their homes. Everyone in the village waited to see if the Bahria Town vehicles and staff would come back to do something with the land they had cleared, but as the weeks inched by there was no sign of them. The men speculated that although the response to Karim's letter had been dismissive, perhaps putting something in writing was enough to scare them off. Tentatively, Karim and his son began to gather funds to rebuild. Jannat's father-in-law, the village elder, Shafi Muhammad, was a gentle man, but he talked about the attack with a quiet steeliness that she had never seen before. They needed to plan, he said, in case the Bahria Town people and the police came back. 'We will not sell a single inch of our land and we will not surrender. If we have to die defending it, we will die. We will not give them our land.'

Later that year, Jannat gave birth to another baby boy, Muhammad, and spent her days nursing him and helping her mother stitch the outfits for Bushra's wedding. Despite the attack on Karim's land, no one begrudged Bushra's fiancé for continuing to work for Bahria Town. Everyone understood that he needed a job. The house he was building for Bushra was beautiful, with neat stripes of pastel colour painted on the exterior and real wooden-framed sofas inside, not just cushions on the floor. It was an especially impressive house to make up for the long wait.

Usually, it was easy enough to push the dread aside amid the noise of the children marauding around the village after school and the steady pressure of daily tasks. Now that she had three children, two of them very small, Jannat found it more difficult to get everything done. She was still caring for the goats and the cattle, as well as cooking the meals, but she felt tired, as if she was dragging her body through the motions. Ghulam was out at work for long hours, but he was increasingly anxious about the situation in the village. His anxieties came out in strange ways. His mother got sick and he decided that all of them – he, Jannat, his mother, the children – had to stop drinking water from the borehole and use only bottled water from now on. Jannat thought it was an unnecessary expense; they were all used to borehole water. But Ghulam was emphatic: bottled water only. In the face of frightening changes beyond the borders of their village, it was one way for him to feel he had control over keeping his family safe.

When the day of Bushra's wedding finally came, hundreds of guests gathered from the surrounding villages. The women were decked out in their fanciest clothes, with darkly stained henna patterns on their hands and forearms. They danced the *jhumra*, standing in a circle and clapping hands with the person in front of and behind them. Bushra muttered that sitting still while everyone else celebrated gave her a headache. But underneath the complaining, Jannat could see that her sister was happy. Her life was beginning in earnest.

During Ramzan, it was a challenge for Jannat to fast. It fell in the month of June, one of the hottest times of the year. As a breastfeeding mother, Jannat was not religiously obliged to fast, but she wanted to observe the holy month. She fell into long, sticky sleeps in the afternoon, weak from hunger and still physically drained from childbirth. The swarms of flies that gathered in the village in the summer months buzzed so loudly that in her half-sleep they blended with the sounds of Bahria's thrumming machines.

Everything slowed down during Ramzan. People whiled the afternoons away in sleep or prayer until it was time to get up and fetch the firewood to make the evening *iftar* meal. There were a lot of people in the village and *iftar* was a huge production – much more work than making a normal dinner. On one of these afternoons, Jannat put the children to sleep and said her prayers before lying down to rest. She lay in the darkened room, but couldn't quite fall asleep. She did not know how long she had been lying there when she heard a commotion – the unmistakable sound of adult voices shouting. She felt so weak that it took her a while to get up. Then she heard what they were saying: 'The Bahria Town vehicles have come.'

Jannat pulled herself up and staggered blinking into the glaring sunlight. Everyone was running around in a panic, but she could not see any police cars or bulldozers. Quickly, she realized what they meant: the vehicles had come to the second cluster of houses that made up Lal Baksh Goth, a few kilometres away. This was an extension of their village, but because the facilities – the school, the borehole, the mosque – were all here, around the place where Jannat lived, not many people built houses over on the other settlement. The only reason they maintained property there was to keep some oversight of the land, as it was closer to most of the poultry farms. Jannat's father-in-law, Shafi Muhammad, had a house there, and there was an *autaq* – a single-room structure which anyone in the village could use if they needed to receive guests or to socialize outside their homes. Jannat looked around and saw that the man who used his Datsun pickup truck as a taxi for people to get around the area was ushering villagers onto the vehicle without taking a fee, urging them to hurry. People piled on, some still clutching their prayer rugs, others obviously just woken from sleep like Jannat, with hair askew. Still dazed, Jannat broke into a run and got onto the truck, leaving the children behind. The truck started up and they drove.

The Bahria Town vehicles had arrived an hour or two earlier, at this remote corner of a remote village. Some people in the village said there were fifteen bulldozers and thirty-five police cars, others doubled this number, others still put it far lower. Typically, this second settlement of houses was empty, but on this particular day, Shafi Muhammad had called together a group of men, including Dildar, Bushra's brother-in-law. That was because there had already been an incident in the village, in the early hours of the morning, when everyone was asleep. A bulldozer escorted by a number of police cars had driven to a cluster of poultry farms owned by Kachehlo men and smashed down two farms owned by Dildar and his six brothers, and two others next door. One small mercy was that they were empty of chickens; the men had just sold their last batches to market traders in Karachi and had not yet restocked with baby chicks. But because there were no chickens there, no one had been at the farms to alert the village to what was happening. It was only when Dildar went to do a routine check on the premises later in the day that he found them completely destroyed. It would cost tens of thousands of rupees to repair the damage. No one had approached them at any point to ask about purchasing their land and they couldn't understand why this was happening. So they gathered together with Shafi Muhammad to plan what they would do if their land was attacked again. They had not expected another assault on the same day.

As they talked, they had heard a sound, and came out of the house to see the bulldozers lined up like alien invaders. Dildar ran over to them, yelling, 'Why are you coming here? This is not your land. We have not given it to anyone.'

The driver of one of the vehicles wound down his window. 'This is not your land. This land belongs to Bahria Town,' he said.

'It's ours,' Dildar shouted, but the bulldozers were advancing.

First, they ploughed into the *autaq*. What stuck with the Kachehlos later was not the destruction of the guest house itself, though it had been there for decades. It was that no one, not the police, not the Bahria Town bulldozer drivers, stopped to check if anyone was inside before they drove their metal claws into its surface, smashing it into the ground.

Everyone had come out of their houses by now – around ten or twelve people, not just men but women too – and they watched in horror as the *autaq* was crushed. No one knew who started lobbing the rocks that littered the uneven ground at the police cars, but soon everyone joined in, picking up stones and throwing them with all their might at the bulldozers. Someone was sent to the main settlement of Lal Baksh to fetch backup.

Jannat arrived to see everyone throwing stones, a violent hailstorm raining on the police cars. The police were still some distance away. Suddenly gunshots rang out and everyone screamed. The smell of gunpowder cut through the dusty air, but the stones did not stop.

The police were firing into the air to try and disperse the villagers. Shafi Muhammad shouted that they should not be afraid. 'The police will not attack us directly because there are women among us,' he called out. Jannat naturally respected authority and was terrified of the police. But now, when she saw the attack on her land and heard her father-in-law suggest that she, as a woman, might be able to help, she gathered the last of her energy, ran out of the truck and joined her people. She picked up a rock and threw it. It was exhilarating, terrifying. She remembered what Shafi Muhammad had said: 'If the time comes, we will die for this land.'

More gunshots rang out. The police advanced with batons. Jannat saw Shafi Muhammad being seized and roughly handled, and felt sick. She heard screaming and saw that Fatima, a woman from the village, had fallen to the ground. Fatima had a slight, frail build. A police officer had struck her with his baton and she was bleeding from the head, dark red blood oozing from a deep cut along her hairline. Some of the women clustered around her to help. Above them, the stones continued to fly. The windscreen of a police car smashed. The Datsun pulled up with another truckload of people. As the crowd grew, the atmosphere changed. The Bahria Town workers and the police got back into their cars to shield themselves from the hailstorm of stones. Just as quickly as they had come, they drove away. They were gone.

Jannat and the other women clustered around Fatima. They cleaned her head wound and carried her inside to rest. Her eldest daughter, Gulshan, a softly spoken teenager, cried when she saw her mother's injury. In the chaos, no one checked on Fatima's youngest daughter, who was six. Suddenly, someone realized that she was missing. Everyone rushed to search their houses to see if she was hiding inside somewhere, but she was nowhere to be seen. The people of Lal Baksh were frantic that a child was out alone in this wilderness, with those terrifying machines and unknown men lurking. It took two hours to find her. The sound of her sobs led them to where she was cowering, terrified, under one of the big trees in the area where the women went to gather wood.

In the days that followed, Lal Baksh was gripped by a strange mix of terror and jubilation. The teenage girls practised fighting with each other using their pillows, saying that they needed to be prepared if the Bahria Town people came back. Some of the women laughed giddily as they described how they had scared the policemen away. They shrieked as they repeated the stories – 'I came there', 'I picked up a stone', 'I shattered the window glass', 'Did you see the stone I picked?' – their voices building on each other's, creating a vivid shared memory. It was intoxicating, the sense that even though they were small people, they had chased away these powerful forces. But there was a manic quality to their laughter. The children had nightmares, waking up sweaty and tearful. The steady chugging of the faraway machinery at night haunted the village. Everyone knew that the machines could come back at any time. The men were particularly troubled by what the driver had said to Dildar: 'This is not your land. This land belongs to Bahria Town.' But the days inched by and the bulldozers and police cars did not come back. Someone had made a video of the assault and it had been shared on Facebook and WhatsApp, forwarded on from person to person. People from other villages in the district came to offer their congratulations that they had fought off Bahria and to ask their advice on how they could do the same. Jannat was proud when these visitors came. But she was also afraid in a way that was bigger than she could articulate. It was not just the destruction of the *autaq* or the poultry farms. It felt like nothing would ever be the same again.

Shafi Muhammad was shaken. He kept repeating, 'In all my sixty years, the police have never come here.' He had rallied everyone to be brave that day and they would never have fought off the bull-dozers without him. But Shafi Muhammad did not recover from the shock of the assault. When he fell ill a few months later and was taken to the hospital, the doctors diagnosed a heart problem. He died within a few weeks. There was no doubt in anyone's mind that it was Bahria Town that killed him.

12

AFTERSHOCKS

With the Karachi Operation in full swing, Safdar was often called to the aftermath of police and Rangers encounters to collect the dead or injured, with strict instructions not to ask any questions. He did not mind this. The thought of an innocent person being killed distressed him and he preferred not to know if that was what had happened. Gradually, the Lyari street battles, the targeted political killings in Orangi and the terror attacks began to recede. They did not disappear altogether, but for the first time in years it was possible to pause and breathe in between. Safdar's mother and wife no longer whispered prayers for his safe return every morning when he set off for work.

He suddenly had long breaks during shifts, periods when he was simply waiting for a call to come in. He stayed close to the main Edhi office in Tower at these times, but liked to leave the confines of the building and settle into one of the nearby cafes. There was the biryani stall that dished up heaps of fragrant, steaming rice and meat to drivers, who sat on grubby plastic chairs on the street outside; the tea shop that offered an enclosed space to sit, a relief from the sun in the hot summer months, its battered white wallpaper adorned with small blue fleur-de-lis; the 'juice bar' next door, newly decorated with white walls and bright orange plastic seats, selling fried chicken and canned drinks. Safdar was friends with the staff and sometimes, if it was a particularly slow day, he would go into the kitchen there and cook something for the other drivers. He loved to cook, but for years he hadn't had time to indulge this passion. All these places were close enough to the control centre and the parked ambulances that if a call came in he could leap into action.

When he was fresh on the job, his colleagues had laughed affectionately at the way he treated every call – even a routine transfer of a patient who needed to get home from hospital – as an emergency. Even after more than a decade on the job, this was still his attitude. Safdar had never forgotten the long hours he and his family had spent waiting to get his brother Adil home from hospital during his polio surgery. If it was in his power, Safdar never wanted to make anyone else wait that long. Sometimes he got into trouble with his managers for using his siren inappropriately. Whatever was happening, he wanted to get there as soon as he could.

In July 2016, Abdul Sattar Edhi died. The old man had been the guiding light of the foundation ever since he started it in the 1950s. The news hit Safdar hard. He cried as if he was grieving for his own father. Edhi was declared 'Pakistan's Father Teresa' in the international media and was given the rare honour of a state funeral. It was held at Karachi's National Stadium. Safdar knew that Edhi would not have expected this pomp and ceremony, but he still felt a surge of pride when he saw soldiers carrying Edhi's coffin. Safdar held the army in the highest regard and seeing Edhi honoured in this way made the tears stream down his face afresh. The body was wrapped not in the black and white shrouds of the Edhi mortuary, but in the green and white of the Pakistani flag. Sometimes, on his days off, Safdar drove out to Edhi's grave. He rarely sat still, but at the graveside he felt a kind of peace. He prayed quietly and spoke to Edhi, repeating the same promise: 'We are going to take forward all the work you did for humanity.'

As a teenager Safdar had been forced to abandon his dream of joining the army because of his poor literacy. But his work as an ambulance driver had allowed him to serve his country in a different way. Safdar is full of bravado, constantly joking and always ready to dismiss others as stupid or incompetent. ('I can tell what kind of a person someone is simply by looking at his legs,' he once told me.) The only time I ever saw him looking self-conscious was when he had to sign his name. By contrast, when it came to his medical knowledge, he lit up. Safdar rattled through the procedure to follow in the event of a heart attack, electrocution, broken bones, fire bombs. He had developed tricks for lifting particularly heavy people and improvised methods of propping people up to keep their airways open as he drove. Like all ambulance drivers, he had received only a few days of basic instruction when he started. Drivers who showed aptitude then got further training from doctors on an ad hoc basis. Safdar loved these sessions. He asked questions constantly, checking if the methods he had developed were acceptable. Once, he told me proudly, a doctor asked how long he had studied medicine for. 'It seems like you've studied for a long time, because you know the right questions to ask,' Safdar remembers him saying. Instead of responding verbally, Safdar showed the doctor his thumb, which signifies illiteracy – those who cannot sign their name often use their thumbprint for official documents. The cruelty of the city – its violence and its poverty – had stopped him from completing his formal education, but it had also given him an astonishing level of professional expertise and, perhaps even more importantly, a driving sense of purpose.

In late 2018, I went to Safdar's family home for a meal. On the main road were rows and rows of motorbikes parked up next to each other, workers' vehicles parked outside the factories that proliferate in Landhi. We turned onto a bumpy side street, before parking and going the rest of the way on foot through a maze of densely popu- lated alleys, past the barber's shop where Safdar and his brothers all got meticulous Bollywood-style haircuts. The house – a few rooms built around a small, cement-floored central courtyard protected by a loosely strung-up curtain – was packed full of people. The entire family was there to celebrate. Adil's wife had just given birth to their second child, a daughter. As the family members argued over the best name for the new baby, Safdar picked her up, his entire face changing as he cooed over her, rubbing his nose on hers. 'Babies smile, because the angels are with them,' he told me.

I ate the chicken and naan that was served to me along with slices of guava, and my plate kept getting replenished. I protested that I was so full I was getting uncomfortable.

'You will finish it,' Safdar said, his tone mildly menacing. 'When you come to a Pashtun's house, you will eat until you sweat.'

I gritted my teeth and continued to eat.

Safdar's youngest siblings, Fatima and Nadir, came into the room. They were in their late teens now, both in their final years of school. They joked that Safdar was the 'boss brother' and said they hoped to go on to further study. Safdar, who looks older than he is, with sun- worn skin and teeth discoloured and cracked from years of chewing paan, smiled proudly.

I thought of something Safdar had said to me once, several years earlier. We were sitting at the side of the road next to his parked ambulance as the streets filled up for a religious procession. The Edhi Foundation was providing medical backup, as it always did. Trucks kitted out with loudspeakers blaring religious music drove past, as people gathered and walked along the streets. I asked what it was like to work at these processions, after experiencing the destruction of suicide bombs ripping through crowds.

Safdar thought for a minute. 'I don't think about it too much,' he said. 'I don't dwell on my memories. Memories are a prison.'

As I watched him with his entire family gathered around, bickering about the best name for the newest member, it was obvious that he was focused, instead, on his future.

The Karachi Operation undoubtedly meant that some people had the space to breathe again, as terror attacks and gang violence reduced. But there was also a dark side to the crackdown, a human cost to this tentative peace. The Edhi mortuary, which predominantly caters to the poor, is in Sohrab Goth, set back from a main road so busy that even the scant trees planted at the edge of the road appear to be covered in a thin film of dust. In front of the mortuary is space for ambulances and cars to drive through and unload or collect bodies. For a very low cost, Edhi workers carry out the traditional rites to prepare the body for burial. Families who cannot bury their dead straight away, perhaps because they are waiting for relatives to arrive from further afield, can pay a small fee for the body to be kept in the cold-storage unit, protected from the overwhelming heat. The mortuary has another, sadder function too. It cares for the thousands of unidentified dead bodies that turn up on Karachi's streets every year. When someone spots a dead body anywhere in the city, they call the Edhi ambulance service to collect it. If the hospital or police cannot identify the dead person, they are brought here. Edhi mortuary staff take three photographs of the face: one from the front and one from each side. These are filed along with a serial number that marks the shroud. Staff send their fingerprints to the national ID card database. If this yields a result, they track down family members. If there is no result, or they cannot reach the family, the body is taken to the Edhi graveyard, a few kilometres away. It stretches out over the space of several football pitches. The bodies are buried by Edhi staff. Each grave is marked by a wooden tag bearing the same serial number as the photographs of the corpse, so that even years later, if a relative comes looking, they will be able to find their grave.

In the summer of 2018, I spent several weeks at the Edhi mortuary, working on a documentary about unidentified bodies. During long hours waiting to film, I sat on the stone benches that lined the central hall, next to grieving relatives and staff members on their breaks. This atrium was open to the street and the dank humidity of the July air filtered in. To the left was a room where Edhi staff washed bodies. To the right was the cold-storage unit where corpses were kept. I was occasionally hit by a blast of icy air from the unit, freezing gusts that carried the faintly sweet smell of death under an overpowering blast of disinfectant.

A steady trickle of people arrived, looking for their loved ones. Some walked in uncertainly, unsure of where to go or who to speak to. Two young men came in one day, saying that their cousin from a village near Multan had gone missing after coming to Karachi to work. No one had heard from him for months. The Edhi staff were matter-of-fact and pulled out the photo albums – a bulging pile containing photographs of dead faces, one after another. These bodies had not been prepared for an open-casket viewing. Their faces bulged and swelled, their lips were blue. Some were distorted by gashes or blasted by bullet holes, faces frozen in expressions of horror. As the young men turned the pages, their whole bodies appeared to shrink. They did not find their cousin.

For years, the mortuary and its workers had been grim witnesses to the ravages of the city. Staff told me that during the worst of the violence, they collected 3,000 unidentified bodies a year. These might be low-ranking gang members whose families were too afraid to collect them after a reprisal killing, or migrant labourers caught in the crossfire without their identity cards on them. After the Karachi Operation began, this number halved. Each tragedy that afflicted the city meant a rush of bodies to the mortuary: the mutilated remains after a suicide attack, the swollen corpses killed by water shortages during the brutal 2015 heatwave. During my visit, there was another cause: a steady stream of people looking for loved ones who had been questioned by Rangers or police and then were never heard from again. Blinking back tears, one young man told me that his brother had been picked up by the Rangers for questioning four months earlier. No one had heard from him since. His brother was forty-five when he disappeared and had been involved with the Muttahida Qaumi Movement at a junior level when he was in his twenties, although he was no longer affiliated. He had only ever been a 'nobody' in the Party, the man said, but the family could not think of any other reason why he would have been questioned.

'We won't make a fuss if he's found,' he said. 'We won't complain to anyone. I just want to know for my own peace of mind, for my own heart. I want to know if he's alive.'

I had been told many different versions of this story. There was the missing fifteen-year-old Afghan boy who lived in an area known as a militant hotspot, picked up for questioning and never heard from again. There were scores of young men from MQM-dominated areas, poor people who had never risen to a high rank, who had disappeared into thin air. In the absence of any other information, each week their families quietly came to the Edhi mortuary. They asked to see the photo album. They leafed through page after page of frozen, dead faces, unsure whether to hope to see their loved one there or to pray for continued uncertainty. Not knowing was painful, but at least it allowed a shard of hope.

*

Zille was not convinced that the Karachi Operation had made the city safer – not really, not in a way that would last. Sure, it was easier to get around. There were fewer terror attacks, the gang war had dwindled into inactivity and even the police encounters he had so exhaustively covered over recent years were slowing to a halt. But the city still appeared to him a dark tapestry, with threats stitched into every street. He was in touch with Lyari's gangsters by phone and knew that they continued to work, running their drugs businesses in Karachi from overseas. The top command from each of the main terror groups had escaped too, to Pakistan's northern areas or to Afghanistan. No one knew when they would come back. It was all very well to be told that he was on a hit list, but no one ever rang up to tell him he no longer needed to worry. Perhaps that time would never come – not when peace was so fragile. He had lived like this for so long that certain things had become habit, so ingrained into his daily routine that he barely even noticed them. He did not let his wife, children or parents travel in his car. He went out for dinner sometimes, but mostly with friends in the police, other people who were on hit lists and occasionally with journalists who at least understood the heavy weight that hung over him. He had long since stopped pushing his other friends for invites when they went to play cricket or took trips to the seaside with their families. His four daughters were getting older now and two of them were in school. One asked him, 'Baba [Daddy], why don't you ever come to my school? I want you to come.' He did not explain that the head teacher had told him his presence posed a threat to the safety of the children. He smiled and promised that he would come soon, in full knowledge that he could not.

After the disaster with Bol TV, Zille had found another job, as a senior crime reporter with News 24. The channel was not as well established as Geo, but at least they were paying salaries. He got stuck in straight away, covering police encounters, and was pleased that he had kept his contacts fresh during his months of unemployment. But as the Karachi Operation dragged on for months and then years, these raids became less frequent. Public interest in this violent spectacle waned too, as crime began to have less of an impact on people's daily lives. Infuriatingly, alongside his ever-present, low-level fear, Zille was bored. Since starting as a crime reporter over a decade earlier, there had been more or less daily incidents to cover – gun battles, police stories, terror attacks. Now there was the occasional shooting, an incident that killed two or three people here or there – nothing really significant. There were stories about jail conditions and routine police work, long-running corruption or murder cases. These stories took days, sometimes weeks, to break and involved sit-down interviews and long, soporific days at court. There was no buzz or excitement. Zille was accustomed to worrying about his position after years of frantic competition to be first on the scene. Now the anxiety took on a new focus. If crime rates were so reduced, would there be any need for a crime reporter at all?

Zille had always loved to travel, and now that his working weeks were so much quieter, he took trips as often as he could. He had friends in London whom he visited at least once or twice a year. At one time he had loved being recognized in Karachi, the sense that everyone knew his face, but now that he was on a hit list he was conflicted. In London, he did not have to look over his shoulder or move on quickly from public locations. He liked being able to walk around on streets where he was truly anonymous. While his hosts were at work, he took the red double-decker buses to random places, took selfies of himself at shopping centres and tube stations, in cafes and next to statues. He walked around endlessly, feeling free. I met him on one of these trips at a cafe in Euston in the autumn of 2018. Over the years I had known him, Zille was usually keen to meet and talk, but cagey and evasive when it came to the details. In London, he was like a different person. We sat in the busy coffee shop, where the tables were practically piled on top of each other, and he spoke expansively about his past and his current situation.

'Here, I can move easily, I can walk around,' he said. 'In Pakistan I can't do this. It's home to office, office to home.'

'Isn't Karachi a lot safer now?' I asked.

'The city is safe, but it's not . . .' he paused. 'We can't say the city is peaceful. The situation is under control, but it is not peace.'

A few days later, Zille was woken up in the middle of the night by a call from a gangster contact in South Africa and then by calls from the news desk and police in Karachi. Ghafar Zikri, the gangster who had long controlled the area around Parveen's childhood home, had been killed in a police encounter. Zille was frustrated that he was not there to cover the story. From his friend's house in a London suburb, he sat with his two phones, coordinating communication between the gangsters and his colleagues. He told me wistfully that it was the first major story from Lyari that he had missed in over a decade.

That year, Pakistan's general election had delivered another change in government. Imran Khan, the former cricket star, was the new prime minister, but the general consensus was that the army was really pulling the strings behind the scenes – even more than usual. Rival politicians had their speeches and footage of rallies expunged from major cable networks. Critical journalists were picked up by the all-powerful security forces. Zille was not worried that he would be targeted by the military establishment. He had excellent links with the police, including some who were closely connected with the security agencies, like Rao Anwar, the face of the Karachi Operation and the officer most associated with the Bahria Town clearances. But the effect on his industry was devastating. Viewers tuned out. Advertisers stopped investing. Profits plunged. Newsrooms shed staff by the hundreds. Zille clung on to his job, but he wondered what to do next. He started thinking, again, about starting afresh.

When I saw him in Karachi a few months later, he was back to his usual, cagey self. I accompanied him on a visit to a police station and, midway through, he abandoned his car and called a friend to come and collect us, never explaining what the security risk was. He talked about investing in property and getting out of the media altogether. But we both knew that was unlikely.

'It's been twenty years,' he said. 'It's hard to start over.'

In 2018, Parveen and her siblings returned to Lyari. Now that the area was safer, they wanted to be at home again, close to their extended family. But they did not contemplate moving back into the family house in Kalri that their father had built. Their sister Samreen still lived there, with her husband and children, and begged them to join her there, saying that they were scared rattling around in that big house. But Parveen knew it was impossible. The thought of its bullet-pocked walls, the discarded bloody corpses after the gangsters' occupation, the memory of how many nights there had passed in terror – it was all too much. Her sister Nasreen and younger brother Faheem silently agreed. Her eldest brother, Naeem, who was usually less emotional than the others, repeated what Parveen had once said to me: that he wouldn't live there again even if someone paid him. Instead, they rented a big house in Baghdadi, a bustling district of Lyari close to the yellow arches that marked the entrance to the area. The house sat on a busy alleyway blanketed, as all of Lyari was, in discarded rubbish. The house stretched upwards over several storeys, its plastered exterior painted in bright patterns, the door protected by a metal grille.

Coming home to live in Lyari was complicated for Parveen. In a sense, she had never really left. Even during almost fifteen years in Kiamari, she had spent long stints staying with relatives in Lyari, and she had always been fixated on improving the area. But now Parveen was back, she missed Kiamari. She sometimes felt claustrophobic, as if everyone was watching her. It was not an unfounded paranoia. Often when I visited her house, we sat in the reception room on the ground floor, separated from the narrow street outside by a thin wall. The interior of the house was as brightly coloured as Parveen's clothing – in the reception room, the walls were bright orange on one side, with a pale yellow and blue pattern on the other. Thin carpets in clashing patterns were spread over a hard concrete floor, with cylindrical Baloch cushions strewn around in lieu of chairs. The sounds and smells of the street drifted in from outside. Parveen likes to talk and she does not watch her words. She railed against the evils of marriage, of creeping religious extremism, about the fact that even one of her own brothers, Naeem, had become immersed in what she called 'mullah-ism' and was trying to prevent his daughter from going to school. Occasionally, though, she would catch herself. If she had something to say about particular gangsters or specific religious groups that were active in Lyari, she would first stand up and close the small windows that opened onto the street outside. She would click the window shut, then sit back down and, in lowered tones, launch into whatever she wanted to say. That was the thing about Lyari. The battles had not taken place in some far-off war zone: the gang war had been waged here, on their homes, their bodies, their families. The Karachi Operation was being fought on the same territory.

For years, Lyari's streets had been stripped of their life because people were too afraid to sit outside. The children had stopped playing football in the alleys, the old men had stopped sitting on plastic chairs outside chai hotels to argue about politics, the women had stopped squatting outside their homes together to peel garlic and potatoes and trade stories. Now, despite the heavy Rangers presence and the frequent raids, it seemed like some of the old ways of life were coming back. Whole alleys were taken over by football matches orchestrated by eager young boys and occasionally girls. Young men set up pool tables out on the street and played raucous games before an audience. Old men passed newspapers around. Old women sucked deeply on hookah pipes and chopped vegetables over heavy-bottomed pans. But although the street culture was returning, Parveen was not confident that the damage wrought by years of brutal violence had been undone. She looked back on her childhood with rose-tinted glasses, thinking of the spirit of volunteerism that had made people set up the street schools for no financial gain, the residents who had gathered money together to help out a neighbour in financial difficulty. The way she saw it, that spirit of doing things for yourself had been co-opted and destroyed by the gangsters. They had monopolized any positive community work with their criminal cash, at the same time as the violence had obstructed people from starting out on their own.

Parveen was keen to get this community spirit going again. She had so many ideas that it was energizing to listen to her – if sometimes hard to keep up. She and her younger brother Faheem, along with a friend, had founded an NGO called Meherdar, which performed street theatre around Karachi and Balochistan to raise awareness about early marriage and domestic abuse. They set up travelling libraries for under-served communities. The reception room at her Lyari home was full of piles of books and shelving that she'd procured to take to different villages. They were starting the Lyari Literary Festival to platform local poets, activists and journalists.

Parveen is a force of nature. No injustice is too big or small for her to take on – from supporting a female friend ostracized after a divorce to organizing protests against state abductions of activists in Balochistan. But the battles of the area had been wrought on her mind and body too, just as much as they had on anyone else's. There were times when it came over her like a wave, leaving her barely able to come up for air. She had helped to organize a series of protests outside Karachi's Press Club about forced disappearances in Balochistan. She was in regular contact with the families of the missing, and while their grief and distress drove her to continue coordinating the protests, it also clattered around her head until it threatened to deafen her. In the midst of this, I went to see her. She had told me vaguely that she was unwell, but I assumed she meant a cold or a stomach bug. I was shocked when I saw her. Her voice shook and her whole demeanour was heavy. 'What about all the people who no one can hear or see?' she asked me. 'When torture is perpetrated on them, what happens to them? Who is there to listen to their screams?' As her nephews and nieces passed in and out of the room, she mustered a smile for them, but it was clearly an effort.

Uzair Baloch might have been in custody, but Parveen did not believe he would stay there indefinitely. There were sightings of some of his associates in Lyari, men who had fled overseas when the operation was in full flow, and Parveen wondered if that meant an imminent return. She heard stories about the wives of some of the biggest gangsters taking over the drugs empires in their absence, managing shipments of *charas* and heroin from their homes. The sheer injustice that many of the most prominent gangsters were free to live in luxury overseas while the low-ranking foot soldiers were rounded up and arrested, or tortured and discarded on the street as Nasir had been, enraged Parveen. Sayed, the cousin who had pointed a gun at Parveen's head, had quietly relocated out of Lyari, hoping to escape the scrutiny of the Rangers. In the years since their altercation, Parveen had seen him only once, at her younger brother's wedding. Other than that, she avoided him, staying away from family events that he was likely to attend. It did not come naturally to her to hold her tongue.

One day, Parveen took me with her to visit her cousin Aisha, Sayed's sister, who still lived in the house opposite Rehman Dakait and Uzair Baloch's now abandoned mansions. Aisha and other gathered relatives were excited to see Parveen, who rarely came to visit them. They said they'd been waiting all morning. Parveen looked uneasy. The house carried memories for her – a happier time in childhood marred by the horror of her meeting at Uzair's. I sat cross-legged on the floor, eating hot, crumbly samosas filled with potato, picked up fresh from a street stall outside. Suddenly, a tall man with a greying beard walked in, looking uncertain. Parveen clutched her head in her hands for a moment before standing up. The man embraced her.

'Hey, bro,' she said, pushing his shoulder in a playful show of bravado, but avoiding eye contact.

'I was visiting my mother and I heard you were coming so I stayed,' he said, speaking quickly, looking anxious and emotional. 'You haven't come to see us in a long time, Parveen.'

It was Sayed. I don't know what I was expecting, but it certainly wasn't a man who looked to all intents and purposes like the civil servant he was. It was hard to imagine him holding a gun to Parveen's head. The other relatives looked on. They wanted the bitter divisions and bad decisions of the gang war to be in the past. But history cannot be so easily erased. Soon afterwards, Parveen said hasty goodbyes and we walked quickly to the car. As she reached for the door, I saw that her hands were shaking.

She coped as she always did: by doing more. When I saw Parveen again a few days later, she was back to full energy, frenetically scribbling down ideas for new projects in a notebook. She was surrounded by boxes of books, planning another library.

In December 2018, a few months after the attempted land grab on Lal Baksh Goth, I drove to Kathore to meet a local land rights activist, Hafeez Baloch. It was late and the sky over Kathore was completely black apart from the thin crescent of a new moon, a misty shroud of pollution hiding the stars. As well as being an activist, Hafeez was a shopkeeper, and we met at the shop where he sold biscuits and soft drinks imported from Iran. He has greying black hair, a heavy moustache and a harried air. He was stressed. After years of agitating for official action on the Bahria Town development that threatened to engulf his home, something was finally happening. Back in 2016, Karim Baksh's letter may have gone unheeded, but a series of other court cases had gradually been working their way through the Supreme Court and the National Accountability Bureau. The Pakistani courts system is notoriously slow, and while the cases plodded on, construction of Bahria Town continued at a rapid pace. Then something unexpected happened. In May 2018, the Supreme Court ruled that much of the land had been illegally procured. In December 2018, it ordered a halt on all construction. Hafeez was desperately trying to turn this temporary stay on construction into a more permanent decision. He wanted people from the area to give testimony to the Supreme Court. It was a tough ask. People were afraid of repercussions. Malik Riaz, the owner of Bahria Town, was one of the richest people in the country, with friends in high places, and no one knew how long the court's decision would hold. Hafeez told me that forty-eight villages had already been affected by the Bahria Town construction. Some had actually seen their houses bull-dozed to the ground. But almost all had lost their agricultural and grazing land, which made continuing to live there all but impossible. 'If the land goes, everything goes,' he told me. He was not optimistic that the construction would stay halted for long: 'The state sides with people who have money. If we lose this battle for our villages, we are the ones who will be considered thieves and beggars, not those who have done the stealing.' He showed me a map of the planned expansion of Bahria Town. It went right over Kathore.

The next day, Hafeez took me to see some of the damage for myself. We drove over scrubland, past thorns and thatch-roofed shacks. Standing out against the ochre vista was a sparkling white cluster of buildings in the distance. Hafeez nodded towards it: 'Malik Riaz's empire.' Lal Baksh Goth was not the only village that had been attacked; those that were closer to the development were fighting off bulldozers almost every day. In one village, I saw a partially destroyed graveyard, small stones sticking roughly out of the earth. An enormous, smooth white wall had been built over half of the graveyard. Behind the wall was an incomplete water feature with garish metal birds standing in a fountain. This was to be the entrance to the 'farmhouses', the most exclusive properties on offer at Bahria Town, built over dead bodies. Later, we stopped the car and walked up a hill. Hafeez wanted to show me the gravestone of Gohar Bano, a female warrior who featured heavily in local Baloch folklore, so that I could see how their stories were deeply embedded in the earth. Dust clouds swirled like living entities. Clusters of thorn branches clamped onto my feet like animal traps. When we got to the top, I admired the battered stone that marked Gohar Bano's grave. From this vantage point, I could see into the Bahria Town development, a cookie-cutter model village that had been dropped onto the wilderness. On the way down, we encountered an old man standing alone as wind billowed his salwar kameez, his face spotted pink with vitiligo. Hafeez asked what he was doing out here on his own. 'I'm just roaming around,' he said defensively. 'It's my land. It's all of our land.'

While people in the district saw Bahria Town as a terrifying invading force, many in Karachi had a very different view. Bahria Town's properties were heavily advertised, with glowing accounts of the amazing facilities it would offer. It was planned to span over 45,000 acres (around the size of Washington, DC), with space for a million residents. Malik Riaz had already built much smaller Bahria Towns (property developments bearing the same name) just outside Lahore and Islamabad. They were sprawling residential compounds that offered a way out of urban chaos, promising private supplies of electricity and water, smoothly paved roads and functional street lights. Riaz had a penchant for the ridiculous – alongside tidily mown grass and well-equipped playgrounds were imitations of architectural icons, with a Taj Mahal here, a miniature Parthenon there – but it was the convenience that appealed so widely. Allegations of illegal land appropriation had hovered around all of these projects, but without much repercussion. When I spoke to family and friends about Bahria Town – people from the comfortably upper or middle echelons of society – most of them viewed it as a potential investment opportunity, even when the court verdict came out. It was far away from the gangs and the terrorists and the mafias, a place where you could have a reasonable guarantee of safety, a place where you wouldn't have to spend hours on the phone to procure a tanker of water.

I drove to Bahria Town from downtown Karachi one morning, keen to get a sense of why so many people were drawn to it. The motorway was edged by a flat expanse of sandy, dry-looking earth, punctuated by petrol pumps, massive lorries and rusting electricity pylons. We paid a toll to enter Bahria Town – a small fee, but enough to make the compound inaccessible for people like the Kachehlos. The roads were noticeably smooth and free of potholes, edged by neatly trimmed hedges. Lush green lawns filled the spaces between intersections, an unusual sight in a city plagued by water shortages.

The site was full of half-finished houses and apartment blocks. There were road signs pointing to the hospital, the cricket stadium, Sports City, Golf City and Cine Gold, the cinema complex. One round-about bore a sculpture of two bears poised over a log, then another soon afterwards, an elephant. Signs everywhere urged you to KEEP BAHRIA CLEAN. In the distance, gigantic plastic lettering reading I ♥ BAHRIA TOWN loomed. Construction was still suspended, and although some people already lived there, much of it was empty or half-finished. It felt like stepping into a ghost town. As we drove, sometimes roads tapered off into nothingness, merging into the dusty scrubland of the villages beyond. My driver wasn't sure where we were and wanted to ask for directions, but we drove for more than fifteen minutes before encountering anyone. 'How hard is it to find a human round here?' he muttered. Eventually, we came to the Dancing Fountain, a pool of water as large as a lake, sparkling in the sun, surrounded by floodlights. I looked at the complicated system of pipes and pumps designed to make the water spurt and 'dance' during an event, and thought about Jannat filling up jugs from the borehole, her arms aching when the power was off and she had to use the hand pump. We drove to the Eiffel Tower, which was partially constructed. It sat atop a mountain of sand, surrounded by steelworkers, sparks of welding flying from its joints, despite the fact that construction was halted. I stopped for a moment to stare at it, overwhelmed by the utter incongruity of a fake Eiffel Tower surrounded by freshly planted palm trees and piles of sand. The development stretched out as far as the eye could see, half-built roads that led nowhere dissolving into the sandy earth. It was so big already. It was unstoppable.

The Supreme Court decision was reversed within a few months. In March 2019, it was agreed that Riaz would pay an immense sum – 460 billion rupees (£2.3 billion) – to the court, in return for being

able to resume construction. Soon after the decision, I visited Lal
Baksh Goth. Given Jannat's obsession with my unmarried status, I
was excited to share the news that I had got engaged since I saw her
last. She clapped her hands in delight.

'Has your groom built you a house yet?' Bushra wanted to know.

'It doesn't really work like that in London,' I explained. 'We don't
have a lot of space for new houses to get built.'

'Don't worry,' said Jannat, not missing a beat. 'There's a lot of
space in Bahria Town. Why doesn't he build you one there?'

No one in Lal Baksh knew what was going to happen to them.
They could not afford to rebuild their poultry farms, which sat there
destroyed, the rubble disintegrating in the wind. In the few months
that the construction was off, the machinery that bothered Jannat
so much at night had been inactive. Now it was back, humming
and beeping. When I visited, the dust stuck to my tongue and made
my eyes itch. Jannat saw me wiping my phone screen and told me
that this fine, persistent dust was because of the construction. The
Bahria bulldozers with their police escorts had not returned yet, but
everyone in the village assumed that it was a matter of when, not if.

Jannat was pregnant again and she was wearier than ever. Looking
at her, I wondered if she might have anaemia, which is endemic in
parts of Pakistan where women have multiple pregnancies and limited medical oversight. I knew all about anaemia and its life-sapping
misery; I have suffered from it in one form or another for most of my
adult life, but access to free healthcare in the UK means I've been
able to manage it with supplements. She told me that Ghulam was
talking seriously about moving away from the village altogether,
going somewhere that the children could get to school easily and
where they could access a doctor. He was waiting until the baby
came, to start looking in earnest. I asked how she felt about the
possibility of leaving Lal Baksh, her ancestral home.

She tilted her head and gave a tight-lipped smile. 'You have to do these things. For your children.' But her voice was small.

Over the six years since Sahiba's murder, Siraj had given scores of statements and attended many hearings. But no one had been brought to justice. The legal process was achingly slow. There were false starts and arrests and a dizzying series of different investigations. It was a painful reminder that justice in Karachi came more easily down the barrel of a gun than through the court system. Sahiba's sister, Aquila, pushed ahead, refusing to let the authorities drop the matter. She was convinced there was a cover-up, that the police had been quick to point the finger at a random person – the young man they had killed in an encounter the very next day – to avoid unpicking the layers of vested interests and powerful people involved in the land appropriation that Sahiba had exposed. 'These people are lying,' Aquila told me. 'They are lying through their teeth.' Tirelessly, she fought for the case to be reopened, re-examined, for investigations to continue. It was the only way she could survive the pain of losing her sister.

Eventually, the police arrested a man called Raheem Swati. He was a local thug who owned premises across the road from the Orangi Pilot Project office. Before Sahiba's death, he'd demanded access to the OPP premises to use part of it as a gym. This dispute was cited by police as a motive for murder. Swati's case came under the auspices of the terrorism court. The session was held in a small, airless room. Siraj and Sahiba's other friends and family came into the room to give their testimony. Swati and his family were sitting right there, staring at them. It was hard not to worry about recriminations. But Aquila was tentatively optimistic that this was progress.

Siraj did not hold out much hope of justice being done. For years, the city had been under daily siege and he had been engaged in a constant process of adjustment and mediation, always trying to find spaces in between the violence to carry on his work. Now, several years into the Karachi Operation, it was easy to travel back and forth to wherever he needed to go. MQM workers no longer patrolled the streets outside the Technical and Training Resource Centre office and religious militants did not restrict access to the schools he worked with in Pashtun areas. But it was almost as if the haze of bullets and explosions had cleared to reveal a sharper picture of the structural injustices that sat behind the street violence. Siraj was acutely aware of the powerful forces that controlled life in Karachi, the same forces that might have led to Sahiba's death. As long as land and water were such valuable commodities, it was difficult to see how things could ever truly change for the better. The people in power – the police, government officials – were making too much money from illegal schemes siphoning off water or grabbing land to meaningfully crack down.

Rather than losing hope, Siraj focused hard on the things that were within his control, working with an obsessive zeal. He helped schools to improve their budgets and buildings; he recruited more women to savings groups so they had a safety net to support their families; he trained young community architects. Even if justice was elusive and money and political connections continued to trump all else, he still truly believed that working with communities could mean something.

Soon after the Supreme Court reversed its decision and allowed construction to resume on Bahria Town, I sat with Siraj in the TTRC office. The ceiling fan whirred overhead as we ate segments of orange sprinkled with salt and *chaat masala* – a tangy spice mix. Dispassionately, he ran through all the things that happened as a result of these major housing developments. It was not just the people displaced to make way for the fancy apartment buildings who lost out; it also meant that water would be diverted to the new development, leaving people in places like Orangi Town struggling. Siraj and his family still had to spend hours frantically filling up their tanks on the one day per fortnight when the taps were switched on.

'Anyone doing anything to make money off basic amenities like land and water is already powerful, and will remain so,' he said, his voice matter-of-fact.

A few days earlier, Siraj had driven over the Banaras flyover, a main road that connects Orangi Town to the city. It is a monument to recent violence, at least partly constructed to keep Mohajir and Pashtun people separate – in more violent times, the Urdu-speakers could drive over the flyover and avoid the Pashtun market below. It was dark as Siraj looked out over the bridge. He saw North Nazimabad, a middle-class district full of busy shopping malls, as well as the cranes and scaffolding that accompanied new constructions. It was full of lights, people moving in and out of shops, cars on the streets. As Siraj drove onwards towards Orangi, he noticed that there were no lights at all, just a heavy blanket of darkness hanging over the area due to load-shedding, broken only by car headlights. In this short distance, there was such a drastic disparity. Siraj worried that, within the next few years, yet more barriers would go up between the affluent and the poor, and that soon people like him, who did not come from money or have a fancy education, would feel embarrassed to even go to the richer parts of town.

After Sahiba's death, the *kachi abadi* project to map unregularized settlements had been put on hold. It never restarted. Siraj was driven by his belief that the act of codifying an area was quietly revolutionary, that it allowed people to prove that they existed and assert their rights. But as more and more land in previously undesirable areas of the city was claimed for expensive redevelopment, to accommodate Karachi's ever-growing population, sometimes he worried that his maps might be used as a template for developers only interested in scoping out what was there for them to destroy. The seemingly unstoppable force of Bahria Town showed how closely some developers were tied to the police, the army or the political parties. It was conceivable that a map and the legal leases to the land would not always be enough for poor people to defend what was theirs.

All Siraj could do was to keep his faith in the power of incremental change. His contribution was there in each small improvement to a school's architecture, a family's budget, a map of a formerly unmapped area. Etching the shifting boundaries of the city into a permanent record created something lasting in the tumult, the implicit affirmation: we are here.

AUTHOR'S NOTE

Everyone who appears in *Karachi Vice* is a real person, although I
have changed some names; Jannat and Bushra are pseudonyms. For
reasons of privacy, I have also changed the names of some other
people who feature only briefly in the narrative. The stories are
based on in-depth, in-person interviews with Safdar, Parveen, Siraj,
Jannat and Zille, which took place during extended trips to Karachi
between 2015 and 2019. This is a work of narrative non-fiction,
not history, and as such it is rooted in the subjective experiences
of these five people. They were deeply generous with their time,
sharing sometimes extremely painful recollections. Memory – particularly memories of a traumatic event – can be a slippery thing
and occasionally people gave me contradictory or varying accounts
of the same event over time. Where possible, I sought to verify
events either by corroborating with other people who were there
or through my own independent enquiries. During the research for
this book, I got to know the families, friends and colleagues of the
five people whose stories I have told, who helped hugely with my
reconstruction of events. I also got to know the areas where they
live and work, which gave me a fuller understanding of how wildly
these areas differ from each other and how they slot together into a
chaotic, energetic whole.

I have been spending time in and writing about Pakistan for over ten years, and the various stories I have reported on informed my descriptions of the wider social or political context I have included in this book. Over the course of the past decade, I have interviewed politicians, policemen, lawyers, activists and terrorist recruiters. In 2015 and 2016, as the Karachi Operation was in full force, I spent time in the city's police stations and following officers out on patrol; my account of police attitudes to extrajudicial killings is based on what I observed. I have accompanied Safdar and other Edhi ambulance drivers on numerous emergency call-outs around the city and have seen first-hand the way they operate.

In addition to interview material, I consulted as many sources as possible surrounding the events that feature in the book – from contemporaneous news reporting to academic studies. At different points I referred to the work of Nida Kirmani and Sarwant Viqar on Lyari, and Nichola Khan on the MQM and Mohajir militancy. *Rural Karachi: Facing an Existential Threat*, edited by Farhan Anwar (Shehri, 2014), informed my discussion of the degradation of land around Kathore. *Cityscapes of Violence in Karachi: Public and Counterpublics*, edited by Nichola Khan (Hurst, 2017), was a wonderful resource that I returned to repeatedly. And Laurent Gayer's masterful *Karachi: Ordered Disorder and the Struggle for the City* (Hurst, 2014), which expertly codifies the different power dynamics at play, deserves special mention. Anyone seeking a more detailed, academic analysis of the city should read it immediately.

ACKNOWLEDGEMENTS

First and foremost, thanks go to the people who feature in this book: Safdar, Parveen, Siraj, Jannat and Zille. They shared their stories, opened their homes and workplaces, and put up with relentless, often repetitive questioning with good humour and grace.

This book would not exist without Haya Fatima Iqbal: translator, friend and slave driver. She offered a wealth of knowledge about Karachi and made the research not just collaborative but a lot of fun. I am grateful to my agent, Sophie Lambert, for seeing the potential in this project and helping to shape it, and to my editors, Laura Barber and Ka Bradley, who transformed the manuscript with their sharp insights. Thanks to the whole team at Granta for helping to craft my idea into the book you are holding.

Senior management at the Edhi Foundation allowed me to observe their work over a period of years; thanks to Anwar Kazmi (who sadly passed away in 2019), to Faisal Edhi and to Imran and Bilal. I came to know about Lal Baksh Goth only through Hafeez Baloch, a faultless host and an indefatigable activist working against unimaginable odds. In Orangi Town, Salma Mir was insightful and unstinting with her time. Aquila Ismail gave me invaluable background on her sister, Perween Rahman, and access to the Orangi Pilot Project's archived reports. Zia Ur-Rehman – a fountain of knowledge – was always generous with advice and contacts. Thanks also to Meher Ahmad and Zoha Waseem for generously sharing their expertise to give laser-sharp notes on the manuscript.

This book originally grew out of two newspaper features. Particular thanks to David Wolf at *Guardian* Long Reads who kick-started it all by commissioning me to report on Karachi's crime reporters in 2015 (and who came up with the headline that is now this book's title), and to Louisa Saunders, then at *Mosaic*, who commissioned me to write on Karachi's ambulance drivers a year later.

Friends and family in Karachi made the city a home from home, providing copious food, wry humour and endless advice. I owe particular gratitude to my aunt and uncle Sumayra Ayazuddin and Ayaz Fakir, who welcomed me into their house in 2012, as a newly freelance twenty-five-year-old with scant Urdu and little idea how to navigate Karachi or its security problems. Thanks also to Samar Husain, Imran Husain, Amin Fakir, Aziz Fakir and Satish Anand.

Many people have supportive parents; I have the rare good fortune of being born to two writers and experts on my chosen field. My father, Christopher Shackle, instilled in me an appreciation for Pakistan's rich linguistic and literary culture, and gave remarkably quick and incisive notes on the first draft. My mother, Shahrukh Husain, is always my first reader and sounding board. She has read every iteration of this manuscript, and it would be far inferior without her wisdom and gift for words. Mum, Dad, thank you for encouraging me so unconditionally.

My writer friends Cal Flyn, Rosa Rankin-Gee, Alex Christofi and Caroline Crampton all gave feedback and boosted morale at different points. Edwina Kelly offered astute, thoughtful comments on the finished manuscript. Jasmine Shackle lifted my mood. My uncle Aamer Hussein has always championed my writing. When

I was struggling to write, long conversations with Katherine Ross helped to order my thoughts – thanks, always, for your insights and patience. At the *New Humanist*, Daniel Trilling and Dan Hancox were supportive and considerate colleagues. Louis Brooke and Alex Lawrence-Archer were princely hosts, and I wrote parts of this book at their beautiful house in Norfolk. Thanks also to the MacDowell Colony in New Hampshire, USA – it was a gift to complete the manuscript in such a creatively nourishing environment.

In-depth foreign reporting is expensive, and this book wouldn't have been possible without the support of grants from the Society of Authors' K. Blundell Trust and MacDowell's Calderwood Foundation, and a media fellowship with Columbia University's Center for the Study of Social Difference (a programme which also provided a wonderful critical framework for thinking about representations of women).

My husband, Owen Kean, has travelled with me to far-flung places with little regard for his own digestive health, been my loudest cheerleader and put up with sometimes long absences as I researched this book. Six months after we met, you travelled with me to Karachi and helped me find my own place in a city that had seemed bewildering. Thank you, Owen; you are the best person I know.

The last word belongs to my beloved, supportive, sparkling aunt Safinaz Bhai, who passed away soon after I finished the first draft of this book. *Khala*, I miss you every day and I hope I made you proud.

GLOSSARY

abba	father
amma	mother
baji	older sister
beta	child
bhai	brother
bukhar	fever
chaat masala	tangy spice mix often used as a garnish
chacha	paternal uncle
charas	cannabis
dada	paternal grandfather
dadi	paternal grandmother
goth	village
haleem	thick stew made from meat and grains
iftar	evening meal with which Muslims end their daily fast during Ramzan
kacha/kachi	unfinished
kachi abadi	informal settlement, shanty town
khala	maternal aunt
mamoo	maternal uncle

maulana	learned or pious person
meetha pani	fresh water
nana	maternal grandfather
nani	maternal grandmother
naswar	moist, powdered tobacco; snuff
nikah	religious marriage contract
pukka	finished
sahib	sir
sahiba	madam
salan	light, often tomato-based, meat stew
sardar	leader
tamasha	scene, spectacle